The Self-sufficient
HOUSE

The Self-sufficient HOUSE

Brenda and Robert Vale

M

Design by Robert Updegraff
Drawings by Brenda and Robert Vale
Photography by Robert Updegraff, John Ritson,
and Brenda and Robert Vale

The publishers thank the National Centre for Alternative Technology
at Machynlleth, Powys, for their kind permission to photograph examples
of their equipment.

First published 1980 by Macmillan London Limited
London and Basingstoke

Associated companies in Delhi, Dublin,
Hong Kong, Johannesburg, Lagos, Melbourne,
New York, Singapore, and Tokyo

Typeset and printed in Great Britain by
G. A. Pindar & Son Ltd., Scarborough

Vale, Brenda Alison
  The self-sufficient house
  1. Dwellings — Heating and ventilation
  2. Dwellings — Power supply
  I. Title II. Vale, Robert James Dennis
  696   TH7222

ISBN 0-333-25868-1

Contents

Introduction

In 1973 we mortgaged ourselves to the Abbey National and bought a house with a large garden: our intention was to put into practice the theories of alternative technology. This book is based on the results of our experiences to date. Neither of us feels we have yet tried everything we want to do, and there are probably several more projects that we have not even if it is only a door that opens, and then the enough practical experience to be able to establish a few principles for alternative technology in its application to the home.

The first is that the simpler the idea and its method of application, the more likely it is to work. Introduce something that has to move, even if it is only a door that opens, and then the trouble starts. So the complete insulation of a house, walls, roof and floor, carefully carried out, will be a potentially very effective if unglamorous piece of alternative technology. On the other hand, our experience of high speed windmills, so kinetically exciting and obviously alternative, is much less happy: there is so much that can go wrong with a windmill, and eventually something always does.

This observation about insulation versus the windmill also illustrates another fairly obvious principle that we have established from our experience: it is much easier to conserve energy than to make it. For this reason many of the projects described will involve principles and methods of energy conservation, although we have also included methods of collecting ambient energy which are as cheap and simple as we could devise.

Money is always the impediment to carrying out alternative technology schemes since building is inevitably expensive even if you provide all the labour yourself. However, if you do not build properly then many alternative technology projects will never be cost effective. The thorough insulation of a building will pay back its cost through fuel savings within a few years; but, for the more fun projects of solar panels and solar cookers, you will have to build well or your device may have fallen to pieces before you have met your capital expenditure through the value of fuel saved. We hope though that you do not get bogged down by cost effectiveness but rather become enthusiastic about alternative technology for its own sake. We have derived a lot of enjoyment from what we have done and learnt something about building. Alternative technology becomes a habit after a while, so that you cannot stop trying out different ways of collecting and conserving energy. On an overcast winter's day in December we may occasionally suffer cold feet but there is always the remedy of an extra pair of woolly socks.

Part I
THEORY

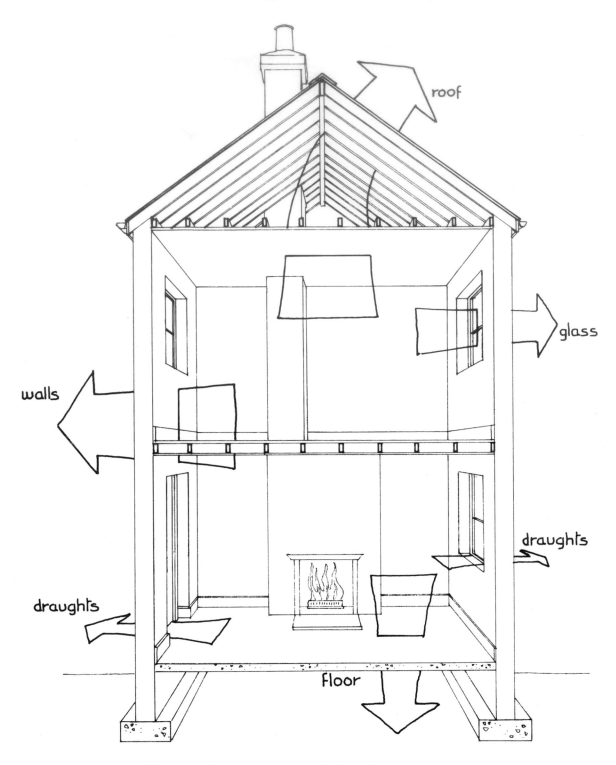

heat losses from an uninsulated house

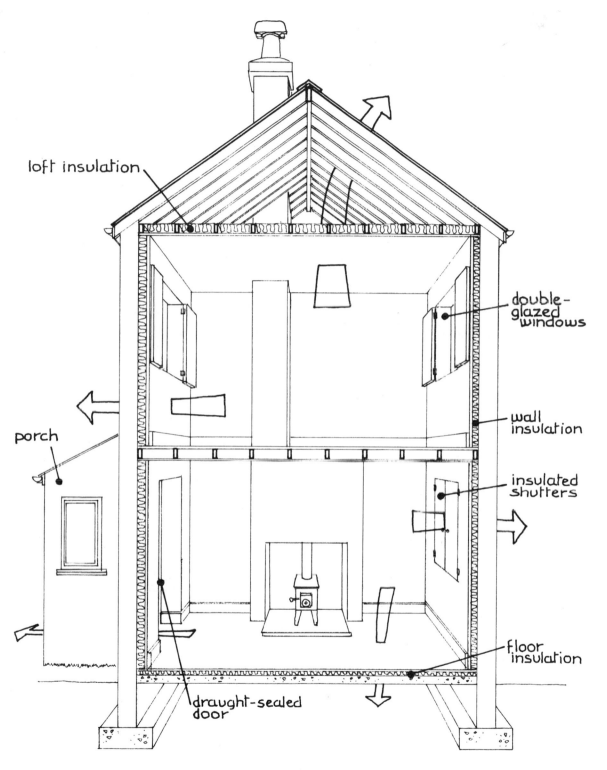

loft insulation

double-glazed windows

wall insulation

porch

insulated shutters

floor insulation

draught-sealed door

the same house insulated

1 The Importance of Orientation

Few of us ever get the chance to analyse the orientation of a house before it is built. Usually we have simply to make the best of what's already there. Architects and builders rarely seem to consider the way the sun moves round a building, how much extra heat could be gained through the windows or whether the building will be constantly exposed to the cooling effect of the wind. It is common to see rows of new houses with the same large picture windows facing both north and south on either side of a road. Because of this lack of foresight you will have to take a careful look at the orientation of your home before you apply any of the schemes described in this book.

Windows

To start with, you will need a compass to find out which side of the building faces south. Once you know, you can see if there are any south-facing windows that might be made into collectors of solar energy. A single sheet of glass is a very poor insulator, even when covered with curtains at night; windows are more usually considered to be a major cause of heat loss from the warm house to the cold outside than a way of adding heat to the inside. In winter, more heat is lost from the house through a single-glazed, south-facing window than is gained to the house from the sun shining through the glass. But if the same window were double-glazed and fitted with insulated shutters, which were kept closed during the hours of darkness, it would act as a solar collector and useful energy could be gained over the winter months.

A house could be designed to obtain a large part of its space heating through the windows alone. The house would need a very massive structure, insulated on the outside, to store heat and even out variations in outside temperature. For this reason the effect of energy gains through large windows may not be so apparent in an existing house, and you would need to be sure that your house was suitable before deciding to increase the number or size of south-facing windows. More details on this subject can be found in the chapters on windows and shutters.

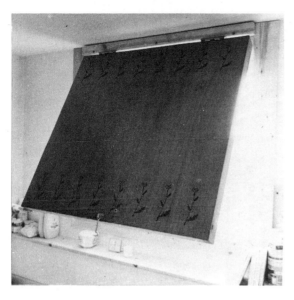

Insulating shutter on a south-facing window

The shutter open during daytime

Any glass facing north, or indeed anything other than almost due south, will cause net heat loss even if the sun shines through it during part of the day. If there are large areas of glass facing north, such as floor to ceiling windows, it would be worth reducing them. A floor to ceiling window could be boarded up to a more normal sill height and the new solid area insulated to a high standard.

Any reduction in the number or surface area of windows will have to comply with local building regulations. In the UK, these require that the area of glass in the window or windows of a room shall be not less than one-tenth of the floor area of that room, to ensure adequate daylighting, and that the total area of openable window shall be not less than one-twentieth of the floor area of the room, to ensure adequate natural ventilation. It should also be noted that any north-facing window in the roof will lose more heat than a similar window in the vertical wall as the former is completely exposed to the sky. At the same time a south-facing window in the roof will fail to collect as much energy in winter as a vertical south-facing window: the low winter sun will strike the vertical window directly whereas it will be reflected off the sloping glass of the roof window.

Rooms

Having examined the outside of your house, it would then be worth considering the layout inside. If there are any rooms which are to be heated to a lower temperature, only heated

An insulated door keeps the larder cool

7

A conservatory porch

occasionally or even left unheated (such as spare bedrooms, larders, storerooms and workshops), it would be best to try and place these against the north wall of the building. These rooms would then form a buffer between the heated part of the building and the cold outside. Although the buffer zone is unheated, its temperature is higher than the outside temperature: hence the temperature difference between the heated space and the buffer zone is less than that between the heated space and the outside – this also happens with the unheated attic space of a house.

Conservatories

It might now be worth looking round to see if there are any south, south-west or south-east walls against which a lean-to conservatory could be built. A conservatory will form a buffer zone and act as a collector of energy. Even on an overcast day the temperature inside the unheated conservatory rises and thus reduces the heat loss through the walls of the building.

To build a conservatory less than 50m^3 in volume you will need to comply with the building regulations, but you will not need planning permission. Traditionally the conservatory has always been added on to the back of the house where this faces approximately south, although its role as a buffer zone has perhaps been less appreciated than its use for growing seedlings and storing wellington boots; but there is no reason why a conservatory built over a south-facing front door should not act as a useful entrance porch.

Roofs

The compass will also enable you to find out in which direction the roof slopes. A solar device will collect energy not only from the sunlight striking it directly but also quite considerably from the indirect radiation reflected from the whole sky (see Chapter 7). This split in the directions from which energy is received has some bearing on the orientation of solar collectors. If your roof faces south it is the obvious

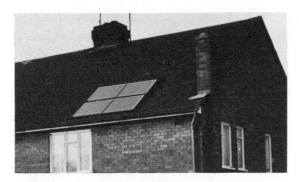

Solar panels mounted on a roof

site for a collector, although a wall facing south would also be suitable. However, a roof system collects more energy than a wall one, even in winter when the rays of the sun shine almost straight into the vertical wall-mounted collector. This is because the roof collector is visible to a greater expanse of open sky and hence receives more scattered indirect radiation.

This has another bearing on orientation when considering a roof slope that does not face south. Very little difference in the amount of energy collected by a roof-mounted collector will be found if the roof points up to 30° either side of due south and even at 50° either side of south only a 10 per cent reduction will occur. However, a wall collector will be far less effective if it does not face due south, as it will be cut off from the direct rays of the sun for a greater part of the day as well as being sheltered from indirect radiation.

Because the arc made by the sun across the sky changes from summer to winter, solar panels required for hot water heating in the summer only (the hot water coming from another source in winter) could be placed on a vertical wall facing east or west where the rays of the sun will be more nearly perpendicular to the collector. Such an orientation would, however, be of little use in winter. If the roof slopes east or west and a collector is required for winter operation, some other site will have to be found, such as the roof of a back extension. You might add some kind of structure to the roof on to which a well orientated collector could be built; but this might be expensive as well as worrying to local planning authorities and building inspectors. A better alternative is to use a free-standing fixture in the garden.

Vegetation

Even in a cool climate, if your house has large areas of glass facing south, overheating can be a problem in the summer. This can be controlled by well placed vegetation, which brings us to another way of modifying the climate around the building. Deciduous trees will provide shade in summer, as will trellises with roses and honeysuckle growing over them, whilst the same trees and trellises, free of leaves in winter, will let the sunlight through to the house. Careful planting can modify the exposure of the building to the wind. As the wind blows across the building it increases the amount of heat lost from it. This is demonstrated by the relative heat losses of windows in sheltered and exposed sites (see page 25).

In coastal areas and on hill tops, where the prevailing wind directions are easy to work out, planting shelter-belts or windbreak hedges upwind of the building may help. A solid barrier would not be as effective as is a hedge or a row of trees which let some wind through: it would produce eddy currents on the downwind side rather than a reduction in wind speed. As can be seen from the diagram, the sheltered zone

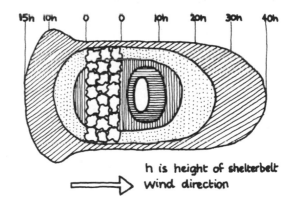

h is height of shelterbelt
→ Wind direction

80% reduction in wind speed
60 - 80% reduction in wind speed
40 - 60% reduction in wind speed
20 - 40% reduction in wind speed
20% - 0 reduction in wind speed

9

can extend to thirty times the height of the belt but for practical purposes it will be between five and ten times the height of the barrier.

A true shelter-belt, the most effective windbreak, consists of two or three rows of trees planted in a staggered pattern; it is perhaps usefully applied only to a large building or to a group of houses. For a single house a suitable hedge, which will grow faster than the trees, will provide protection from the wind sooner. Care must be taken that the windbreak hedge doesn't grow to overshadow a carefully positioned solar collector, although in some cases the overshadowing may be useful. For example, the prevailing wind direction in most parts of the UK is south-westerly, so a screen of deciduous plants might provide useful shade in the summer; in the evening it will also prevent the low summer sun entering rooms facing south-west or west and overheating them. Another possible use of vegetation is to grow a dense evergreen creeper up the walls: this will trap a layer of still and therefore warmer air against the side of the building.

Windmills

You will need your compass again if you are planning to buy or build a windmill and produce your own electricity. Obviously the windmill must be directly in the path of the prevailing wind. You may be in a position to build a tower to raise the height of the windmill above that of the house or any other obstruction; but the ideal height of 15 metres may not appeal to your local planning authority. However, as long as the machine is sited between the house and the direction of the prevailing wind – which can be found from local weather data and plotted on site with your compass – the presence of the building will have little effect on wind speed. If your house is surrounded by large trees all carrying a preservation order, you will have to compromise and perhaps site the machine further from the building than might be ideal.

In fitting many of the devices and systems described in this book you will sometimes have to compromise, but it is precisely this challenge of adapting the schemes to suit your own house, rather than using blanket solutions, that is so exciting. So examine the climate, and the individual characteristics of your house and its site, and decide how modifications can be made to improve it. Finally, do not forget to site the compost heap downwind of the back door!

2 The Efficiency of Different Fuels

Basic energy units

The electrical and mechanical energy we use daily for heating is measured in many ways but this book is unashamedly metric, so we will discount all those British Thermal Units, horsepower and therms, and deal instead in kilowatt-hours (kWh). To be scientifically correct all measurements of energy in this book should be in Joules, Kilojoules, Megajoules and Gigajoules. But we are dealing with buildings, and the building trade has used kilowatt-hours since it went metric, so we will stick to them to avoid confusion. The advantage of the kilowatt-hour is that it is the unit on electricity bills so most people are familiar with it.

The kilowatt is a unit of power, rather than of energy, which means that kilowatts or watts measure the rate at which energy flows. A 1kW electric fire can give out 1kW or 1000W of heat energy. If it runs for an hour it will produce 1kWh or 1000Wh of heat energy and of course consume 1kWh or 1 unit of electricity. If you run the fire for a whole day it will consume 1×24=24kWh, and so on. Similarly a 100W light bulb run for ten hours will use 100 × 10 = 1000Wh = 1kWh; it will also put 1kWh of heat energy into the room, since a light bulb gives out its energy almost entirely as heat.

Primary energy

The use of fuels such as gas, coal or electricity as sources of energy raises the question of efficiency. An electric fire is said to be 100 per cent efficient, as all the electrical energy it uses is converted into heat. In an open coal fire only 20 per cent of the energy contained in the lumps of coal goes to keep you warm; the remaining 80 per cent is lost up the chimney. In a gas or oil central heating system or a modern solid fuel heater up to 70 per cent of the energy contained in the fuel may be usefully employed for heating, so it is said to have an efficiency of 70 per cent.

At first glance it would seem that electricity must be the best fuel because it is so efficient. But to obtain a complete picture one must look at how fuels are produced. To make electricity, fuel such as coal or oil is burned to heat water in a boiler to make steam which drives a turbine which turns the generator which makes the electricity which lights the house that Jack or Jill built. Each step in this process is less than 100 per cent efficient and the result is that less than half of the energy in the coal or oil comes out in the form of electrical energy. Further losses are incurred in the transmission of the electricity because of heating effects in the wires of the National Grid. The final result is that the consumer receives about 27 per cent of the energy contained in the coal. This raises the question of the use of electricity as a fuel for space heating, as overall the efficiency is hardly better than that of a coal-burning open fire. The problem is one that will have to be dealt with on a national scale as most consumers are more concerned with their own bills than with national energy consumption.

The energy used to produce a fuel, for example the energy that is required to mine coal, clean it and transport it to the consumer, or the energy needed to extract oil from oil wells, transport it and refine it into heating oil, is termed 'primary energy'. When politicians and others talk of 'national energy demands' or 'energy consumption', this is what they are referring to. All fuels need a certain amount of primary energy for their production, and in the UK the Building Research Establishment gives the efficiencies for the manufacture of various fuels as follows:

electricity from fossil fuels	27%
manufactured fuels (such as smokeless coal)	71%
substitute natural gas made from coal (estimated)	79%
oil	93%
natural gas	94%
coal and wood (estimated)	98%

Note: substitute natural gas or SNG will have to be made from coal when *natural* natural gas supplies cannot keep up with the demand.

To put it another way, to make 1kWh of electricity requires 3.73kWh of primary energy, but to make 1kWh of coal requires only 1.02kWh of primary energy.

When these efficiencies are combined with the efficiencies of conversion to useful heat in a building it turns out that overall, the most efficient way to heat your home is to burn coal in a closed stove or room-heater, which can be 69 per cent efficient in terms of primary energy. The least efficient is off-peak electric heating which has an efficiency of only 19 per cent in its use of primary energy. Other typical efficiencies of primary energy use are:

wood-burning stove	59%
natural gas central heating	57%
oil central heating	56%
coke-fired room-heater	46%
on peak electric heating	27%
coal in an open fire	20%

Net or useful energy

As a consumer you are more likely to be interested in the efficiency with which fuel is burnt in your house. If you heat a room with an open fire at 20 per cent efficiency you will burn £5 worth of coal or wood for every £1 worth of heat or 5kWh for every 1kWh. If you burn the same £5 worth of coal in a stove that is 70 per cent efficient you receive £3.50 worth of heat, or 3.5kWh.

To put it another way, you might calculate that your house would need 8000kWh to heat it over the whole winter (see Chapter 5 for how to calculate energy demand). This is about the amount of energy contained in 1 tonne of coal. However, if you plan to heat with an open fire you will need 5 tonnes of coal to give out 8000kWh of useful heat energy, because the open fire is only 20 per cent efficient. The 5 tonnes of coal contains 40,000kWh (5×8000) of energy: this is the 'net' or delivered energy demand of the building. The 8000kWh you need to keep the place warm is the 'useful' energy demand. If the same house were heated with a coal burning room-heater which might be 70 per cent efficient, the net energy demand would be 11429kWh (8000kWh useful energy divided by 70 per cent or 0.7) which would be a little less than 1.5 tonnes of coal. For the same amount of useful energy the house with the open fire uses more than three times as much coal as the house with the more efficient heater.

The comparative study of the primary, net and useful energy consumption of various types of heating systems shows, in our opinion, that houses with electric central heating, even if fully insulated, use far more primary energy than a conventionally insulated house with gas or oil central heating; but, because the insulated house has a reduced useful energy demand, you pay no more for the heating than someone with a gas or oil system. If such all-electric houses were to become commonplace and replace other forms of heating the national primary energy consumption might increase although the demand of each house had been reduced.

Once a building has been properly insulated the best fuel to burn is one that requires little primary energy to produce it, such as wood, coal, oil or gas, leaving electricity to be used for lights and electrical appliances. In the long term coal or substitute natural gas are likely to become the most widely used fuels, so if you are planning a conventional heating system these are probably the fuels you should be considering.

3 Insulation

The Building Research Establishment has estimated that up to 50 per cent of the total primary energy consumption of the UK is used to service buildings: for heating, lighting, providing hot water, cooking, and running appliances. Of this energy use about half is required to keep the buildings warm. It seems obvious that the reduction in energy used for space heating is the most important area to tackle first if the aim is to reduce a building's energy consumption.

At the individual level the bills for heating a house always seem to be the largest fuel bills, with those for cooking, heating water and lighting, if you can distinguish between them, being far smaller. This supposition is borne out by the BRE whose figures show that in a typical centrally heated house the energy use is divided as follows:

space heating	71%
water heating	18%
cooking	8%
TV, lights, etc	3%

These figures are changed somewhat for an average house, as only about one third of houses in the UK have central heating, giving the average as:

space heating	64%
water heating	22%
cooking	10%
TV, lights, etc	4%

The difference between the two sets of figures comes from the fact that centrally heated houses are usually kept warmer than those without central heating, so the energy used for space heating is greater.

One way of using less energy is to turn down the heating; but this method is unlikely to appeal to most people whose houses are at present under-heated. The best way is to reduce the rate at which the heat in a house is lost to the outside air. When you heat your home, the heat that you put in continually passes from the warm interior to the cold outdoors and you keep putting in more heat to make up this loss. A typical 1930s semi-detached house loses heat as follows:

450mm insulation in walls, roof and floor

through the walls	35%
through the roof	25%
through the ground floor	15%
draughts	15%
through the windows	10%

A more recently built house with very large windows might lose more heat through the windows, an old house might be draughtier. But all buildings will lose heat because heat will always flow to a cooler place; if it was not cold outside you would not need the heating and there would be no flow.

Although this flow of heat cannot be stopped it can be slowed down. This means that less heat will be lost in a given period, so less energy will be needed to replace it; and less energy means lower fuel bills. The way to slow down the rate of heat loss is to use insulation materials in the fabric of the building. It is clear from the table that the walls and roof are likely to be the first parts to be insulated, as they make up the largest part of the total heat loss. Draughts however can be stopped up cheaply (see Chapter 15), so they will also be a high priority simply on the grounds of cost effectiveness.

Where to insulate

The position of insulation in a building is quite important. A house with internally insulated masonry walls, with a timber frame or built with other lightweight materials, is said to be thermally 'light' and to respond quickly to heating. The insulated surfaces of the rooms

External insulation with a rendered finish

15

A thermally massive solar-heated school

have little mass and therefore require little heating to make the building warm. But when the heating is turned off the building will cool quickly because the materials do not store heat.

A thermally 'heavy' house, made of dense masonry materials, insulated on the outside, will take a long time to heat up because the massive materials have a high thermal capacity and will need a lot of heat to bring them up to the required temperature of the building. The house will store casual energy such as the heat given off by the occupants, by electric lights and appliances and by the sun shining through the windows. When the heat source, whether intentional or casual, is removed, the heat that has been stored in the heavy walls is released slowly to the rooms as they cool down, just as an electric storage heater gives off heat during the day after it has been heated up at night.

The reason people say that old stone cottages with walls half a metre thick are warm in winter and pleasantly cool in summer has nothing to do with the insulation value of stone, which is very poor; it has to do with thermal mass. The thick walls store the heat put into the building and even out variations in the

internal temperature. If the weather becomes very cold the stored heat will delay the time when the effect of the lower temperature is felt indoors. Conversely in summer the building heats up very slowly and will therefore tend to feel cooler than a building with a quicker response.

The position of the insulation depends to some extent on the way the house is to be used. For example, if you are out all day and need heat only in the morning and evening, and at weekends, a structure with a quick response may be more appropriate as the house could be heated quickly when you come home. On the other hand a thermally heavy structure is more appropriate for a building that is to be heated more or less continuously.

In the real world nothing is straightforward and in the conversion of an existing building it may well be that other factors than the intended occupancy will determine the position of the insulation. Do not worry overmuch about this; it is perfectly possible to heat a light-weight structure continuously, although less easy to heat a heavy one intermittently. However, a lightweight structure will tend to over-heat if you design it to absorb solar energy

16

External insulation clad with boarding

through the windows, while a heavy structure will soak up this extra energy to be given out later. If you hope to make use of casual solar gains it is a good idea to try to achieve as much thermal mass as possible, using exposed quarry tiled or concrete floors with edge insulation, masonry internal partitions and external wall insulation.

Condensation

Wherever the insulation is it must be protected from condensation. Cooking, washing clothes, running a bath, using a gas cooker, and simply breathing, produce water vapour. The vapour produced by an average household each day is equivalent to about twelve litres of water. It diffuses through the building and as long as it remains as vapour there is no problem. The difficulty arises when the water vapour diffuses through the structure of the building to the outside, where the vapour pressure is lower. Warm air can hold a lot more water vapour than cold air, and when warm moist air

is cooled there comes a point where the air is saturated with vapour and will not hold any more. This is called the dewpoint. Any cooling below the dewpoint will cause the vapour to condense into water.

In winter the outside temperature may well be below the dewpoint for the warm moist air within the building. As the water vapour seeks to balance the difference in vapour pressure between inside and outside by diffusing through the structure, it will reach a point where the temperature in the walls is cold enough for the vapour to condense into water. If this point occurs within a material that may be damaged by water the result can be disastrous. Insulating materials work by trapping layers of still, dry air within them; and if they get full of water they cease to insulate, as water is a good conductor of heat.

To overcome the problem of water in the insulation it is essential to put a vapour barrier on the *warm* side of any insulating materials used in a building. It is also a good idea to arrange a ventilated cavity behind the insulation wherever possible, so that any water that passes through is evaporated by the air. A vapour barrier is any material that prevents the passage of water vapour, for example aluminium foil, heavy gauge polythene sheet with joints folded and taped, or even two coats of oil-based gloss paint. The gloss paint is not reckoned to be very effective as a vapour barrier and under no circumstances must it be applied to expanded polystyrene ceiling tiles, where it will become a fire hazard.

When a building is insulated the temperatures of the surfaces of walls, ceilings and other elements are raised, and if the temperature is above the dewpoint there will be no condensation on the surface. However, if there is no vapour barrier, condensation will occur within the wall (interstitial condensation), and once the insulation becomes saturated the condensation will spread to the inside wall, and may cause mould to grow. Insulation will therefore relieve the problem of condensation in your house, but there must be a vapour barrier and it must be in the right place, if the insulation is to reduce heat loss and condensation.

The advantages of insulation

Insulation is definitely the most effective way of saving energy in your home; the more exciting solutions, such as wind or solar power, are useful only when the demand for space heating and hot water have been minimised by the use of insulating materials. People sometimes worry about the amount of energy used to manufacture these materials, but, even if a relatively high technology material such as glass fibre is used, the energy that went into its manufacture will be paid for by the energy it saves in one winter, or at most two. For the rest of the building's life, provided that the insulation has been installed correctly it will be saving energy.

If a building is thoroughly insulated it will need a much smaller, simpler and cheaper heating system than the same building when not insulated. If you move into an old house, it is much better to spend money on insulating it to the point where you can heat it with a single stove rather than spend the same money on a conventional central heating system. The running costs of the insulated house will be very low compared with a centrally heated house with no insulation; yet the house will be kept just as warm. If you decide to put in central heating as well as insulation you will find that you can use a very much smaller boiler and smaller radiators; so you will pay less for the central heating system than if the house were not insulated.

Internal insulation before the plasterboard is fixed, showing the battens and polythene vapour barrier

Finally, it is worth pointing out that, in our view, a programme of complete insulation of all existing houses in the UK combined with the abandonment of electric space heating could reduce the national primary energy demand by about 10 per cent.

4 U values

Methods have been devised to provide an accurate picture of how heat is lost from a building by calculating the amount of heat lost through each part of the building. Using these methods, which are simple if rather tedious (a pocket calculator is a great help when it comes to the detailed calculations), the rate at which heat is lost through walls, floors, roof, windows, and so on can be worked out, and the results added together to show the heat loss from the whole house.

The figure which represents the heat loss rate of part of a building is called its U value. For example, a typical single-glazed window has a U value of about 5 Watts per square metre degree Celsius (centigrade). This means that every square metre of window will lose heat at a rate of 5W for each degree of temperature difference between the inside and outside. In other words, if the temperature inside is 20°C and the temperature outside is 19°C each square metre of window will lose 5W; if the temperature outside goes down to 0°C (freezing point) and the inside is kept at 20°C the heat lost through the glass will go up to

$5 \times 20 = 100W$. To maintain the temperature in the house 100W of heating will have to be provided for every square metre of glass.

Some typical U values for parts of buildings are shown in the first table on page 20. The lower the U value, the better the insulation value of the construction.

Example

To find the heat loss from a brick cavity wall with a single glazed metal-framed window, multiply the U value of the wall by the surface area of the wall, and the U value of the window by its own area. If the wall is 5 metres long and 2.3 metres high, with a window measuring 1 metre by 1.2 metres, the area will be $5 \times 2.3 = 11.5m^2$ minus the area of the window, $1.0 \times 1.2 = 1.2m^2$, giving a total wall area of $10.3m^2$. The heat loss through the wall will be 10.3×1.7 (the U value taken from the table)$=17.51W/degC$; the heat loss through the window will be $1.2 \times 5.6 = 6.72W/degC$; so the total heat loss through the wall will be $17.51 + 6.72 = 24.23W/degC$ for each degree of temperature difference.

19

Walls

	W/m² degC
225mm solid brick wall, plastered on inside	2.67
brick cavity wall, plastered on inside	1.70
cavity wall with outer leaf of brick and inner leaf of insulating blockwork	1.00
brick cavity wall with cavity filled with 50mm thick urea formaldehyde foam	0.45

Pitched roofs

tiles or slates on battens, roof space and plaster ceiling	3.18
tiles or slates on battens on felt, roof space and plaster ceiling	1.70
tiles or slates on battens on felt, roof space and plaster ceiling with 50mm glass fibre between ceiling joists	0.50

Flat roofs

three layers of felt on boards on joists, plaster ceiling	1.82

Ground floors

boards on joists:	detached house	0.68
	terraced house	0.53
concrete slab on hardcore:	detached house	0.76
	terraced house	0.48

Note: because all four edges of the floor of a detached house are exposed to the outside air, the floor has a greater rate of heat loss than the floor of a terraced house, of which only two parallel edges are exposed.

Glazing

single-glazed, severe exposure	6.7
single-glazed, average exposure	5.6
double-glazed, average exposure	3.4
double-glazed, south facing, sheltered exposure	2.8
triple-glazed, average exposure	2.5

elements	surface emissivity	direction of heat flow	m²°C/W
walls	high	horizontal	0.123
	low	horizontal	0.304
roofs and ceilings	high	upward	0.106
	low	upward	0.218
floors	high	downward	0.150
	low	downward	0.562

width of cavity	surface emissivity	resistance in m² °C/W	
		heat flow horizontal or upwards	heat flow downwards
5mm	high	0.11	0.11
	low	0.18	0.18
20mm or more	high	0.18	0.21
	low	0.35	1.06

Standard U values — floors and walls

A problem obviously arises in the calculation of heat loss if the type of construction in which you are interested is not listed in any table of U values or if you want to find out the effect on a known U value of adding some extra insulation. To deal with this you will need to find out how U values are derived from more basic information. The following section is based on the calculation of so-called 'standard U values' which are used to allow comparison between one building or method of construction and another. These calculations can be used to find the U values of walls and roofs but ground floors and windows are treated separately later in this chapter as they cannot be worked out from first principles.

The 'standard' means that various assumptions are made about moisture contents of materials, solar radiation and convection effects, and rates of air flow in ventilated cavities. In real life all these factors can change with the weather, the degree of exposure of the building and other variables, but for the calculation of standard U values, which are a fairly close match to reality, the variables must be standardised.

The formula
The U value of any construction is the reciprocal of its resistance; thus, $U = \frac{1}{R}$. The total resistance, R, is the sum of the resistances of each element of the construction. Thus:

$$R = R_{si} + R_{so} + R_{cav} + R_1 + R_2 \ldots + R_n$$

In this equation the symbols have the following meanings.

R_{si} is the resistance of the internal surface; this is the insulating property of the thin layer of still air that is immediately next to the material. This layer is still because it is held by the roughness (sometimes microscopic) of the surface, and as it is still it does not convect the heat away. As you come further away from the surface the air begins to move, adding convection heat losses to those caused by conduction and radiation across the layer of still air.

The internal surface resistance is affected by the emissivity of the surface, this being the ability of the material to reflect or absorb radiant energy. All building materials including glass are assumed to have high emissivity: the low emissivity values in the table which gives some values for R_{si} (centre, opposite) should be used only for unpainted metal surfaces such as aluminium, stainless steel, galvanised steel, and so on, which reflect radiated heat.

R_{so} is the resistance of the outside surface layer of still air. This value is often assumed to vary with the degree of exposure of the building, but for standard U values these variations (which make very little difference to the final answer) are ignored, and the values in the table below are used:

element	surface emissivity	m² °C/W
wall	high	0.055
	low	0.067
roof	high	0.045
	low	0.053

Note: a floor which is exposed to the open air on the underside, a floor over an archway, or one that projects out from a building, should be considered as it were a roof in terms of the R_{so} value.

R_{cav} is the resistance of any cavity in the construction. If, for example, a cavity has aluminium foil on both sides, its insulating value will be improved because the heat loss caused by radiation will have been reduced. If there is more than one cavity then a value for R_{cav} is put into the equation for each one. The standard values are as shown in the third table, opposite. The 'surface emissivity' column refers to the emissivity of the materials which make up the sides of the cavity.

These values apply also to roof spaces which have a small amount of ventilation to prevent condensation and to the cavities in normal cavity walls, but for air spaces which are ventilated the values in the table overleaf should be used.

element	m²°C/W
loft space between flat ceiling and tiled, but not felted, pitched roof	0.11
air space between tiles or slates and roofing felt on a pitched roof (the value for the attic space can be found in the table of cavities (p.20)	0.12
air space behind tiles on a tile-hung wall	0.12

R_1, R_2, etc., are the resistances of the materials used in the construction. These are worked out by dividing the thickness of the material in metres (remembering that 1mm=0.001 metres) by its thermal conductivity or k value.

The k values of most common building materials have been worked out in laboratory tests, and where these materials are used in a dry condition the k value can be read from the table and used directly in calculations. However, masonry materials that are constantly exposed to rain, such as the exterior walls of a house, will lose some of their insulating value because of the moisture. The table below gives some examples. The 'dry' values should be used for masonry in the inner leaf of a cavity wall and the 'wet' values for the outer leaf. Values for densities not given can be obtained by interpolation.

Some examples of typical dry densities for various masonry materials available in the UK are given immediately below. These can be used with the previous table to work out the k value of the material.

material	kg/m³
ordinary bricks in cement mortar	1600–2000
engineering bricks	2000–2400
concrete blocks (dense), reinforced concrete	2000
'Lignacite' solid blocks	1400
'Thermalite' aerated concrete blocks	730
sandstone (York, millstone grit, etc.)	2200
limestone (Bath, Cotswold, Ketton, etc.)	2000–2200
granite	2600

If the wall has no cavity there will be no gap between the dry and the wet sides, so the k value for a wall exposed to the rain should be used.

Finally, to calculate U values, you will also need the list of k values (opposite) for non-masonry building materials, which include insulating materials.

Example
Using these values and the formulae given earlier, you can now calculate the U value of almost anything. As an example, consider a

bulk dry density	brickwork protected from rain, 1 per cent moisture	concrete or stone protected from rain, 3 per cent moisture	brick or concrete or stone exposed to rain, 5 per cent moisture
200	0.09	0.11	0.12
400	0.12	0.15	0.16
600	0.15	0.19	0.20
800	0.19	0.23	0.26
1000	0.24	0.30	0.33
1200	0.31	0.38	0.42
1400	0.42	0.51	0.57
1600	0.54	0.66	0.73
1800	0.71	0.87	0.96
2000	0.92	1.13	1.24
2200	1.18	1.45	1.60
2400	1.49	1.83	2.00

The percentages at the top of the columns show the moisture content expressed as a percentage of volume.

k values for building materials	W/m²°C
softwood	0.13
hardboard, standard	0.13
plywood	0.14
hardwood	0.15
wood chipboard	0.15
gypsum plasterboard	0.16
polystyrene (solid not expanded)	0.17
vermiculite plaster	0.20
glass-reinforced plastic	0.23
PVC flooring	0.40
asbestos cement sheet	0.40
gypsum plaster	0.46
steel	0.50
sand–cement render	0.53
water	0.58
asphalt roofing	0.58
aluminium alloy	160.00
copper	200.00

k values for insulating materials

expanded polyurethane	0.026
urea formaldehyde foam	0.030
extruded polystyrene	0.034
expanded polystyrene	0.035
fibreglass quilt and resin-bonded slab	0.036
expanded polystyrene beads	0.04
mineral wool mat	0.042
mineral wool loose fibres	0.045
felt underlay	0.045
foamed glass	0.05
carpet	0.055
vermiculite granules	0.065
cork flooring	0.085
cellular rubber underlay	0.10
wood wool slab	0.10
strawboard	0.11

---

wall which has an outer leaf of brick 100mm thick, a 50mm cavity and an inner leaf of 100mm aerated concrete blocks with 12mm of plaster as an internal finish. Remembering that $U = \frac{1}{R}$ and that

$$R = R_{si} + R_{so} + R_{cav} + R_1 + R_2 \ldots + R_n$$

it is easy to substitute the values given in the tables into the equation as follows:

$R_{si} = 0.123$ because the wall has a high emissivity, as it is not made of polished metal, and the heat will flow out horizontally (because it is a wall).

$R_{so} = 0.055$ because it is a wall of high emissivity.

$R_{cav} = 0.18$ because the cavity is more than 20mm wide, has high emissivity sides (brick and concrete), the heat flow is horizontal and the cavity is not deliberately ventilated.

$R_1 = \frac{0.1}{0.96}$, where 0.1 is 100mm expressed in metres and 0.96 is the k value given in the table for ordinary bricks (1800kg/m³ bulk dry density) if they are exposed to rain, as they will be in the outer leaf of a cavity wall.

$R_2 = \frac{0.1}{0.21}$ The thickness is as before, and the k value is for concrete protected from rain. As the table gives no value for the density of 730kg/m³ of aerated concrete, a value midway between those for 600kg/m³ and 800kg/m³ is used.

$R_3 = \frac{0.012}{0.46}$ The thickness is 0.012 metres, and the k value is that for gypsum plastering from the table.

Adding up all these figures the result is:

$$R = 0.123 + 0.055 + 0.18 + \frac{0.1}{0.96} + \frac{0.1}{0.21} + \frac{0.012}{0.46}$$
$$R = 0.123 + 0.055 + 0.18 + 0.104 + 0.476 + 0.026$$
$$R = 0.964$$
$$U = \frac{1}{0.964} = 1.037 \text{W/m}^2\text{degC.}$$

Having obtained this value and having seen that it is not going to give you very much insulation, you may perhaps decide to try the effect of filling the cavity with urea formaldehyde foam. To calculate the effect of this, you needn't go back to the beginning and add up all the internal and external surface resistances; you simply take out the cavity and add the foam to the U value just calculated.

First the total resistivity is obtained. As $R = \frac{1}{U}$ and in our example $U = 1.037$, R is 0.964. From the previous calculation R_{cav} is 0.18, so the resistance of the wall minus the cavity is $0.964 - 0.18 = 0.784$. The thickness of the foam will be the same as that of the cavity, 50mm or 0.05 metres, and the k value from the table is 0.03, so the resistance of the foam will be $\frac{0.05}{0.03} = 1.667$. When this is added to the R of the rest of the wall the result is $0.784 + 1.667 = 2.451$ which gives a U value $U = \frac{1}{2.451} = 0.408 \text{W/m}^2\text{degC.}$ The foam has more than doubled the insulation value of the wall.

Ground floors

This technique for adding to or altering known U values is very useful when it comes to dealing with heat losses through ground floors. The U values of ground floors, which lose heat to the earth under a building, cannot be calculated from first principles as can walls and roofs, but the Building Research Establishment has published tables of U values for ground floors of differing dimensions. The dimensions are important because the floor loses heat most rapidly round the edges, whereas the earth under the middle of a very large building may be more or less at the same temperature as the building.

The first table relates to ground floors made of concrete. The thermal conductivity of earth is similar to that of concrete so the thickness of the slab is not important as the slab and the earth are assumed to be acting as one. The presence of a layer of hardcore under the concrete also makes no difference to the U value for the same reason.

dimensions of floor in metres	U value for floor with four exposed edges
over 150×30	0.16*
×15	0.28*
× 7.5	0.48*
150×60	0.11
×30	0.18
60×60	0.15
×30	0.21
×15	0.32
30×30	0.26
×15	0.36
× 7.5	0.55
15×15	0.45
× 7.5	0.62
7.5× 7.5	0.76
3×3	1.47

*These values also apply to floors which are losing heat from two parallel edges, so if you live in a terraced house which measures 7.5 metres from front to back and has a concrete ground floor, the floor will have a U value of 0.48W/m²°C.

If you live in a short row of houses or in a semi-detached house, the dimensions used for finding the U value of your floor should be those of the whole group or pair of houses, not just of your own house.

The next table gives the U values of suspended timber floors, both bare or with vinyl or lino, and covered with fitted carpets or cork tiles.

dimensions of floor in metres	bare or with vinyl or lino	with carpet or cork
over 150×30	0.18	0.18
×15	0.33	0.33
× 7.5	0.53	0.52
150×60	0.14	0.14
×30	0.21	0.21
60×60	0.16	0.16
×30	0.24	0.23
×15	0.37	0.36
30×30	0.28	0.27
×15	0.39	0.38
× 7.5	0.57	0.55
15×15	0.45	0.44
× 7.5	0.61	0.59
7.5× 7.5	0.68	0.65
3×3	1.05	0.99

These U values can be modified as described earlier (see page 23) so that the effect of adding extra insulating materials can be calculated. All the U values for floors given here are used with the full temperature difference between inside and outside; it is not necessary to make any allowance for the earth being warmer than the air.

Windows

There are also published U values for different types of windows, single, double and triple-glazed. The table shows that the insulating value of double-glazing increases as the gap between the two panes of glass is increased up to a maximum of 20mm; after that the U value is not affected. The table opposite, above, gives the U values of windows through the glass only and does not include the frames.

glazing	exposure		
	sheltered	normal	severe
single	5.0	5.6	6.7
double: gap 3mm	3.6	4.0	4.4
6mm	3.2	3.4	3.8
12mm	2.8	3.0	3.3
20mm or more	2.8	2.9	3.2
triple: each gap 3mm	2.8	3.0	3.3
6mm	2.3	2.5	2.6
12mm	2.0	2.1	2.2
20mm or more	1.9	2.0	2.1

The degrees of exposure of the windows are as follows:

sheltered: houses in town centres
normal: most suburban and country areas
severe: tower blocks, hill tops and coasts

The U values relate to clear or transparent glass, not to the mirrored heat reflecting types, which reduce heat loss through radiation. Data for these types of glass are best obtained from the manufacturers.

Because windows usually have frames, the area of the frame must be considered when calculating the U value of the window as a whole. Metal window frames have roughly the same U value as glass, unless they are designed to incorporate a 'thermal break' to reduce the heat flow through the metal. Wooden frames offer some degree of insulation as is shown in the following table of U values for windows and frames.

For individual windows the area of glass and the area of the frame can be measured and the U value of each worked out separately if you really want an exact figure, but the values in the table will give a useful first approximation.

Total structural heat loss

Using the measured areas of the doors, windows, roofs, walls and other elements of your house, and the calculated U values (or values from tables) for each different element, you can work out the total structural heat loss from your house by multiplying the U value of each element by the area of the element, and then adding the results together to give a figure in Watts per degree C. When multiplied by the difference between the inside and outside temperatures this figure shows the heat energy required to balance the heat lost through the fabric of the house.

window type	percentage of total window area occupied by frame	exposure		
		sheltered	normal	severe
single glazed				
metal casement	20	5.0	5.6	6.7
wood casement	30	3.8	4.3	4.9
double-glazed 20mm gap				
metal with thermal break	20	3.0	3.2	3.5
wood	30	2.3	2.5	2.7

5 Ventilation and Heat Loss

Draughts

As shown in Chapter 3, a typical house may lose up to 15 per cent of its heat through draughts. The warm air inside the house is replaced by cold air from outside coming through the gaps that inevitably exist in any building around doors and windows. The incoming cold air must then be heated if the temperature of the house is not to drop. The more cold air that comes in the more energy must be used to heat it, so clearly it is worth trying to reduce draughts. Draughts are a form of accidental ventilation, so the heat loss they cause is called ventilation heat loss. A completely sealed building would have no ventilation heat loss but after a while the occupants would die through lack of oxygen!

Ventilation rates, whether intentional or accidental, are measured in terms of 'air changes per hour' (ac/hr). If a house is said to have a ventilation rate of 1 air change per hour, it means that in one hour all the air in the house is exchanged for air from outside. It is not easy to measure air change rates without a lot of very complicated equipment, and even if you can measure the rate it won't be much use, as ventilation varies with windspeed, degree of exposure, type of house, standard of construction and other variable factors. The BRE have measured ventilation rates in apparently identical houses on a new estate and have found that one house could have twice the rate of another, even with all the windows and doors shut. As a very rough guide, a Victorian house might have a ventilation rate of 2ac/hr or more, a modern house a rate of 1ac/hr, and a well draught sealed house a rate of 0.5ac/hr.

In spite of the belief left over from Victorian days that fresh air is a Good Thing, a well sealed building will be much easier to keep warm, and provided the windows can be opened if necessary, the building regulations will not be contravened. In a house with good structural insulation the loss of heat due to ventilation may well be as much as that lost through the structure, and this is as good a reason as any for doing all you can to reduce draughts.

You are very unlikely to be able to seal a house so well that there would not be enough

A shutter is used to draught seal a window

air to breathe; you need only 6.8m³ per person per hour of fresh air, which in a house with a volume of 410m³ would be about 0.016ac/hr. A large closed woodburning stove with a fuel consumption of 1kg of wood per hour needs 20m³ of air per hour, so even five people plus a big stove would need only 0.13ac/hr. You are unlikely to be able to achieve a lower ventilation rate than 0.5ac/hr, so there is little need to worry unduly about being unable to breathe, and if you have a party you can always open a window if people start gasping.

However, you must not reduce the ventilation rate by draught sealing any room which has a heating appliance with no flue, such as a gas geyser, paraffin stove or calor gas heater. You run the risk of being suffocated if you use one of these, particularly the gas types, in a room with insufficient oxygen. Open fires, although they have flues, are so inefficient that they need a lot of air to work successfully, and may not burn well in a building with too low a ventilation rate.

Ventilation can be reduced first and most simply by keeping doors and windows shut; even a window that is just ajar can let in a lot of cold air. The second simple control is to draught seal all doors and windows as described in Chapter 14, for the gap round an average door is equivalent to having a whole brick missing from your wall. Finally, draughts can be controlled by porches, which act as air locks (see Chapter 21).

The formula

The formula used to calculate the heat loss through ventilation is $Q_v = 0.36 \times V \times N$.

Q_v is the ventilation heat loss in W/degC.

0.36 is derived from the 'volumetric specific heat' of air, which is the heat required to raise the temperature of one cubic metre of air by 1 deg C. The specific heat of air is 1300 Joules per cubic metre degree Celsius (J/m³ degC); but if this figure were used in the equation the result would be in Joules per hour. To obtain an answer in Watts, which are Joules per second, 1300 is divided by 3600, the number of seconds in an hour, to give $\frac{1300}{3600} = 0.36$.

V is the volume in cubic metres of the space being heated.

N is the number of air changes per hour. This will have to be guessed, but as stated before, a very rough guide would be to take a house that feels cold and draughty as having a rate of 5ac/hr, a Victorian house as having a rate of 2ac/hr, a more modern house a rate of 1.5 or 1ac/hr, and a well draught sealed house a rate of 0.5ac/hr.

Example

As an example consider a bungalow, recently built, with an internal floor area of 81m² and a floor to ceiling height of 2.3 metres. The volume is $81 \times 2.3 = 186.3m^3$ (the roof space is not considered part of the volume, as you are not trying to heat it). As the bungalow was recently built, and assuming that it does not feel too draughty, N could be taken as 1ac/hr. Putting these values into the ventilation equation gives the following:

$Q_v = 0.36 \times V \times N$

$Q_v = 0.36 \times 186.3 \times 1$

Q_v = approximately 67W/degC

Thus for every degree of temperature difference between inside and outside it would take about 67W to replace the heat loss caused by ventilation. If it were freezing outside and you wanted the house to be at 20°C you would need more than one kilowatt in order to replace the heat being lost to cold draughts $(67 \times 20 = 1340W)$.

Condensation and smells

It can be argued that reducing ventilation will lead to condensation and stale air. Provided that draught sealing is combined with insulation which incorporates the correct vapour barriers as described in Chapter 3, the reduction in ventilation should not cause condensation. If condensation does occur it can be dealt with at source, usually in the kitchen or bathroom, by installing an extract fan controlled by a dew stat. This is a device which turns the fan on only if condensation is likely to form, thus avoiding unnecessary ventilation. An easier solution is to open a window a little bit if you find the condensation a nuisance, but remember to shut it again as soon as the condensation has cleared. Smells can be dealt with in the same way.

Finally, it is not worth doing all this draught sealing to cut down ventilation loss if you leave windows or doors open. As your awareness of the ways a building loses heat increases you may find that you develop a greater 'energy consciousness' and that habits like shutting doors and turning off lights become automatic.

Selecting a heating system

Once you know the structural heat loss and the ventilation heat loss the two figures can be added together to give the total heat loss from your house. As an example, consider a house which has a structural heat loss rate of 225W/degC and a ventilation heat loss rate of 75W/deg C. By adding together the two figures you reach a total heat loss rate of 300W/deg C. This figure can then be used to work out the size of the heating system and the amount of energy that will be consumed in a season's heating.

Your heating system, be it gas, solar or wood powered, must be able to supply enough energy to keep the building warm in the worst possible conditions: it is no good trying to heat a room with a 1kW fire if the room loses heat at a rate of 2kW in very cold weather. The energy which the heating system must be capable of supplying is therefore based on the maximum likely difference between inside and outside temperatures. In southern England the value used is often 20°C or 21°C, but in the north of Scotland or other areas known to be cold it might be 25°C or more. The use of too high a value for the temperature difference would result in a heating system that is too big for the job it has to do; it would work at under capacity and inefficiently almost all the time.

Taking the example of a house with a total heat loss of 300W/deg C, and assuming a temperature difference of 20°C, the chosen heating system must be able to supply $300 \times 20 = 6000W$ or 6kW.

A 6kW heater does not supply heat at a rate of 6kW all the winter; if it did you would be too hot most of the time, and the fuel bills would be enormous. A properly designed heating system supplies enough energy to maintain the temperature of your house at the desired level; if it is warm outside the system will provide little energy, if it is cold it will provide a lot.

Degree days

To estimate the energy you might use over a whole heating season (usually assumed to be from 1 October to 30 April), you need to measure the way the outside temperature changes from day to day because it is this variation that determines the energy required. The daily change in temperature can be allowed for by the use of 'degree days' which give a measure of the variations between inside and outside temperatures.

The degree days used by the Department of Energy assume a base temperature of 15.5°C: if the average outside temperature over 24 hours is 14.5°C (i.e., one degree less than 15.5°C), that is one degree day. The figures given by the Department of Energy are actually based on a constant indoor temperature of 18.3°C, but the figure of 15.5°C used to calculate the number of degree days allows for the heat gains to the building from the sun, electric lights, cookers and of course people.

These so called 'casual gains' are not insignificant, particularly in a well insulated house. As an example, a 100W light bulb gives out 100W of heat, an adult male is worth 114W if seated and at rest, 144W if eating, and 264W if dancing. The figure of 18.3°C may seem slightly low as an average temperature for a house but the Department says it is 'considered comfortable for normal domestic purposes'. In fact, most houses are not heated to this level at night but might be kept warmer in daytime, so the temperatures average out.

In the UK, degree day figures are calculated by the Meteorological Office, and if you want to know how they do it, all is explained in a free Department of Energy booklet called *Fuel efficiency booklet 7, Degree Days* (see Bibliography). The numbers of degree days per month and per year (on an average of twenty years) for different regions are given below. The figures range from 2605 degree days for North East Scotland, to 1822 for the South West, with most parts of the UK being surprisingly similar to each other at about 2200.

Example

Degree day figures can be used to find the estimated energy consumption of a building over a whole winter's heating season. Taking the

	Sept	Oct	Nov	Dec	Jan	Feb	Mar	Apr	May	Total
Thames Valley (1)	56	132	256	336	346	304	282	197	113	2,022
South Eastern (2)	84	161	280	359	370	329	310	224	145	2,162
Southern (3)	76	144	258	331	339	307	294	214	141	2,104
South Western (4)	55	114	215	278	293	272	267	197	131	1,822
Severn Valley (5)	69	143	259	332	344	311	292	209	129	2,088
Midland (6)	92	172	290	362	371	335	318	233	152	2,325
West Pennine (7)	79	155	280	350	359	323	304	222	139	2,211
North Western (8)	95	168	296	361	366	333	319	239	163	2,340
Borders (9)	108	183	300	364	376	343	332	259	193	2,458
North Eastern (10)	87	170	296	364	374	334	317	234	154	2,330
East Pennine (11)	77	156	282	353	362	323	304	217	139	2,213
East Anglia (12)	74	153	283	363	378	334	315	232	143	2,275
West Scotland (13)	106	179	303	359	368	335	316	235	163	2,364
East Scotland (14)	106	185	308	371	379	343	326	252	189	2,459
North East Scotland (15)	124	199	322	384	396	359	345	270	206	2,605
Wales (16)	72	138	239	304	323	301	292	228	156	2,053
Northern Ireland (17)	100	171	288	347	359	325	311	237	167	2,305

The figures in brackets refer to the map overleaf.

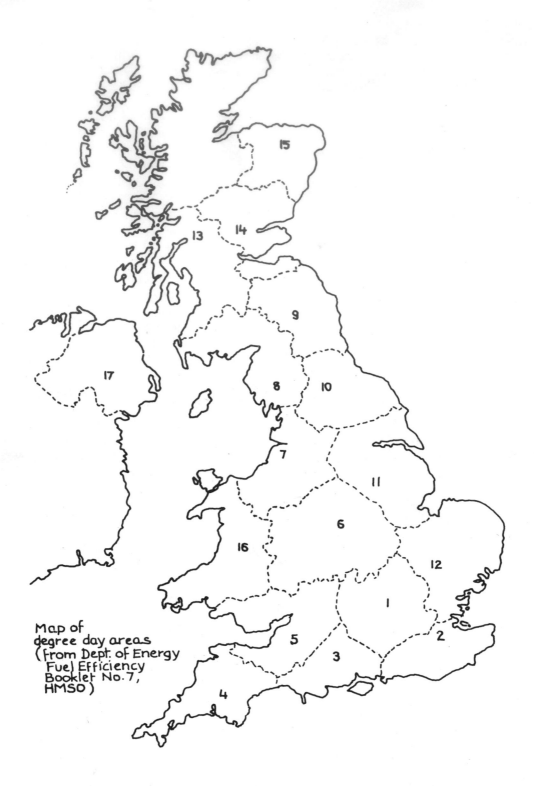

Map of
degree day areas
(from Dept. of Energy
Fuel Efficiency
Booklet No.7,
HMSO)

example we used earlier of a house where the heat loss was 300W/deg C, this heat loss is multiplied by 24 (the number of hours in a day) and then by the number of degree days in the area where the house is sited. The answer is divided by 1000 to give the answer in kilowatt hours. Assuming the house is in the Midland region, which has 2325 degree days, the total energy required will be:

$300 \times 24 \times 2325 = 16740000Wh = 16740kWh$.

The same house in the South West would use 13118kWh, while in North East Scotland it would use 18756kWh, or over 40 per cent more energy than the house in the South West. To obtain more details, the monthly degree day figures can be used and daily figures are available from the Meteorological Office.

You are now in a position to work out the energy you use for space heating at the moment, the energy you could expect to save by insulating and the amount of useful energy on a daily, monthly or annual basis that you will need to keep warm.

6 Comfort Temperatures

It is easy enough to measure the air temperature of a room with a thermometer but it is far more difficult to say at what temperature a person feels comfortable in a room. Whether internal good feeling predisposes us to comfort and emotional upset causes us to be more critical of our environment is something that cannot be gauged. Watching a good late-night thriller on the television you may not notice the drop in room temperature that has occurred since the central heating automatically switched itself off at 10 pm. The film is absorbing, the chair ensures that your body is relaxed, the elderberry wine is of a particularly promising vintage and you finished the autumn digging in the morning.

All the scientists are able to do is measure the physical conditions within a room, such as air temperature, humidity, the surface temperature of walls, floor and ceiling, and the spread of draughts within the room and then, noting how the people are dressed and what they are doing, they ask them how comfortable they feel. By doing a survey in a large enough sample of buildings they can produce a range of conditions within which people engaged in certain activities can be said to be comfortable. This in turn leads to official tables of recommended temperatures to be achieved in various buildings: to find these, in the UK, refer to *The Shops, Offices and Railway Premises Act* and the Parker Morris recommended temperatures for Local Authority housing.

The environmental measurements that can be taken within a room relate to how people lose heat from their bodies. Unless you are ill your body temperature should be around 37°C. This relatively high temperature means that each person continually loses heat to the surroundings. Heat is generated within the body as food is digested. The more work we do, the more heat is generated and the greater is our need for food. Sawing wood for two hours on a frosty Sunday afternoon will produce a better appetite for tea-time crumpets than sitting reading in front of the fire. However, because most of our calorie intake is used simply to keep the body functioning we still need to eat even in hot climates. At rest you give off a little over 100W and this can rise to around 250W for work such as scrubbing the floor.

Providing the conditions that suit a given level of activity remain constant, you remain comfortable. When conditions change, most people's bodies, except those of the very young, the ill and the very old, compensate automatically by altering the rate at which heat is lost from the skin's surface. If these compensatory mechanisms are not adequate you might increase your insulation by putting on a jumper when the sun goes in, or you might increase the rate at which air movement removes heat from your skin surface by opening a window on a hot day. The only time you are unable to practise this type of automatic compensation is when you are asleep. Going to sleep with three blankets on and the window open on a frosty night may cause you to wake hot and clammy the next morning when the weather has changed to a warm muggy drizzle.

The 100W rate of heat loss at rest is determined by two main factors: one is the temperature difference between your skin and the surrounding mass of air (which governs the heat lost by convection); the other is the difference in temperature between your skin and the surface temperatures of the walls, floor, furniture of the room (which governs the heat lost by radiation). The amount of water in the air of the room, the humidity, has very little effect on the heat loss balance and, therefore, on comfort. It is only when you are already hot and sweating that humidity has any effect. This is why we tend to feel uncomfortable on hot, humid days.

Quality of heating

The fact that we lose heat by both radiation and convection also has a bearing on the different types of heating that can be used within a room in order to maintain comfortable conditions.

If you are sitting in a room where the air temperature is very low, but you are near a source of radiant heat (such as a stove which was lit early in the morning), you may still feel comfortable. You are gaining more radiant heat than you are losing and, even though the heat

Radiant heat from a stove

lost to the cold air may be considerable, the total heat loss rate is still in balance.

The amount of heat lost from your body will also remain constant if you sit near an electric fan heater. Here you will be hotter than the warm air which might be at 20°C and you will continue to radiate heat to the air and the surrounding surfaces of the room (which are at less than air temperature); but there will be very little heat lost by convection to the warmed air.

A more normal central heating system with water-filled radiators both warms the air by setting up convection currents and radiates out heat to anyone standing near the radiators, as the surface temperature of a radiator is higher than that of skin. Interestingly, many people will say that they feel more comfortable when seated next to a source of radiant heat (a coal fire or a stove) than in a room with central heating.

33

A centrally placed stove

Insulating to control room temperature

By insulating your house you alter how comfortable you feel within it. Apart from reducing the heat loss which may mean that the building can be heated with, say, a single, centrally placed stove, the insulation will affect the temperatures of the surfaces surrounding you within a room. When the room is heated these surfaces will be at the same temperature as the air within the room and providing the

Draught sealed windows with shutters

The shutters closed at night

windows are covered with insulated shutters there will be no very cold spots to which you will be losing heat through radiation. Less heat will be needed to keep you feeling comfortable. At the same time, if you have stopped up all the draughts, there will be no cold air to increase your heat loss by convection. Draughts, which usually only blow about the feet, induce a feeling of discomfort as they cool only a part of the body.

What you may lose in setting up a house that consumes little energy is the control of separate room temperatures that some forms of central heating now give. It would not be possible to pre-set temperatures in an insulated house heated by a single source of radiant heat such as a woodstove. The room containing the stove would be the warmest but the stove would also warm the room above it, and, to some extent, those around it, allowing for the fact that warmed air would rise up the stairwell. The only way you could control the heating of a room would be by opening and shutting doors. Such a system might be suitable for a house that was continuously occupied. At the other extreme where the insulation is placed on the inside walls, each room can be very quickly

warmed up by using a gas fire in each; such a system might suit a household out at school and work each day. If you do some hard physical work in this type of insulated room you may end up feeling rather hot; but work leading to a heat loss rate of 175W (moderate housework such as changing a bed) is generally done only for a short time in most rooms, except perhaps the kitchen.

The table on page 36 shows four types of work, the rooms with which they are associated and the recommended temperatures for those rooms in local authority housing.

What the recommended temperatures do not allow for are different patterns of use, such as bedrooms which children might use as playrooms during the day or as study rooms in the evening. Using systems such as central heating often with pre-set temperatures also tends to pre-set the ways in which the house is used. In an insulated house which is continuously occupied, it is much easier to keep all the rooms at a reasonably comfortable temperature which may free the way in which they are used. If a room is warm you will use it whereas you may be unwilling to suffer half an hour

	recommended temperatures in °C	heat loss rate in Watts, female (male 20 per cent higher)			
		65 (sleeping)	90 (sitting)	125 (light work)	175 (moderate work)
kitchen	13			x	x
living rooms	18		x	x	occasionally
bedrooms in daytime use	18	x		x	x
stairway/hall	13			x	x

reading in discomfort while you wait for a bedroom to warm from 15°C to 20°C.

Clothing

It is far easier to alter the amount of clothing you wear than it is to adjust the temperature of a room. Today the levels of insulation of our clothing are less than was usual at the turn of the century; we have become accustomed to having our buildings heated and to wearing less. We also vary the amount of clothes we wear according to the seasons. If you are wearing a shirt and jeans in the summer you might need a temperature of 23°C to feel comfortable when sitting indoors; but if you wear a shirt and jeans, *and* a sweater, woollen socks and vest in winter, you will need only a temperature of 20°C indoors. The fact that clothing is adaptable solves the problem of varying the temperature of a room to suit the activity. Add an overcoat to your normal winter wear and you could sit happily in a room heated to 17°C, but for the fact that you do not expect to have to wear an overcoat indoors, so that you are unlikely to say that you feel 'comfortable' in one.

For the reasons discussed, any scale of temperatures recommended to give comfort within a building must be fairly arbitrary. However, if you insulate your house and put in some kind of heating system, whether a single stove, central heating or even a low temperature solar-heated water system, you should find some place within the building where you feel comfortable wearing normal clothing. As a general rule, you can leave bedrooms in the insulated house to be warmed by the heat rising through the floor and up the stairs. It is possible (according to the Building Research Establishment) for most people, except for babies, the old and the ill, to sleep happily when the temperature goes below 0°C. But if you are to be able to force yourself out of bed and to dress comfortably in the morning perhaps 15°C would be a better target temperature. The sitting room should contain the source of heat in order to maintain the temperature at a comfortable 20°C; but you can get away with heating the kitchen to only around 17°C.

Bedroom (showing prefabricated chimney)

As mentioned in Chapter 5 casual gains, such as the sun coming through windows, will alter the amount of heat within the building on different days. But if you are willing to substitute the never varying temperatures of a central heating system (with the consistently high bill) for the energy-saving methods of insulation and reduced heating, you may find that you accept more variable temperatures. On cold cloudy days it may be necessary to shut the bedroom doors and wear an extra jumper; but the fact that in so doing you are saving energy may help you to feel both physically and mentally more comfortable.

7 Solar Heating

The Building Research Establishment estimates that the average household uses 170 litres of hot water daily at a temperature of 55°C. This represents a useful energy demand of about 3350kWh per year. Another BRE estimate gives the consumption per person as 50 litres per day, with a useful energy demand of 18kWh per person per week, or about 3750kWh per year for a four-person household. The BRE also reckons that a solar collector with an area of $4m^2$ could supply 1400kWh of useful energy per year, less than half the annual demand of a typical household. Even if the solar energy replaces on-peak electricity, which is the most expensive way to heat water, the value of the 1400kWh of electricity saved will not be very high and the saving in financial terms will not be great.

Before considering solar energy it is worth trying to reduce the demand for hot water, as this will save conventional fuel and allow a solar system eventually to make a greater proportional contribution to water heating. The obvious way to reduce the amount of energy used to heat water is to put a thick jacket of insulation round the hot water cylinder and the hot pipes as described in Chapter 12. A further contribution to energy saving can be made by installing spray taps which use less water. It would also help simply to get into the habit of not washing under running taps and to mend leaking washers (again see Chapter 12).

Only when you have carried out all possible schemes to reduce the need for energy is it worth considering the use of solar energy to heat water. If you do then decide to put in a solar collector you will gain more useful energy from it if you alter your habits to coincide with the course of the sun. Do the washing on sunny days when you collect lots of heat and have hot baths after a day of sunshine rather than on a day of overcast skies. By doing this you will use the solar energy to its best advantage and reduce your need for back-up fuels.

Calculating the energy gained

You may want to calculate how much energy a solar collector will give you. A $4m^2$ average collector, facing south and angled at 30° to the

Commercial solar panels

horizontal, will yield about 1400kWh of useful energy annually in the London area, and will give most of this energy in the summer. Further details are available using data from BRE computer studies based on solar radiation figures for Kew, just outside London. The results show the energy *received* by 1m² of collector surface. To work out how much useful energy is collected, multiply these figures by the collector efficiency which the BRE takes to be 35 per cent over the whole year; so you multiply by 0.35. In the table below, the first figure in each column is the energy received and the second is the useful

energy assuming 35 per cent efficiency. Both figures are in kilowatt hours per square metre per month.

Note: if you think your collector has an efficiency less than 35 per cent you can use the first figure in each column and multiply by your assumed efficiency.

Calculation from first principles

If you live in the North of England or somewhere else a long way from Kew you can calculate the energy collected from first principles. This is a long and tedious job, so it is only worth doing if you are really anxious to know. Because Kew is about the only place with detailed solar data, the details of the behaviour of the radiation in the following formulae are based on averages of Kew figures. For the number of hours of bright sunshine, use figures relating to your *own* site. We do not know if this method of calculation is accurate, but it gives a close tie-in with the BRE figures so should not be too far off the mark.

To start with you need to know the number of hours of bright sunshine per month where you live. The best place to ask is your local public library where they may have a copy of the *Meteorological Office Climatological Atlas of the British Isles* (HMSO, 1952) or perhaps some more recent figures. Failing that, a local

Month	Solar energy at Kew in kWh							
	Angle between collector and the horizontal							
	30°		45°		60°		90°	
Jan	25	9	29	10	29	10	28	10
Feb	38	13	40	14	39	14	35	12
March	82	29	86	30	82	29	67	23
April	100	35	96	34	90	32	65	23
May	133	47	127	44	115	40	79	28
June	143	50	132	46	118	41	78	27
July	132	46	125	44	111	39	74	26
Aug	121	42	117	41	106	37	77	27
Sept	97	34	97	34	93	33	74	26
Oct	65	23	70	24	68	24	58	20
Nov	33	12	36	13	38	13	35	12
Dec	24	8	26	9	28	10	26	9
Total	993	348	981	343	917	322	696	243

RAF station might be able to help, or a university. If you use the *Climatological Atlas* you will have to use the data from the weather station nearest you.

There are two separate calculations to be made for the solar energy received by a collector, one for direct radiation (which is self-explanatory) and one for indirect radiation, which is that part of the radiation that is scattered off clouds, reflected from the ground and comes from the whole sky rather than just from the sun itself.

The formula for direct radiation

In a given month a solar collector will *receive* $0.698 \, \mathrm{I} \, \mathrm{n} \sin(\theta+a)$ kWh of direct radiation per square metre.

I is the average monthly intensity of direct solar radiation on days of high radiation, measured in calories per square centimetre per minute on a surface normal to the radiation. You do not have to worry too much about that definition; here is a table of values for I. The figure of 0.698 in the formula converts the cal/cm²/min to kWh/m².

Jan	0.41	Jul	0.63
Feb	0.49	Aug	0.71
March	0.62	Sep	0.63
April	0.65	Oct	0.57
May	0.76	Nov	0.46
June	0.77	Dec	0.41

n is the number of hours of bright sunshine in the month. θ is the angle between the collector and the horizontal. a is the average solar altitude in the month under consideration: this is the apparent angle of the sun above the horizontal and will vary according to your latitude, as shown in the table below.

These values are the altitude of the sun at 10 am and 2 pm rather than at noon, to give a more accurate figure. We hope they are fairly accurate but do not write in and tell us if they are not, as they were worked out on a rather crude sun angle calculator.

To use the formula, find your latitude on a map and use the nearest value for a from the table above. You will have to do the calculation twelve times to obtain the direct solar radiation on the collector for each month.

The formula for indirect radiation

The next step is to work out the indirect radiation on the collector. In a given month a collector *receives* $0.698 \, \mathrm{i} \, \mathrm{n} \, \frac{1}{2}(1+\cos\theta)$ kWh of indirect radiation per square metre.

i is the average monthly background diffuse radiation intensity, measured in calories per square centimetre per minute on a horizontal surface. Values for i are shown in the table opposite.

The values are near enough in a straight line relationship for you to find the value for i of angles not in the table by simple interpolation. For example, the value of i for an angle of 52.5°, which is half-way between 50° and 55°, will be half-way between 0.36 and 0.40, i.e., 0.38.

n is the number of hours of bright sunshine in

Latitude (North)

	50°	51°	52°	53°	54°	55°	56°	57°	58°	59°	60°
Jan	14°	13	12	11	10	10	9	8	7	6	5
Feb	23°	22	21	21	20	20	19	18	17	16	15
March	33°	32	32	31	31	30	29	29	28	27	26
April	43°	42	41	41	40	40	39	38	38	37	36
May	51°	51	50	50	49	49	49	48	48	47	47
June	57°	56	55	53	52	52	51	51	50	50	49
July	51°	51	50	50	49	49	49	48	48	47	47
Aug	43°	42	41	41	40	40	39	38	38	37	36
Sept	33°	32	32	31	31	30	29	29	28	27	26
Oct	23°	22	21	21	20	20	19	18	17	16	15
Nov	14°	13	12	11	10	10	9	8	7	6	5
Dec	10°	10	9	8	7	6	5	4	3	3	2

Solar altitude	i cal/cm²/min	Solar altitude	i cal/cm²/min
10°	0.07	40°	0.29
15°	0.11	45°	0.325
20°	0.15	50°	0.36
25°	0.185	55°	0.40
30°	0.22	60°	0.44
35°	0.255		

the month. This value is put in because the indirect radiation can usefully be collected only during periods of bright sunshine when there is sufficient direct radiation for the collector to be working.

θ is the angle between the collector surface and the horizontal.

Combining the two results

The indirect radiation is calculated for each month and the result added to the respective monthly direct radiation figure that you worked out earlier. This gives you the total number of kWh of solar radiation falling on one square metre of the collector each month. All that

remains is to multiply the figure by the total area of the solar absorbing surface in the collector and then by the assumed efficiency, say 35 per cent (or 0.35) for a homemade solar panel and 30 per cent (or 0.3) for a trickling solar roof (see Chapter 20).

These efficiencies are on the pessimistic side: the solar radiation figures assume that the collector will be operating only during periods of bright sunshine when efficiencies should be higher than the BRE's annual average figure. But it is safer to make a conservative estimate rather than a wildly optimistic one. At least the installation then has a chance of performing better than you expected. When you have multiplied your results by the collector area and the efficiency you will end up with an estimate of the useful energy that the collector will give you each month.

Hot water solar collectors

A typical solar hot water system consists of a solar collector to heat the water, an insulated hot water storage tank, and pipework to con-

A low-cost PVC-covered solar roof

Cottages with solar collectors

nect the two together. Most systems will also incorporate a pump, and a temperature differential controller, an electronic device that turns on the pump only when the collector is hotter than the water in the storage tank.

The plate

The flat plate solar collector consists of a blackened plate, over which or through which a fluid, usually water, can be passed (other fluids used include air and special oils). The black plate has a clear or translucent cover which allows solar radiation to fall on the plate. Because the plate is black it absorbs radiation very effectively. If you doubt this try touching the bodywork of a dark coloured car and a white car that have both been parked in the sun: the dark car will be hotter because dark colours absorb more solar radiation than light colours, and matt black absorbs the most.

The cover, usually of glass or clear plastic, reduces the loss of heat from the absorbing surface while allowing the solar radiation to reach the surface. Without the cover the collector would lose so much heat that it would never become hot enough to be of any use. An increase in the number of covers, through double-glazing, increases the temperature of the collector and therefore of the hot water, but adds to the cost and the complexity of the construction. Double-glazing will also reduce the amount of radiation reaching the collector surface because some radiation is absorbed in each sheet of glass and some is reflected off each glass surface. Most solar collectors for domestic hot water supply in the UK are single-glazed. Behind the black plate a thick layer of insulation is used to reduce heat losses from the plate and the fluid passing through it.

The tank

The hot water storage tank can be either an open tank of glass reinforced plastic or a conventional copper hot water cylinder. It should be an indirect system: in other words the solar-heated water should flow through a coil of pipe (or heat exchanger) inside the hot water tank so that the heat from the solar water passes into the water in the tank through the walls of the pipe. The disadvantage of this system is that there is a loss of energy in the exchange of heat between the water in the coil and the water in the tank.

This can be overcome by using a direct system where the water from the tank passes through the solar collector and back to the tank without going through a heat exchanger. In such a system the water in the tank is constantly being topped up with fresh water from the mains. In an indirect system the same lot of water goes round and round the collector and is not replaced by fresh water. The air that is dissolved in water when it comes out of the mains accelerates the corrosion of solar collectors, pipes and tanks, even if these are made of copper. In a direct system fresh water is constantly being introduced, encouraging corrosion; but in an indirect system the dissolved air and any other impurities in the water are not continuously reinforced by fresh supplies so they do less damage.

In the simplest set-up, the hot water flows from the collector to the tank and back again by 'thermosyphoning': hot water is less dense than cold water so it rises and creates a flow round the circuit. When the sun stops shining the water cools and stops flowing. There are two main problems with a thermosyphoning solar installation.

The first is that the bottom of the hot water tank must be at least 900mm above the top of the collector for the flow to work properly. This often makes it difficult to find a suitable location for the collector, which usually cannot go on a roof because there would not be room above it for the storage tank. One answer is to put the collector on the south-facing roof of a porch or garage so that it is lower than the main roof and the tank can then go in the attic.

The other problem is that the water in the collector can freeze on cold nights, because the black surface which is so good at collecting solar radiation in the daytime will lose heat quickly to the sky on a cold clear night. You can overcome this problem by using anti-freeze in the solar collector circuit, which must then operate on an indirect system to avoid contaminating the hot water supply to the house.

Thermosyphoning collectors at low level

The pump
Most solar hot water installations use a small pump of the type used for central heating to push the water round the circuit. This gives considerably more freedom in locating tanks and collectors, and allows smaller diameter and therefore cheaper pipe to be used for connecting them. The pump is often switched on and off by a temperature differential controller which turns on the pump when the temperature of the collector is higher than that of the water in the hot water storage tank. This ensures that the collector is not operated unless there is some useful energy to be collected.

Getting the most out of the system
The best way to use a solar water heater is as a pre-heater for a conventional supply. This requires the use of a solar hot water storage tank, the water from which forms the 'cold' feed to the existing hot water tank. When there is plenty of sunshine the water coming into the existing tank will be hot enough for direct use; when there is only a little sunshine the water coming into the tank will be at least a bit warmer than mains temperature, so the boiler or other water heating system will use less fuel to heat the water as required. The most efficient systems have a valve worked from the pump controller: this allows water from the solar tank to be used directly if it is hot enough before it passes through the existing tank.

Solar space heating

With collector and tank
Solar energy can be used to heat your home as well. One way is to use a large area of collector and a large hot water storage tank. The rule of

Collectors for space and water heating

thumb is to allow 50–60 litres of thermal storage per square metre of collector area, although some people might suggest up to 140litres/m^2. For example, a tank containing 3000 litres or 3m^3 of water (i.e. a tank 1m×1m×3m) will hold 87kWh if it starts at 50°C and cools to 25°C. This assumes that you have a heating system that can use water at low temperatures such as underfloor heating with pipes buried in a concrete floor.

This calculation is based on the specific heat of water which is about 1.16Wh/l deg C. This means that one litre of water cooled through 1 deg C will give out 1.16Wh of stored heat. The 87kWh stored in the 3m^3 of water, which will weigh 3 tonnes, would heat a *very* well insulated house for about 2½ days. Such a storage tank would need a collector area of 30–60m^2 depending on the efficiency. The cost of · tanks, which must have a very thick layer of insulation round them to keep the heat in and must not be liable to corrode or leak, is only one factor which makes this type of heating system very expensive.

Through windows

A much simpler way to take advantage of the sun is to use your windows as solar collectors. The BRE figures at the beginning of this chapter show that a vertical window facing south will receive about 700kWh per square metre per year, or just over 300kWh during the winter heating system (1 October to 30 April). If the window is double-glazed about 70 per cent of the solar radiation reaches the inside of your house, providing about 200kWh. The same window will lose about 150kWh over the same period if it is not protected. But if it is covered with insulated shutters for sixteen hours a day, the heat lost will drop to about 75kWh, giving a useful gain to the building of 125kWh per square metre over the heating season. Providing the building is thermally heavy, with externally applied insulation on heavy masonry walls, a concrete floor and brick internal partitions (see Chapter 3), this solar heat gain will be stored in the structure and given out slowly into the interior.

This sort of passive heating system, which

requires no mechanical parts and uses the house itself as the collector and storage system, can reduce the need for conventional fuels. However it is not easy to control and requires everyone's cooperation. For this reason cheap, reliable and elegantly simple passive systems have found little support from architects and engineers building experimental projects; they prefer to install the maximum number of pumps, thermistors, electronic controls and motorised valves to give their schemes technological sophistication. One argument is that people do not want to be involved in operating solar collectors and the complex systems are supposed to be as unobtrusive in their operation as gas central heating.

Lean-to conservatories

Another source of passive solar heating is the familiar conservatory or lean-to south facing greenhouse. A conservatory can reduce the heating load of a building in several ways. First the air in the conservatory becomes warm when the sun shines because of the so called

Passive solar gain through a south-facing window (above) and conservatory (below)

'greenhouse effect'. The wall against which the conservatory is built will then lose less heat because the temperature difference across its two sides will be less than that between the inside of the house and the outside. In the spring and autumn the conservatory may well become hotter than the inside of the house and there will then be a flow of heat through the wall to the inside of the building. Any heat flow can be improved by putting vents into the house near the top of the conservatory where the hottest air will collect. If the vents have insulated covers they can be opened when the air in the conservatory is warmer than that in the house, thus providing a source of solar-heated air. Finally, the conservatory, even at night when there is no sunshine, will trap a layer of still air against the house. The effect of wind increases the heat loss from the surface of a building so the trapped layer of air will have an insulating effect.

It is not easy to evaluate the contribution made by a conservatory as much will depend on variable factors such as the size of the conservatory, the construction and insulation of the house to which it is attached, the type of glazing and how airtight the conservatory is, as well as the number of hours of sunshine. Estimates of energy contributions range from 10 to 60 per cent of a building's total space heating demand. The good thing about conservatories is that they are not just solar heaters. You can grow figs, grapes, peaches and apricots as well as tomatoes, aubergines and melons in a conservatory and you can use it as an extension to the house on sunny winter days or wet spring ones. You cannot do any of these with a solar panel.

8 Windmills

Windmills are the piece of alternative technology hardware that seems to create the most enthusiasm in their designers and users. Part of their appeal is visual: they move in response to the wind, unlike solar collectors which lie quietly absorbing heat from the sun (if you are lucky) or insulation which you cannot even see. Windmills have some of the charm of early aeroplanes with their spinning blades and light construction; and they offer ample opportunity for the amateur engineer to try out his or her theories, and perhaps invent some new or improved method for harnessing the energy of the wind. In East Anglia model windmills, ranging from mass-produced plastic ones to large-scale replicas of old corn mills, rival gnomes as garden ornaments in rural areas, suggesting that the sight of revolving blades brings pleasure to many.

Alternative technology windmills are most commonly used to make electricity; they are often given names which are somewhat more technological than 'windmills' (Don Quixote has a lot to answer for) such as wind turbines, aerogenerators or even 'wind energy conversion systems'. Except in very windy areas, windmills used to make electricity are not really economic if you need batteries to store the electricity, because the cost of batteries and their replacement is so high, but if you live in an isolated house with no mains electricity and you want electric lights and say a radio, television or stereo set, a windmill may be the practical answer. If cost effectiveness is not your concern, or if you can obtain scrap materials, go ahead and build a windmill anyway. They are fun, a splendid symbol of alternative technology, and a kinetic demonstration of the use of natural sources of energy.

Selecting a site

The formula

Before building or buying a windmill you need to know if the site where you intend to put it is windy enough to make it worthwhile. The energy available from a windmill can be calculated using a formula devised by Dr R. Rayment at the BRE, whereby E is approximately equal to $10 V_{50}^3$.

E is the energy available in the wind in kWh per year per square metre of swept area, the swept area being the circle or other shape described by the rotating blades of the windmill. The equation allows for the loss of energy from very low and very high speed winds which the mill will not be able to use.

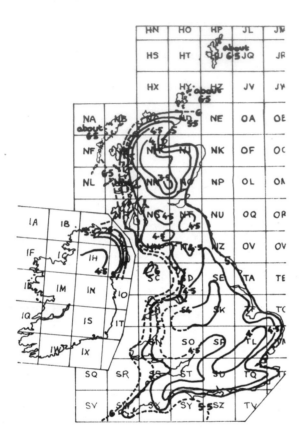

V_{50} is the wind speed exceeded 50 per cent of the time. The map shows values of V_{50} for different parts of the UK, and these values should be multiplied by the following factors to take account of the proposed site:

city	0.7
suburban	0.8
open	1.0
coastal	1.1
hilltop	1.2

The values for V_{50} on the map will give you a rough idea of what you are likely to obtain in the way of energy in the wind, which is *not* the same as the output from the windmill. However, an individual site may be 50 per cent more or less windy than it appears from the map depending on topography, the presence of trees, and other factors. If you are serious about windpower you must choose the proposed site carefully and then measure the wind there.

The general principle when choosing the site is to find the most exposed one possible. The best place would be a bare hilltop, preferably a smoothly rounded hill which tends to accelerate the wind over it; the worst possible location would be in a forest clearing. Try to choose a location where the windmill will be at least 150–200 metres from any trees or other obstructions, as these will block the wind and cause turbulence that may tend to damage the windmill. If you are going to use the windmill to generate electricity it will have to be fairly close to your house, or the cost of the cable linking windmill and house will be excessively high. Most sites are not large enough to allow much scope in the placing of the windmill and the chosen location usually involves some compromise.

Using an anemometer
To establish most precisely the amount of energy available at a site you will need an anemometer, preferably a 'cup anemometer'. This is a device which is blown round by the wind: as it revolves it turns a counter like the mileometer of a car. This clocks up the number of kilometres or metres of wind that have been past the anemometer. For example, if you set the thing up and after an hour the counter reads 10km the mean wind speed during that period has been 10km per hour. If you read the anemometer each day you can then divide each result by 24 hours to give a daily mean wind speed in km per hour. The figure clocked up in a year, divided by 8760 (the number of hours in a year), will show the mean annual wind speed, which is fairly close to the V_{50} speed. If the speed is in km per hour it can be converted to metres per second for use in the equation by multiplying it by 0.28 – similarly

figures in metres per second can be divided by 0.28 to convert them to km per hour. Using the mean annual wind speed and the daily mean wind speed, you will have some idea of the distribution of wind energy throughout the year.

Selecting a windmill — size and power

The rated speed

Most people are unlikely to bother with buying an anemometer: if you want to build a windmill you will probably simply go ahead and build one. What you need to know is how big to make it and how much power it is likely to produce. The first thing to consider is the 'rated speed' of the windmill. This is the wind speed at which the machine produces its maximum output. The BRE suggests rated speeds for values of V_{50} as follows:

V_{50} in m/sec	rated speed in m/sec
3.0	7
3.5	8
4.0	9
4.5	11
5.0	11
5.5	13
6.0	14

The value for V_{50} for your site can be taken from the map if you do not plan to set up an anemometer and take measurements over a year. The rated speeds in the table are chosen to give the maximum output per year from the windmill for the values of V_{50} shown. If you make the rated speed too high or too low you will fail to collect the energy from low or high wind speeds so you will collect less overall than if you use the values in the table. Say you design a windmill for use in an area where the map suggests that V_{50} is 4m/sec. According to the table, the rated speed will need to be 9m/sec if the machine is to be efficient.

Generators and alternators

The starting point for the design must be the use to which the machine will be put. If it is for generating electricity the important factor is your choice of generator or alternator. The alternator will determine the maximum output of electricity from the windmill, and this is the output that must be generated at the rated speed. For example, if your alternator has a maximum output of 500W, you must size the windmill to produce 500W at its rated speed, which is 9m/sec in this example.

However, whatever alternator you choose it will not be 100 per cent efficient in its conversion of the mechanical energy of the windmill shaft into electricity. Most alternator manufacturers give a figure for the power absorbed to drive the alternator at a given number of revolutions per minute, and a curve showing electrical output related to revolutions per minute. The output in Watts at a given speed, divided by the power input in Watts at the same speed, gives the efficiency.

For example, if the power input is given as 1kW at 3500rpm, and the electrical output is 500W at 3500rpm, the efficiency is $\frac{500}{1000}=0.5$ or 50 per cent. Some alternators have the power absorbed given in horsepower, and you will have to multiply this figure by 746 to convert it into Watts. If the output of the windmill is to be 500W and the alternator is 50 per cent efficient the windmill will have to be able to produce $\frac{500}{0.5}=1000W$ at its rated wind speed. If you can find a 70 per cent efficient alternator the windmill will have to produce only $\frac{500}{0.7}=714W$ to provide the same amount of electricity.

Gearboxes and V belts

The amount of energy the windmill will have to produce will increase if the gearing is inefficient. A properly designed gearbox used to increase the speed of the windmill shaft is likely to have an efficiency of about 94 per cent, while a V belt on pulleys might have an efficiency of 90 per cent. If the windmill uses more than one set of pulleys or a gearbox and V belts, the efficiency of each set must be allowed for in the calculation of the total energy that the windmill will have to produce. Gearboxes that will step up in a ratio of 1:20 are available, but V belts are not practicable for an increase greater than about 1:7.

The power formula

Let us suppose you calculate that your windmill must produce a total power of 1200W to allow for the inefficiencies of gears, V belts and alternator, so it is to have an electrical output of 500W. Your job now is to calculate the diameter of windmill required to produce 1200W at the chosen rated wind speed, in this example 9m/sec. The power obtained from a windmill at a given speed is calculated from the formula $P = 0.00064 \times A \times V^3 C_p$.

P is the power output in kW. A is the swept area of the windmill in square metres. V is the velocity of the wind in m/sec.

C_p is the coefficient of performance: this is the amount of power that the windmill can extract from the wind. Various people have shown that a 100 per cent efficient windmill could extract 59.3 per cent of the energy in the wind or that it would have a performance coefficient of 0.593. No windmill can, of course, be 100 per cent efficient and typical values of C_p for various types of windmills are as follows:

Savonius rotor	0.15
traditional grinding mill	0.17
Cretan windmill	0.3
steel multi-blade pumping mill	0.3
Darrieus rotor	0.35
high speed propeller	0.45

Selecting a windmill — design

The only type of windmill that we would recommend for do-it-yourself assembly is the Cretan. The Savonius rotor can be built easily from an old oil drum but its C_p is very low so it will not provide much power. The high speed machines, such as the Darrieus and the propeller mills, can be dangerous because of their rapidly turning blades. Conventional wisdom says that a windmill that generates electricity must rotate very fast because a generator must turn fast to produce electricity. If the windmill revolves at high speed there will be little or no need for speed-increasing gearing which would absorb energy and make the whole thing less efficient.

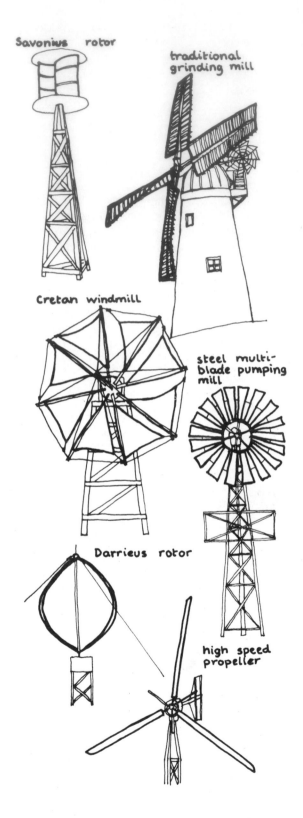

Savonius rotor

traditional grinding mill

Cretan windmill

steel multi-blade pumping mill

Darrieus rotor

high speed propeller

A Cretan windmill at Machynlleth

The problems with high speed windmills are, firstly, that they must be very accurately balanced or they can shake themselves to pieces, and, secondly, that their speed must be governed. If this is not done the propeller would rotate so fast in high winds that it would fly apart. Even commercially manufactured wind generators, seemingly built to withstand hurricane force winds, have suffered blade failures which resulted in pieces of wreckage travelling for hundreds of metres; and the failures of home made high speed machines have been numerous.

To prevent you or your neighbours becoming alternative technology's first martyr we suggest you build only the Cretan type of windmill. This has canvas sails instead of aerodynamically designed blades, and it turns very slowly so that accurate balancing is not important. If it rotates too fast the sails begin to flap and then spill the wind, which slows it down. It needs a lot of gearing to generate electricity; but because it is very cheap to build you can simply increase its diameter a bit to provide the extra power needed to drive the gearing. Finally, if anything does break, it will not send pieces flying about the neighbourhood.

The formula for size

To return to the calculations, we now have all the figures needed to find how big the windmill must be if it is to produce 1200W of power at the shaft (in order to drive a 500W alternator) in a wind of 9m/sec.

Remembering that $P = 0.00064 \times A \times V^3 \times C_p$:
$P = 1.2\text{kW} (1200\text{W})$
A is the swept area in m^2
V is 9m/sec, the rated windspeed
C_p is 0.3 for a Cretan windmill

Detail of the sails

Putting these values into the equation we get
$$1.2 = 0.00064 \times A \times 9^3 \times 0.3, \text{ thus:}$$
$$A = \frac{1.2}{0.00064 \times 9^3 \times 0.3} = 8.57 \text{ m}^2$$

The formula for the area of a circle is $A = \pi r^2$, where A is the area, π is 3.142, and r is the radius; so, we can use A to find the radius:
$$8.57 = 3.142 r^2$$
$$r^2 = \frac{8.57}{3.142} = 2.73$$
$$r = 1.65\text{m}.$$
So the required diameter is 3.3 metres.

Step-up gearing

All that remains now is to find what ratio of step-up gearing you will need to drive the chosen alternator from the shaft of the windmill. All windmills have a characteristic called the 'tip speed ratio' which is the ratio of the speed at which the tips of the blades travel to that of the wind speed. In a windmill with a tip speed ratio of 5 the blade tips will be travelling at 25m/sec in a 5m/sec wind. Some typical tip speed ratios are as follows:

Savonius rotor	1
traditional grinding mill	2–3
Cretan windmill	1
steel multi-blade pumping mill	1
Darrieus rotor	6
high-speed propeller	5–6

Using the tip speed ratio you can calculate the speed at which the windmill shaft rotates at the rated wind speed. In our example the rated speed is 9m/sec and the tip speed ratio is 1: so, at the rated speed, the tip of a blade travels 9 metres in one second. The circumference of the circle swept by the blades is given by πd, where d is the diameter of the windmill, which we know to be 3.3 metres. This gives a figure of about 10.4 metres for the circumference. In one second the blade tip travels 9 metres, so it will take a little over a second to make one full revolution. In 60 seconds it will travel a total of $9 \times 60 = 540$m. Dividing this figure by the circumference gives the number of revolutions turned by the shaft in one minute, i.e.: $\frac{540}{10.4} = 52$ rpm.

You now have to look at the alternator figures to see at what rpm the alternator gives its maximum output. Suppose the answer is at 3500rpm, the gearing-up must be in the ratio $\frac{3500}{52} = 67:1$ to provide the correct speed for the alternator. The best way to achieve such a high ratio is probably to use an industrial gearbox to do the first stage, with a V belt final drive to the alternator, as most vehicle alternators are designed to be driven by belts and pulleys off car engines. If the gearbox gives a step-up of 20:1, you will need in addition a V belt and pulley system that can step up 3.35:1. The step-up values are multiplied to give the final ratio from the windmill shaft to the alternator shaft, thus: $20:1 \times 3.35:1 = 67:1$.

Choosing a tower and maintenance equipment

Having worked out your windmill design you are not finished yet. You will need a tower to mount it on, so that it is able to catch the wind. The ideal tower should be 15–20 metres high, but such a structure would be expensive to build and frightening to climb, so most people settle for something smaller. The cheapest tower is probably a secondhand telegraph or electricity pole, bought as scrap from the GPO or the local electricity board. If they are replacing poles anywhere near where you live they will drop one off at your address for a couple of pounds. If used poles seem in short supply, and sometimes there is a twelve month waiting list, try asking the GPO where they buy the new ones. The price will be higher but the pole will not have been standing out in all weathers for fifteen years before it gets to you. If you buy a new one make sure that it is Tanalised rather than creosoted, as the creosote will rub off on you every time you climb up to oil the windmill.

As well as a tower you will need a safety belt with which to tie yourself on when you reach the top. Try asking the GPO maintenance workers who climb the poles what they use, or look in the *Yellow Pages* under 'Safety Devices and Equipment'. A typical belt is made in the same way as car seat belts and it is attached by a very thick rope to a large hook which can be screwed shut.

Zen and the art of windmill maintenance

You climb the tower, taking care not to trip yourself up with the rope, put the rope round the tower, clip the hook on to a ring on the belt and screw it shut. One sees photos of heroic Swiss windmill repairers, supported by the belt alone and using both hands to adjust the machine; but it is more comforting to hold on to something solid with at least one hand while you wield the spanner and the grease gun. Windmill maintenance is quite an art. The essential thing is to have all the tools and bits you need within easy reach, and to have extras of most things. It is very annoying to drop a vital washer and have to climb down to fish it out of the vegetable garden. Put everything in a bucket before you start, and tie a string to the bucket handle so that you can pull it up once you are at the top and tie it on to the tower.

Installation

If you use a telegraph pole as a tower it will need guy wires to stop it falling over, and these must be anchored solidly into the ground. A machine with a 3 metre diameter might need guy wire anchorages consisting of a hole 900mm deep and 600mm square filled with concrete. For a 5 metre diameter windmill you will need a cubic metre of concrete. It is important to make everything very strong to prevent

disasters during winter storms, but as a final safeguard the tower should be further than its height from your house; then at least if it does fall over it will not come through your roof!

It is best to erect the tower first, then attach the windmill to the top of it, as this prevents damage to the windmill should the tower fall over while you are putting it up. The drawings in Chapter 23 show one way of putting up a tower using only muscle power. You will find that windmill building and installation are best carried out on a cooperative basis, as it is not possible for one or two people to put up a windmill safely by themselves. Ask some people to steady the tower as you pull it into position and to hold it steady until it is finally anchored and guyed. Never try to do any of this on a windy day: even a gentle breeze could blow down the tower before it is secured and someone might be hurt.

As an alternative to a telegraph pole you might consider a self-supporting pylon tower. This type of tower needs no guy wires, and you can more easily fit platforms to it which will allow you to stand comfortably to carry out maintenance on the windmill. Ladders to the platform can be fitted inside the pylon to make the whole business of climbing up and down as easy and safe as possible. This type of tower may cost you more than a telegraph pole because it contains more wood, and it will be more difficult to make, but its advantages make it preferable.

Storing electricity — batteries

Once you have a windmill sitting on a tower you can start making electricity, but you may soon find that you need something to store electricity in for days when the wind does not blow. If you want to use the windmill to heat water with an electric immersion heater, you could have a well insulated hot water storage tank such as you might use with a solar collector, but if, as seems more likely, you plan to use the windmill for lighting, radios and other small loads you will need to store the power it produces in the form of electricity. The only way to do this at present is to use batteries.

Choice of battery

If we leave out the exotic batteries that you will not be able to obtain, such as the high-temperature sodium-sulphur type, you are left to choose between batteries that you fill with sulphuric acid (acid batteries), and those that you fill with potassium hydroxide (alkaline batteries).

Car batteries are always of the lead-acid type, and being mass-produced they are also the cheapest. But they are designed to be portable – which is not necessary for a windmill battery – and to allow very large short-term current drains to operate the car starter motor. The main problem with lead-acid batteries when used with windmills is that they can be damaged both by over-charging and by total discharging. A set of batteries used to store electricity for purposes such as lighting could easily be fully discharged during periods of low wind speeds. Ideally a set of lead-acid batteries should have twice the storage capacity that you think you want, so that with luck they will never become fully discharged. Twice the capacity means twice the price, and it may be cheaper to have a small diesel generator to charge up the batteries if they begin to get a bit low.

Alkaline batteries – the two available types are nickel-iron and nickel-cadmium – are bulkier than lead-acid batteries, but this does not matter if you are not trying to fit them into a car. Their advantage is that neither total discharge nor overcharging damages them; but they are at least twice the price of lead-acid batteries because they are not mass-produced for the motor industry.

Government surplus batteries

Government surplus suppliers are the best source of batteries, and they often advertise their wares in the *Exchange and Mart*. Batteries made for military and other government purposes are much more robust than car batteries and will last longer. They are sold unused and sealed, ready for their first filling and charge, and are very much cheaper than car batteries. If you are lucky you may be able to buy ex-government alkaline batteries, and if you can afford them these will last up to twenty years. It is also worth contacting your local GPO and electricity board headquarters, as alkaline batteries are often used for standby energy storage at power stations and telephone exchanges. If a building is being replaced or modernised they may have a set of batteries to dispose of.

The ideal size

To get some idea of the size of battery you will need you should be aware of your daily electricity demand, and the longest period you are likely to have too little wind to allow the windmill to charge the batteries. Let's say that you will not have any useful output at wind speeds less than 4m/sec. You can contact the nearest meteorological office weather station or RAF airfield for an estimate of the longest period when the winds are less than 4m/sec: now size your battery to cater for this period.

Suppose you want to use a windmill just for lighting. If the windmill produces 24 volts you could use 24 volt DC fluorescent lamps, which use less current than incandescent filament lamps. Each lamp needs about 0.5 amps, so if we assume you use five lamps and they run for five hours a day the total demand will be $0.5 \times 5 \times 5 = 12.5$ah (amp hours). A typical battery set might consist of four 6 volt 100ah government surplus batteries, giving a storage of 100ah at 24 volts (or 2.4kWh, as volts $\times$ amps $=$ Watts), so the batteries would last for $\frac{100}{12.5} = 8$ days. If you find that the periods of low wind speeds are not greater than 8 days you will not run out of stored electricity; but if the batteries are lead-acid you should double the capacity to 200ah to lessen the chance of complete discharge.

Calculating your energy demand

The energy consumption of any set of appliances that you might want to use can be worked out to give you an idea both of the size of windmill required and the size of the batteries. Note that any appliance which uses electricity for heating will have a very high electricity consumption if used for a long period, so you will not if you are wise try to operate an electric cooker from a windmill and batteries.

It is not possible to give figures for electricity consumption of various appliances because these will vary from one appliance to another and from one user to another. The best plan is to make your own estimates based on the wattage of the appliance and the number of hours per day that you use it. The wattage is usually written on the appliance somewhere near the maker's name, but if you are in doubt the local electricity showroom may be able to tell you.

In the case of some appliances, such as refrigerators and freezers which operate on thermostats and do not run all the time, you will have to get an estimate, again from the electricity board. Remember that a fridge or freezer will use less energy if it is in a cool room such as a larder than if it is in a hot kitchen. As a rough guide an average-sized fridge in a normal kitchen will use about 1 kWh a day, and a large freezer will use 3-4kWh a day. In an unheated kitchen a medium-sized fridge, the sort that fits under a worktop, will use 0.5kWh a day. The one way to be certain is to obtain a meter, connect it to the flex of the fridge or other appliances and read it every day for a year.

To calculate how much electricity you use in a day, multiply the wattage of each of your appliances by the number of hours you use them. This will give you the electricity demand in Watt-hours per day (divide by 1000 to give an answer in kWh).

The formula

As a very rough guide the DRE estimate that the average domestic use of electricity for appliances and lights but not cooking, space heating or water heating is 840kWh per household per year, or 2300Wh per day. If you wanted to generate this much electricity in a year in the area used in our earlier example where V_{50} is 4m/sec you would need to work out the size of windmill as follows:

$$A = \frac{E_e}{10V_{50}{}^3 \times C_p \times Eff_a \times Eff_g}$$

A is the windmill swept area. E_e is the required electrical output in kWh per year. The amount of electricity required should be increased by 10 per cent to allow for inefficiencies and losses in batteries and wiring, and to give a safety margin over your estimated requirements. This will give a figure of about 925kWh from the 840kWh average value quoted earlier.

C_p is the coefficient of performance; Eff_a is the efficiency of the alternator; Eff_g is the efficiency of any step-up drive.

Using the 4m/sec value of V_{50} from our earlier example, and values for the other terms as used earlier, we get the following result:

$$A = \frac{925}{10 \times 4^3 \times 0.3 \times 0.5 \times 0.8} = 12m^2$$

So the diameter is 3.9 metres.

The power output at the shaft for a windmill of this diameter can be found at the appropriate rated speed, 9m/sec in this example, using the earlier formula $P = 0.00064 \times A \times V^3 \times C_p$. In this case it will be 1680W; if this figure is multiplied by the efficiency of the alternator and the step-up gearing, the electrical power output can be found, which is about 670W. Since the type of alternator selected will determine the efficiency value used, and you cannot select an alternator until you know the required output in Watts, you may have to do the calculation a few times to work out a reasonably accurate diameter, yearly output and alternator type.

Your average daily electricity requirement can be multiplied by the number of days during which you expect the windspeed to be too low to generate electricity to give the capacity of the battery in kWh or ah. For example, a consumption of 2.4kWh per day for ten windless days would need a battery of 24kWh capacity. This would be 2000ah at 12 volts or 1000ah at 24 volts. A two day battery would be only 400ah or 200ah, and might work out cheaper, if you use a small diesel generator to charge it during longer calm periods. A lot depends on the price you have to pay for the batteries.

For homemade windmills, battery voltage will be 12 or 24 because these are the only alternator voltages that are cheaply available (from the motor industry). The problem with low voltages is that you must have very thick wires to carry the current. For example, at mains voltage a 60W lightbulb has a current demand of only $\frac{60}{240} = 0.25$amp. A normal 5amp lighting cable can carry $\frac{5}{0.25}$ or twenty bulbs at mains voltage. At 12 volts a 60W bulb draws a current of $\frac{60}{12} = 5$amps so a 5amp cable can only operate one bulb.

The ampere rating of cables is determined by their cross-sectional area, the thicker the cable the greater the amperage and of course the cost. At 12 volts even the thick 30amp cable used to connect electric cookers could handle only six 60W bulbs. This problem can be reduced by the use of transistorised low voltage fluorescent lights which are made for caravans and which draw much less current than a conventional incandescent lightbulb of the same light output.

For other appliances it is worth considering buying a transistorised inverter which will change 12 volts DC to 240 volts AC, so you can use normal size house wiring and normal mains voltage equipment. If you decide on an inverter be sure that it produces a mains voltage accurate enough to suit the equipment you wish to operate, and remember that any electric motor when starting draws a current about four times the current it uses when running. The inverter must have the capacity to handle the starting load and not just the running load.

You can see from all this that building a windmill is only the beginning of your problems, but if you really want to do it do not expect it to work properly at once and be prepared for periods without electricity. You will not be able to run an all-electric house on wind power but you should be able to provide yourself with light and perhaps a radio without too much trouble.

9 Collecting Rainwater

We shouldn't have to consider recycling domestic water in the UK, yet, as the recent droughts have shown, the cold tap can all too easily run dry. Nationally, there is enough rain to provide fresh water for everyone but, of course, the centres of population are not necessarily in the wettest parts of the country. Unlike the National Grid which distributes electricity nationwide, there is no total network for distributing water, although suggestions for using a restored canal system have been and may still be discussed. Reservoirs are needed next to cities but the siting of new reservoirs will always be met by public outcry, perhaps rightly so, for they submerge tracts of otherwise useful farmland and often houses or even villages.

You will receive no official encouragement if you do attempt to save or recycle water but since some of the means for doing both are very simple it seems a shame not to have a go. It has been demonstrated that domestic water consumption can be cut (remember those hosepipe bans and plastic bags full of water to put in the cistern?) and an effort to cut our consumption permanently could cancel out the need to build new reservoirs as insurance against the hazards of another drought. It would also be more economical if everyone could reduce their consumption of purified water.

Houses have roofs to keep the rain off, and roofs have to have a way of disposing of this water so, if you have a house, you are already in a position to intercept and catch the rainwater. It will make no difference to tho final destination of the rainwater whether it goes from gutter to surface water drain and so to the river or into your storage tank.

To estimate the amount of water you are likely to collect you will first need to find out the annual rainfall in your area. This figure should be an average of the three driest consecutive years known, if such information is available, so that there is no over-estimation of the amount of rain to be collected. Detailed rainfall information can be obtained from any local institution that collects weather data (such as an RAF station). But, if such information is not available, use two-thirds of the average annual rainfall

57

2030mm and above
1015mm - 2030mm
635mm - 1015mm
under 635mm

rain, the amount of rainfall collected in litres will be equal to the area of the roof, times the corrected average rainfall, times 0.9.

If you intend to use all your collected rainfall, you will need a storage tank and this should be large enough to hold at least 25 per cent of the estimated annual yield. Such a storage volume should prevent any dramatic overflowing during a storm but the storage tank should be linked to a soakaway or watercourse just in case. The estimated figure for yearly rainfall collection will be only a rough guide to the amount of water that might be obtained from a roof; but it is a help when it comes to deciding on the dimensions for a storage tank.

Before considering how to use the collected rainfall it would be well to examine the present patterns of water usage in houses. Different sources of data give slightly different figures but the following list is typical: the figures represent the average water consumption in litres per person per day.

	total	hot	cold
W.C.	43		43
personal hygiene	55	40	15
laundry	21	7	14
washing-up	6	5	1
drinking and cooking	4		4
garden and car	2		2
Total	**131**	**52**	**79**

On top of this total of 131 litres it should be noted that of the total amount of water supplied to us approximately 13 per cent is lost through leaks and bursts in the pipes: this represents not only a waste of water but a waste of purified water, and purified water costs money. Any savings made by you reducing your demand for water will be magnified because less will be wasted.

When it comes to matching rainfall to cold water demand we could imagine a household of four people, living in East Anglia under a roof with a surface area of 50m²:

yearly average rainfall=549mm
2/3 yearly average rainfall=366mm
rainfall collected=366×50×0.9=16470
litres a year.

value for your area as shown on the map. The whole business of estimating rainfall collection is exactly that, an estimation, so worrying too much over the rainfall value is probably inappropriate.

It is worth remembering that 1mm of rain provides 1 litre of water per square metre of catchment area. The catchment area is the area of the roof for a flat roof or the area of the roof in its plan form for a pitched roof. Depending on what you wish to use the rainwater for you may or may not want to collect the first run-off from the roof. This initial water flow from the roof will contain dirt, bird droppings and leaves from the roof and gutters; so, if you intend to use rainwater to wash clothes, this portion might be best avoided. If the rainwater is to be used only in the garden, you can just put some kind of screening at the entrance to the storage tank to collect the worst of the detritus. Assuming that you might lose 10 per cent of the rainfall in initial run-off, evaporation in summer and spillage over the edge of the gutter during heavy

The obvious uses for rainwater from the table of water consumption are watering the garden and washing the car. For the household in our example annual water consumption for garden and car is:

$2 \times 4 \times 365$ litres a year $= 2920$ litres a year. This may be a low assumption since other sources put this figure at ten litres per person per day, which would give an annual consumption for the household of 14600 litres, which could still be met by the rainwater. You may have to use some form of pump, such as a government surplus stirrup pump, to transfer the water from the storage tank to the garden. As a result you will lose the convenience of mains pressure but you will also beat the hosepipe ban.

An excellent use for collected rainwater is flushing the loo. Rainwater itself is too impure to recommend for drinking, especially in towns where it carries not only dust, dissolved sulphur dioxide and other pollutants but also dissolved lead, the product of a motor industry that demands high octane fuels. It could be used for cold water rinsing of clothes, baths, and hair washing. But as we have become so accustomed to thinking that any water coming from a tap is pure enough to drink, it may not be worth the effort and possible risk of actually plumbing in a separate system with an indoor rainwater tap. This is accepted on trains where the wash basins are labelled 'not drinking water', but might be thought strange in a house.

Flushing the loo, however, presents none of these problems and the only drawback is the large quantity of cold water required by the modern cistern. For the four person household the total comes out at 62780 litres a year, a quantity that you might collect on the roof of a large house in Cornwall. However, the quantities of water used for personal hygiene and laundry in the table adequately cover the quantity used for flushing the loo; and it may be that recycling this used water would be a better solution.

The other way to save water is to change the type of appliances used in the house. A bath, depending on its size and the wallowing habits of the users, consumes between 60 and 100 litres of water whereas a shower uses only 4–5 litres per minute: it was once stated that if every person in the UK had a bath once a week there would be a serious water shortage, and this was before the drought. Not only will the use of a shower save water but it will also save hot water and that means a saving in energy, whether you are paying for it or just trying not to deplete your solar-heated water too quickly.

The Building Research Establishment has found that spray taps halve the amount of hot water used in a wash basin. Although these measurements were made in lavatories in office buildings such a saving could still be made in the house. The temptation is to wash one's hands under running water, which is quicker than filling and emptying the washbasin, and this is where a saving in water could be made by using a spray tap. Having installed all these water saving devices you may then find that you do not have enough waste water to recycle for flushing the loo, but it can always be topped up with some of the collected rainwater.

It must be admitted that, unlike people living in other EEC countries, people in the UK have no incentive to save water as it is not metered. We pay our water rate whether we use the average 130 litres a day each or twice that. Some water authorities charge more for an outside tap or unattended hosepipe but for most of us water appears as a 'free' commodity. Whether it will always be so is debatable but attention to water conservation could prevent depleting the reservoirs again next time we have a real summer. This in turn would avoid the expense and inconvenience of flooding more land to store more water, so it must be a good thing. It is obvious that you will save money by installing energy saving showers and spray taps but even if your water supply is not metered, rainwater should not go straight to the drain. At the very least it should be collected and used for watering the garden. If only to grow a lusher and more palatable lettuce, bring back the water-butt.

Part II
PRACTICE

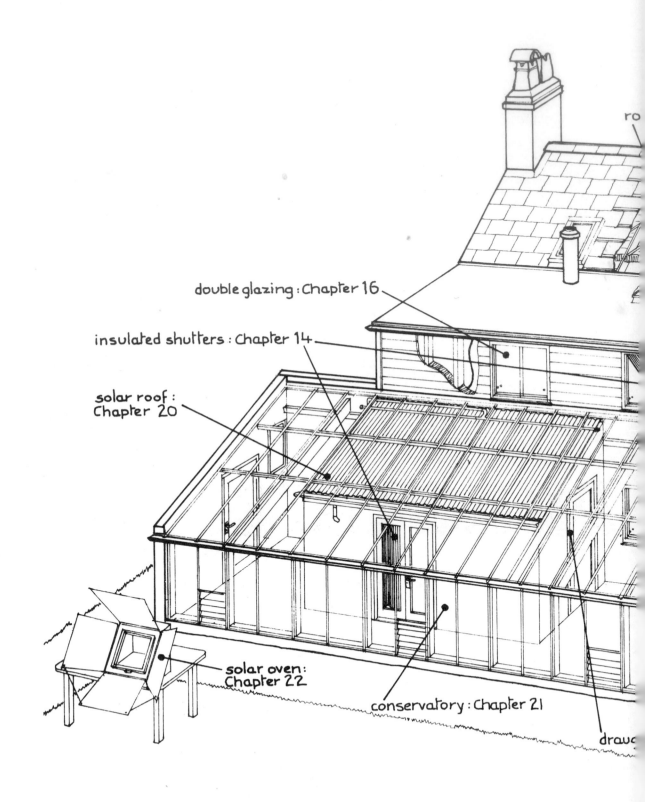

double glazing : Chapter 16

insulated shutters : Chapter 14

solar roof : Chapter 20

ro

solar oven : Chapter 22

conservatory : Chapter 21

drau

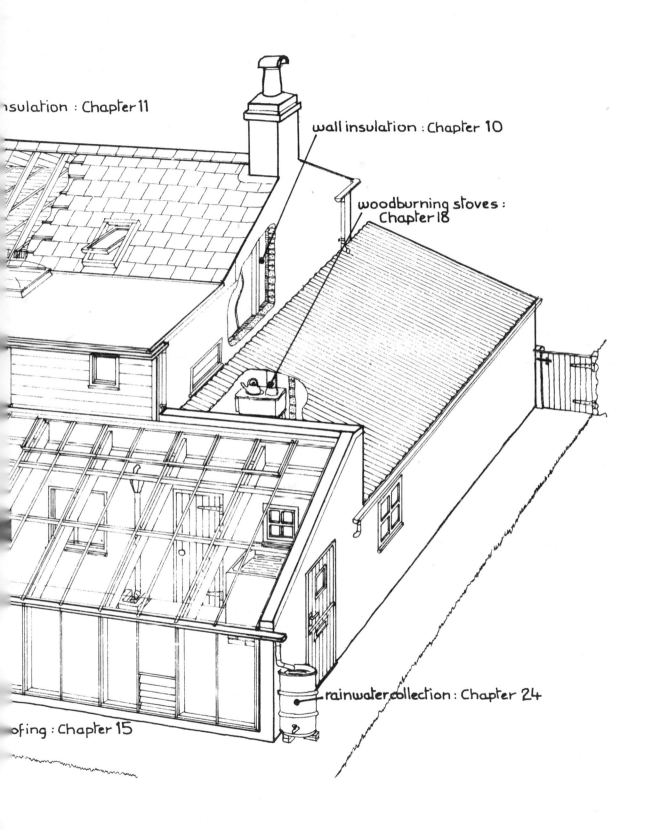

insulation : Chapter 11

wall insulation : Chapter 10

woodburning stoves :
Chapter 18

rainwater collection : Chapter 24

ofing : Chapter 15

10 Wall Insulation

Before you can insulate your walls you must find out what kind you are dealing with. As a rule, houses are built of brick and most recently built homes have cavity walls, which are made of two thin skins of brick with a gap between.

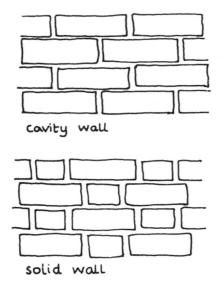

cavity wall

solid wall

These walls can be recognised by their thickness, usually 270mm, made up of two 110mm brick skins with a 50mm cavity between them. If you measure your wall at a window or door opening, it should be about 280mm thick, allowing for 10mm of plaster, if it is a cavity wall. If the wall, with plaster, measures 230mm or 350mm then it is probably a solid wall. A cavity wall can also be recognised by the fact that on the outside there are only stretcher bricks whereas a solid wall will show stretchers and headers.

The legal aspects

No matter what sort of walls you are dealing with, you will need permission to insulate them. In the UK, filling a cavity wall officially contravenes the building regulations unless the firm that does it has a certificate allowing the appropriate regulation to be relaxed. The insulation of solid walls will require full permission according to the building regulations, and perhaps planning permission as well if it changes the appearance of the house.

The best course is to go and see the building inspector at your local council offices, and explain what you are planning to do. The inspector will give you some quite simple forms to fill in and, probably, some useful advice as well. We have found building inspectors without exception to be helpful and friendly, and it is obviously well worth being on good terms with your local inspector rather than treating him or her as a faceless bureaucrat. Of course you have to satisfy the regulations and if you want a detailed explanation of these there is a book listed in the Bibliography (on page 202) that will help you.

If you are contemplating external insulation on a solid wall you will have to talk to someone at your local planning department as the work could change the external appearance of the building. Planning is a more tricky area to deal with as there are no rules — the building inspector must pass an application if it does not contravene the building regulations but a district council under the guidance of a planning officer can refuse anything quite arbitrarily. This is not to say that the council always will; if you ask the planning officer before you apply for permission you may get some idea of local attitudes. If all else fails you can always put the insulation on the inside.

Insulating cavity walls

If you have cavity walls there is nothing you can do to insulate them by yourself, unless you treat them as solid walls as described later. Your easiest solution is to turn to the *Yellow Pages* and look under 'Insulation Contractors'. You will find three common ways of insulating a cavity wall: ureaformaldehyde (or uf) foam, mineral fibre and polystyrene granules. All three methods start with holes drilled in the wall through which the insulation is put into the cavity. The holes made in the wall are mortared up once the job is done and the complete process takes about a day for an average house.

Uf foam is made by mixing two chemicals and blowing the mix into the cavity where it expands to fill the space and sets into a fairly rigid foam. The foam is cheap but not strong enough to be made into sheets like expanded polystyrene; when pumped into a cavity it does not matter that it has no strength as the brickwork will hold it up. Once in place, uf foam cannot be removed without taking down the wall whereas mineral fibre and polystyrene granules have the advantage that they can be removed if problems occur.

Unfortunately damp can be a problem with filled cavity walls. The purpose of the cavity is to stop rain from reaching the inside of the building. Usually the outer leaf of the wall becomes very wet when it rains; the water runs down the inside of this leaf and drains out at the bottom. If you fill the cavity with something you must be sure that whatever it is does not conduct the moisture across the wall to the inside. Because of the risk of damp some kinds of cavity fill are suitable only for sites that are sheltered from driving rain.

Cavity wall insulation is covered by the Agrément Board, a body which tests building materials and their fitness for use. Never go to a cavity insulation firm which cannot show you an Agrément certificate approving the firm and the process used. The certificate grants a waiver of the building regulations which forbid the bridging of the cavity, and it will also show the degree of exposure under which the material can be used. There are some cowboy firms operating in this field, but if you go to companies with an Agrément certificate you should be fairly safe. The best plan is to go to several firms and obtain a free quote from each before you make the final decision.

Cavity wall insulation has the disadvantage that the thickness of the insulation is governed by the thickness of the cavity, usually 50mm or 75mm. If you want a better U value than this amount of insulation can provide (0.4 to 0.5W/m^{2}degC), you will have to apply extra insulation to the wall as if it were solid.

If your house has still to be built you have other options. The width of the cavity can be increased to 100mm, according to the building regulations (Regulations D15 and D16 Schedule 7 rule 12, in case you need to know), provided that you use 'vertical twist type wall ties', spaced 750mm apart horizontally and

450mm vertically. Insulation can be put into the cavity as the wall is built up, allowing slab materials to be used, such as expanded polystyrene or a resin-bonded glass fibre which has been treated with a water repellent to prevent the transmission of moisture across the cavity. The inner leaf of the wall can be built of insulating lightweight concrete blocks to further improve the insulation. If you want more than 100mm of insulation in a new wall the inner and outer leaves of the wall will have to be designed as separate free-standing walls, without conventional wall ties connecting them.

Insulating solid walls

If you can see both headers and stretchers on the outside of your house, your walls will probably be solid and therefore rather more difficult to insulate. Before you try to insulate them you must be sure that they are protected by a damp proof course. If you cannot find one or if you are doubtful, it is worth obtaining a free survey and quote from a damp proofing firm; for addresses see under 'Damp Proofing Contractors' in the *Yellow Pages*. A good firm will offer a guarantee of their system, and your local authority may give you an improvement grant to cover half the cost. The local authority environmental health department, which deals

with improvement grants, may suggest some names of reputable firms, or you can try asking other people for their experiences.

You will have to chip off the damp plaster before the damp proofing is carried out, but if you plan to insulate do not replaster as the insulation can be put over the unplastered wall. If you qualify for a grant this will contribute towards the cost of replastering, or of the battens and plasterboard if you insulate the walls after the damp proofing. Only when the wall is successfully damp proofed can you think of insulating it.

Internal insulation
The cheaper method is to insulate solid walls internally but this will cause a fair amount of disturbance to the inside of your house and it may be best to work on one room at a time. Before insulating internally you must decide what to do about chimney breasts and fireplaces. If the chimney is to be kept in use the insulation should be stopped either side of the fireplace. Any chimney breast on the floor above a stove or fire in constant operation will be a useful emitter of heat and can also be left uninsulated.

If the fireplace is not used you can carry the insulation across it. In this case the stack should be ventilated to prevent any condensation in the closed off flue. To avoid excessive air changes in the building use two air bricks (225mm×225mm), one in the external wall at the bottom of the chimney, and another, if the

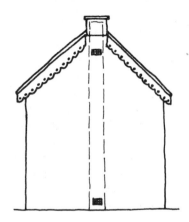

stack above roof level is demolished or capped off, at the top. Of course you can remove the chimney completely but in old buildings chimney stacks act as useful buttresses and their removal may weaken the walls.

All internal wall insulation starts with the temporary removal of skirting boards. The best way to add internal insulation is to leave a ventilated cavity between the insulation and the brickwork. You can do this by building a free-standing framework of softwood studs nailed to a sill on the floor and to a plate at ceiling level, leaving a gap of 25mm between the rear of the studs and the wall. The studs should not be less than 50mm×75mm (which would give 75mm of insulation) or 50mm×100mm; anything thinner than 50mm×75mm will not be strong enough to span from floor to ceiling without bending if you lean against the wall.

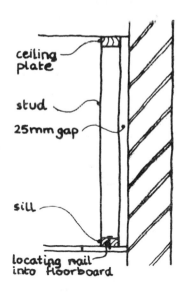

ceiling plate

stud

25mm gap

sill

locating nail into floorboard

It is essential to use timber which has been vacuum treated with preservative (e.g., Tanalised). This is a commercial process so you can buy the wood already treated. A reasonable job can also be made by giving the wood three good coats of timber preservative if you cannot buy it already treated. If you use wood with no preservative it is very likely to rot once it has been built into the new wall.

The studwork is started by laying the sill on the floor at least 25mm from the wall surface. If the floor is timber you can nail the sill to it, using nails long enough to locate the sill but not go through the floorboards in case there are wires or pipes below; 63mm nails would be suitable for a 50mm thick sill. If the floor is concrete you could try to fix the sill down with screws and plugs as described for fixing battens to walls (page 70). If you cannot fix the sill to the floor lay it in position and measure the length required for the end studs. These measure the same as the height from the top of the sill to the ceiling less 50mm which is the thickness of the plate at ceiling level.

Screw the studs to the wall as described on page 70, ensuring that they are vertical and that the gap behind the studwork is maintained. They must be fixed very firmly; use at least five screws per stud. Skew nail the sill to the bottom of the studs with 100mm nails, using a block of wood behind the sill to prevent it from moving when the nails are driven in.

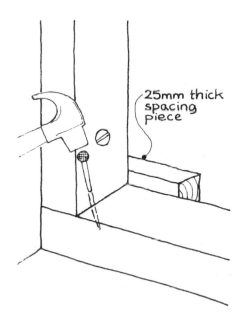

25mm thick spacing piece

Now cut the plate to length, put it in place on top of the studs, and skew nail it to them, again using a spacing piece. Cut the uprights to fit between sill and plate; if they are a tight fit you can put them in at an angle and then tap them into a vertical position with a mallet. They should be skew nailed at top and bottom and should finish up at 400mm or 600mm centres.

Frame round window and door openings (as shown in the illustrations) with vertical and horizontal timbers.

To prevent moisture vapour collecting between the new studwork wall and the old wall, the gap should be ventilated by drilling holes through the existing wall to the outside. These holes should be about 20mm diameter and at about 900mm centres with one row near the top of the cavity and one row near the bottom.

flanged building roll: this is designed to fit between studs and has a flange at each edge to fix it to the timber. If you use the polythene-faced type, the polythene will form the necessary vapour barrier to keep moisture vapour out of the wall (see Chapter 3). It is important to fix the studs at the right spacings to fit the roll, and they should be at 400mm or 600mm centres.

If you use the wider spacings you will need to use thicker plasterboard for the internal lining of the room, 12.7mm rather than 9.5mm; but you will achieve a better insulation value because less of the wall will be taken up with timber, which is not as good an insulator as

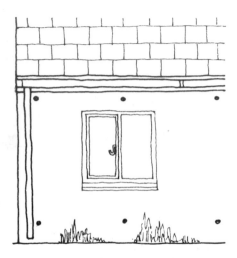

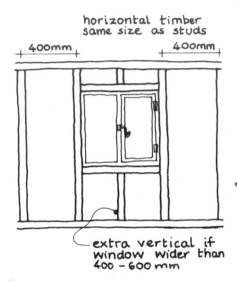

horizontal timber same size as studs

400mm   400mm

extra vertical if window wider than 400 - 600 mm

You can mortar pieces of PVC pipe into the holes for the sake of neatness, and plug them with little pieces of glass fibre insulation to keep out mice. The best way to drill the holes is to hire a hammer drill, the type which delivers very fast hammer blows to the bit at the same time as it rotates, and to use a long, large diameter masonry bit.

You will have to build out the existing frames of doors and windows to take up the new wall thickness and some methods for doing this are shown in the illustration (right).

The insulation must then be placed between the studs, but if there is a cavity behind them there will be a problem fitting the insulation without blocking the cavity. The solution is to use a type of glass fibre insulation called

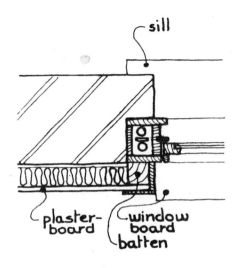

sill

plaster-board   window board batten

polythene
glass fibre

the insulation to position it but the other side must be pushed into place very gently. The expanded polystyrene should have a flame retardant additive (i.e., Type FRA).

The wall should be clad with plasterboard once the insulation is in place. Plasterboard is usually used because it is cheap and gives a low flame spread to the surface of the wall. If you have used flanged roll insulation with a vapour barrier you can use plain plasterboard; otherwise use foil backed plasterboard which will form a vapour barrier. If you choose to use some other sort of cladding you will have to check the fire regulations, and you must staple a vapour barrier of heavy gauge polythene (with the joints folded to make them vapour tight) over the studs and insulation before putting up the cladding.

glass fibre. The insulation is unrolled over the studs and the polythene flange is then stapled to them.

It is also possible to use expanded polystyrene to insulate the wall. In this case the material should be cut to fit tightly between the studs and then pushed very carefully into place. Make sure that the polystyrene does not block the cavity; it should be flush with the face of the studs. You can use your hand at the free end of

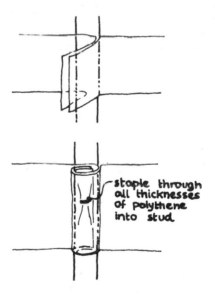

staple through all thicknesses of polythene into stud

If you use plasterboard, nail it to the studs with 38mm long galvanised plasterboard nails spaced about 150mm apart. The sheets of plasterboard should be measured and cut to make a tight fit at floor and ceiling. To cut plasterboard score along the paper with a sharp knife and then bend the cut off piece back to break the plaster core. Finally, cut through the paper on the other side. Plasterboard can also be cut with an old panel saw. Where two

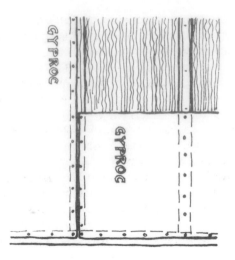

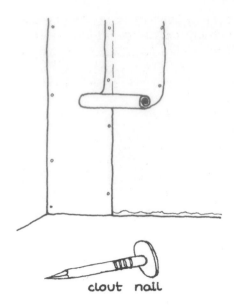

clout nail

sheets of plasterboard meet at a stud try to keep the nails well back from the edges of the board and do not hammer too hard or you will damage the edge. Finally, for a good finish, the surface should have a skim coat of plaster.

The joints between the sheets of plasterboard and the holes made by the nail heads can be filled with special fillers and tapes supplied by the manufacturers. These are supposed to allow the boards to be decorated directly, but the finish is not nearly as good as that given by a skim coat of plaster. It is worth paying a plasterer to do the skim coat, especially as it allows you to use up oddments of board and also means that you do not have to worry if the plasterboard does not go up very neatly; the plaster will cover all mistakes.

If you have not the space to leave a ventilated cavity between the insulation and the old wall, you can apply the insulation direct to the wall surface. In this case the first step, having removed the skirting boards, is to fasten 'breather paper' over the whole wall surface. The paper will allow moisture vapour in the wall to escape through the brickwork, if it is porous enough. It will also prevent any damp or rain that seeps through the brick wall from wetting the insulating material. Fix the paper with 100mm overlaps – you will find it easier to put it up vertically like wallpaper than horizontally. The paper can be fixed to the wall (with the side marked 'outside' facing out) using the short

galvanised clout nails sold for holding roofing felt; all you need is enough nails to prevent the paper falling off the wall while you carry out the next part of the job.

Now screw Tanalised softwood battens to the wall. The battens should be 50mm wide and as thick as the insulation you wish to use. Standard sizes of softwood are 50mm, 75mm and 100mm thick. The 50mm×50mm battens should be screwed directly to the brick or stone wall using 100mm no 12 screws and plastic wall plugs (we have found that the type called 'Plasplugs' are the easiest to use).

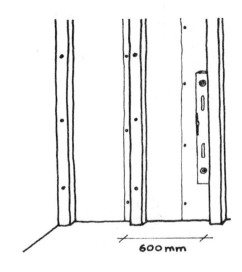

600mm

To put up the battens you will need an electric drill with a 6mm diameter masonry drill long enough to stick out at least 110mm from the drill chuck. Put the batten in place on the wall against the breather paper, check that the

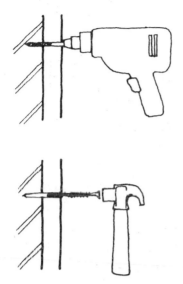

timber is vertical, then drill straight through the wood and into the wall as far as the drill will go. Take a plug and push it into the hole in the piece of wood until it is flush with the surface. Then put the point of the screw into the hole of the plug and tap gently with a hammer to push the plug through the wood to the bottom of the hole in the masonry. Using the biggest screwdriver you can find, tighten the screw and the

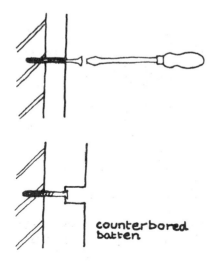

counterbored batten

batten will be held in place. Each batten will need about four screws evenly spaced. This method is much easier than trying to mark the positions of the plugs on the wall separately. Put the battens at 600mm centres on the wall and make certain that they are all vertical, and parallel to one another.

If you are planning to use 50mm×75mm or 50mm×100mm battens so as to have more insulation, the battens will have to be counterbored. This involves drilling holes about 20mm in diameter through the battens with a brace and bit to a point about 50mm from the back of the timber. If you do not do this the screws will not be long enough to go through the timber into the wall. Once counterbored, the battens can be fixed as before, the only difference being that you will need a longer masonry drill as the drill chuck will not be able to go through the counterbored holes.

Once the battens are up you can put in the insulation. This can be mineral wool, glass fibre, expanded polystyrene (Type FRA), extruded polystyrene which is a better vapour barrier than expanded polystyrene, expanded polyurethane if you can afford it, or any other material that is available in sheet or blanket form. Cost is perhaps the best guide to your choice and you will also be limited by what is available locally. Glass fibre or expanded polystyrene are the most likely choices because they are cheap and easy to come by.

If you buy glass fibre in rolls 1200mm wide you can use a saw to cut these (before you unwrap them) into 600mm rolls, which can be fitted between the battens. Glass fibre is very itchy to handle and it is best to wear gloves with gauntlets – bee-keepers' gloves are very good. The manufacturers say that the stuff will not cause lung cancer because the way it is made, by squirting molten glass through tiny nozzles, ensures that the diameter of the fibres is constant, and greater than the diameter of natural fibres like asbestos which are known to cause respiratory disorders. All the same it is quite a good idea to wear a face mask or a farmer's respirator just in case.

Having put the insulation in place you can fix up the plasterboard. This should be foil-backed

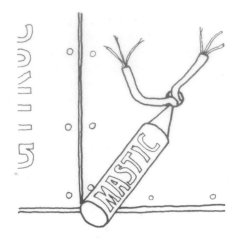

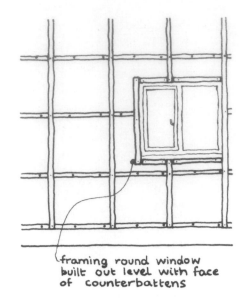

framing round window
built out level with face
of counterbattens

to form the essential vapour barrier to the insulation, and 12.7mm thick if the battens are at 600mm centres. If you plan to have electric sockets or light switches on the insulated wall they should be surface-mounted and the holes where the wires come through the plaster-board should be sealed with mastic. If you made sure that the battens were at 600mm centres, vertical and parallel to one another, you will now find that the plasterboard can be nailed up quite easily. Take care to buy plaster-board 1200mm wide. Finally, you can put the skirting boards back (after the plastering if you have it done) and the job is finished.

External insulation

The most expensive way to insulate a solid wall is to apply the insulation to the outside. The expense is caused by the need to provide a strong waterproof facing to the insulation instead of the plasterboard used internally. The advantages and disadvantages of external insulation are covered in Chapter 3.

Assuming you have decided to go for external insulation, you start by attaching Tanalised or treated softwood battens to the wall exactly as described for internal insulation. The battens should be at 600mm centres. If you want to have very thick insulation you can start with battens fixed horizontally to the wall, and then nail to these counterbattens which run vertically to carry the cladding. The spacing of both lots should still be 600mm centres. At

the base of the wall the external cladding must stop at least 150mm above ground level, and the illustrations suggest two methods of dealing with the junction between the new insulation and the ground which will prevent the cladding from damage when rain splashes up from the ground.

The insulation can be expanded or extruded polystyrene, both of which can be used below ground level, or resin-bonded glass fibre or mineral wool, which should stop 150mm above ground level. Once the insulation has been pushed in between the battens a layer of

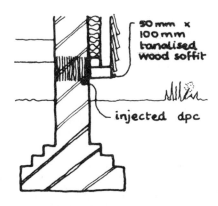

50 mm x
100 mm
tanalised
wood soffit

injected dpc

This will lead to heat loss
through base of wall unless
floor is insulated

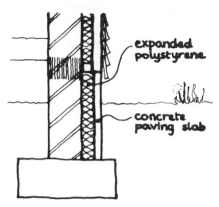

expanded
polystyrene

concrete
paving slab

This detail cannot be used
if house wall is adjacent
to pavement

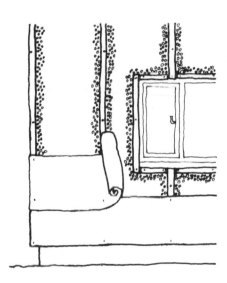

which is easy if you are planning to re-roof the building. For this reason it is perhaps wise to use a lot of insulation, at least 100mm if you apply it externally, otherwise it hardly seems worth the trouble.

At windows and doors there are two possibilities. The first and best is to take out the window and door frames and replace them on the outside of the new wall. If this proves difficult you will have to build a frame of battens round the existing openings and try to make a watertight seal where the new cladding meets the old frames. At the sill you could use two

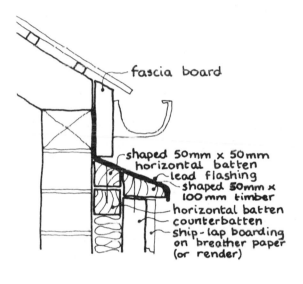

fascia board

shaped 50mm x 50mm
horizontal batten
lead flashing
shaped 50mm x
100mm timber
horizontal batten
counterbatten
ship-lap boarding
on breather paper
(or render)

breather paper should be stapled over the battens and insulation. The paper should be laid horizontally, starting from the bottom of the wall, and the subsequent layers of paper should overlap the lower ones by 100mm. The purpose of the breather paper is to throw off any rain that penetrates the cladding.

Doors and windows will present problems, as will the eaves and gables of roofs. If your roof has a good overhang there is no difficulty but if the edges are flush as they frequently are in Victorian terrace houses, you will have to devise a lead flashing which will protect the top of the insulation from rain. The best solution is to extend the roof over the top of the insulation,

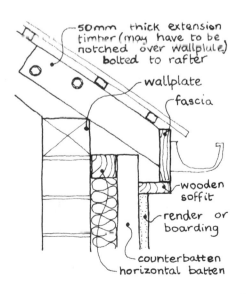

50mm thick extension
timber (may have to be
notched over wallplate)
bolted to rafter

wallplate

fascia

wooden
soffit

render or
boarding

counterbatten
horizontal batten

73

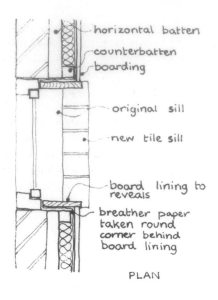

horizontal batten

counterbatten

boarding

original sill

new tile sill

board lining to reveals

breather paper taken round corner behind board lining

PLAN

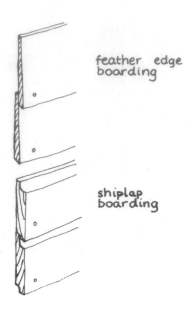

feather edge boarding

shiplap boarding

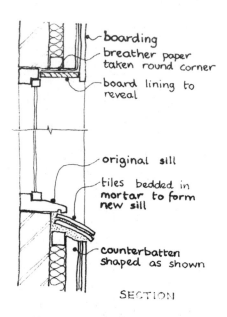

boarding

breather paper taken round corner

board lining to reveal

original sill

tiles bedded in mortar to form new sill

counterbatten shaped as shown

SECTION

There are several possibilities for cladding the external insulation but we will describe only two. The easiest to put up is Tanalised (or treated) softwood boarding, preferably shiplap pattern, as this is easier to use than feather edged boarding. The boarding, which should be at least 16mm thick, is nailed to the battens with 50mm sheradised lost head nails. Start with the bottom board and spend a lot of time making sure that it is fixed perfectly level, as it will then form a base for the other boards. You should check the boards frequently with a spirit level to ensure that they are horizontal. Joints should be made only at battens, and the joints

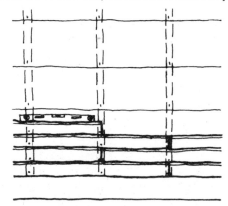

in one course of boards should not coincide with the joints of the boards directly below. Various methods for dealing with corners and

layers of plain tiles laid in mortar with staggered joints on top of the new battens. The new sill must have a good slope on it to throw the water away from the wall as quickly as possible. An alternative method might be to remove the existing sills and cast new larger concrete ones using a mix of one part by volume cement to two parts sand and three parts aggregate (maximum size 10mm). You can see why external insulation is expensive.

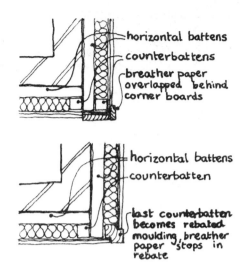

horizontal battens
counterbattens
breather paper overlapped behind corner boards

horizontal battens
counterbatten
last counterbatten becomes rebated moulding, breather paper stops in rebate

the lath to span up to 600mm between supports. The sheets of laths should also be wired together with 1.22mm galvanised wire at 100mm intervals, with the wire ends stuck through the lath so that they do not poke out through the rendering.

The lath should stop at least 150mm above ground level and be terminated with a render stop bead, a metal strip which makes it easy to form a neat drip edge to the rendering. The stop bead should also be used above window and

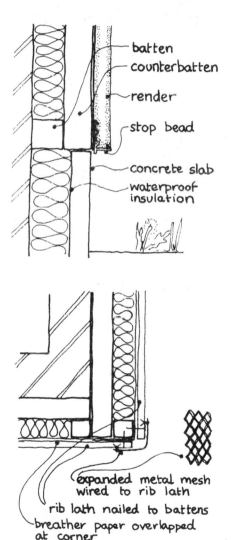

batten
counterbatten
render
stop bead
concrete slab
waterproof insulation

angles are shown in the illustrations. The timber can now be painted or preferably stained with a preservative stain or even creosote, which will not peel or flake like paint.

An alternative for cladding the insulation is cement rendering on a special metal lath underlay. The metal lath, which provides a key for the render, is nailed to the timber battens which have had breather paper stapled to them as before, with 38mm galvanised plasterer's nails through its reinforcing ribs. These ribs are formed in the expanded metal sheet and allow

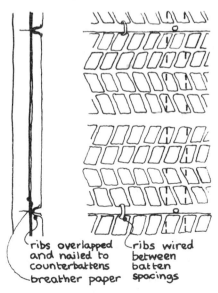

ribs overlapped and nailed to counterbattens
breather paper

ribs wired between batten spacings

expanded metal mesh wired to rib lath
rib lath nailed to battens
breather paper overlapped at corner

door openings. At corners, pieces of bent expanded metal should be used, tied to the lath with wire as above, to carry the rendering round the angle without cracking. The rendering should be applied in three coats, all of a mix consisting of one part by volume (a shovel full) cement, one part hydrated lime and six parts sharp sand.

Rendering is slightly easier than plastering because it does not have to look so flat, but it must be fairly smooth and free from cracks or else it will let the rain through. If in doubt, have a plasterer do the job, or at least ask someone to show you how to do it. If you are determined to do it yourself, mix up a small amount and practise putting it on to the float and then on to the wall – somewhere where it will not matter if it looks a bit rough. A lot depends on mixing the render to the right consistency before you apply it, so be prepared to spend a day getting the hang of it before you tackle the whole wall. When it is finished you can paint the rendering with external paints as sold for painting brickwork. Timber cladding is generally easier than rendering but painted rendering looks more conventional and may be easier from the point of view of obtaining planning permission, especially if you live somewhere like Suffolk where rendering is a traditional finish.

float

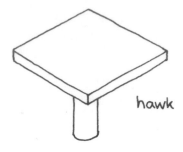

hawk

External insulation is probably best used if you are doing a thorough renovation of an old building. Once you have to take the tiles or slates off a roof because the timbers need repairing and once you have to replace existing rotten and broken windows and even possibly doors, it is much easier to design a scheme that incorporates the insulation on the outside surface of the wall.

11 Roof Insulation

In many cases roofs are the easiest part of the house to insulate, and it is even possible to get a government grant to put in roof insulation. Before you do anything else, go to the local council office and ask about insulation grants; you will not be eligible for one if there is already some form of insulation in the roof.

Pitched roofs

Unfelted

Starting with pitched roofs, there are two main types, those where the slates or tiles are laid on roofing felt and those where they are not. By going up into the attic you can see at a glance what type you are dealing with: if there is no felt you can see the backs of the tiles and usually daylight as well.

It is easy to insulate a roof of this type, as there is no problem with ventilation of the roof space. If you intend to use a material like glass fibre which comes in rolls, you can cut the roll with a normal wood saw into widths that suit the spacing of the joists. Unroll the material and push it lightly into place between the ceiling

joists. You will need to stand on a plank placed across the joists to save having to worry about balancing. Do not compress the material or you will reduce its thickness and therefore its insulating value. If the insulation is wider than the joist spacings you can turn up the edges to make it fit.

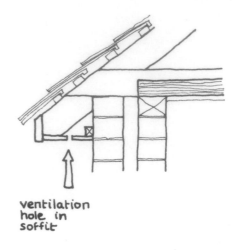

ventilation
hole in
soffit

If you are handling glass fibre or mineral wool it is as well to wear gloves, a boiler suit and wellington boots to keep the itchy fibres from settling into your clothes and on your skin, and if possible a dust mask over your mouth and nose to keep fibres out of your lungs.

The insulation need not be laid right up to the eaves as long as it covers the top of the walls. The thickness is up to you: in the UK, the official recommendation is 100mm in houses, and 150mm is not excessive. But do some calculations before you make your decision. If you want to use the attic for storage the thickness will have to be the same as the depth of the ceiling joists so that you can lay boards across the joists to provide a platform for things to stand on. Many materials are suitable for loft insulation, the main deciding factor being cost and availability. However, if your roof has no felt under the tiles, it is inadvisable to use a loose material like vermiculite or expanded polystyrene granules. On a windy day the draughts that come under the tiles will blow the stuff into drifts and you will find it deep in one place and non-existent in others.

Felted
If there is roofing felt under the slates the insulation of the roof is a bit more difficult because the loft must be ventilated to prevent the dreaded dry rot, which thrives in damp air-

less conditions. Under a felted pitched roof there may be no ventilation and moisture vapour will rise up into the roof from the rooms below; this creates the conditions in which dry rot spores, which are always present in the air, take root and grow. For this reason most felted roofs have small holes or a gap at the eaves to let in enough air for ventilation. The holes are often in the soffit board which covers the underside of the ends of the rafters where they stick out of the wall to form the eaves. The holes may also be in the fascia board to which the rainwater gutter is fixed.

If you have a felted roof and cannot see any holes, go up into the loft on a windy day and see if you can feel any draughts up there. Providing you feel a draught the roof is likely to be well enough ventilated. If there are no holes, or if you relay the tiles or slates of an old roof on felt to provide better rain resistance, you will have to make ventilation holes about 25mm diameter every 600mm along the eaves. It is a good idea to fix pieces of expanded metal mesh over the holes to keep out birds and mice, which will otherwise make their nests in your insulation. An alternative, if the house is detached, is to put a 225mm×225mm air brick into each gable end to provide the necessary cross ventilation (see opposite, above).

When laying the insulation under a felted roof it is essential that the ventilation holes are not blocked up by the insulation. If the ventilation comes through the eaves make sure that

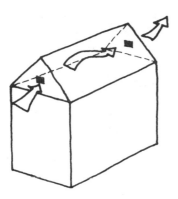

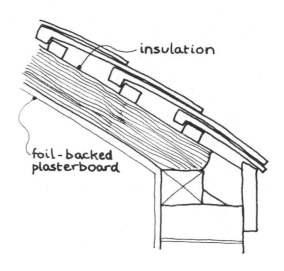

insulation

foil-backed plasterboard

the insulation goes as far as the top of the walls but is not pushed into the eaves where it may stop the flow of air. If there are cold water tanks in the roof – and this applies to any roof space, not just to those under roofs with felt – the insulation must not be put under them: this would prevent heat from the house from reaching them and they could freeze. The insulation should be carried over the top of the tank. The easiest way to achieve this is to build a box of 100mm thick expanded polystyrene held together with 150mm nails pushed into the edges. The top of the box can be lifted off to give access to the tank.

Insulated ceilings

In some houses the upper rooms are built into the roof space and have sloping ceilings, so there is no loft in which to put the insulation. Here, you will probably have to replace the ceiling by one which provides a vapour barrier, such as foil-backed plasterboard. Alternatively,

you can remove the roof covering to put in the insulation, and paint the existing ceiling with three coats of gloss paint (covered with emulsion if you do not like the gloss) to provide a vapour barrier.

The problem is that if there is no felt under the tiles, there is every chance that rain and snow will blow under them; so an insulating material must be used which will not be damaged by moisture. The best materials are expanded or extruded polystyrene or the resin bonded glass fibre used for filling cavity walls during construction. Once you have taken down the ceiling, you can cut the insulation to fit between the rafters and push it into place. It is important to leave no cavities between the back of the plasterboard and the insulation as these could provide a place for dry rot to grow. The use of a vapour barrier in the ceiling will reduce the chance of damp occurring in the roof structure.

If the tiles are laid on felt the insulation need not be waterproof, but it is then essential to fill the whole space between the ceiling and the felt with insulation to prevent the creation of any pockets of stagnant air, and again a vapour barrier on the ceiling is a must. In all cases, as a safeguard against rot, you should cover the roof timbers with three liberal coats of timber preservative once the ceilings or roof coverings have been removed.

Flat roofs

Internal insulation

Flat roofs present a problem because they cannot be entered as can pitched roofs. The only easy way to insulate them — assuming they are made of timber — is to remove the ceiling, fill the space between the underside of the roof and the ceiling with insulation, again

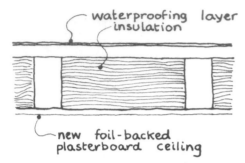

ensuring there are no gaps, and then put up a new ceiling of foil-backed plasterboard to form the essential vapour barrier. The problem with flat roofs is that the waterproof surface acts as a further vapour barrier and any moisture which penetrates the roof cannot escape; so it is

again a good idea to give all timbers three thorough coats of wood preservative while you have the ceiling down.

External insulation

If you do not want to remove the ceiling it is possible to lay slabs of extruded polystyrene on top of the flat roof, assuming that the water-proofing layer is in good condition. The roof waterproofing then acts as a vapour barrier and is protected against the damaging effect of the hot sun by the insulation. The problem with this method is that the insulation must be weighed down either with paving slabs or with 50mm of gravel to prevent it being blown away. This will add a load of about $100kg/m^2$ to the roof joists; most joists will not be strong enough to carry the extra load without contravening the structural requirements of the building regulations. If you plan to insulate a roof this way you should first consult the local building inspector. The manufacturers of extruded polystyrene recommend that this 'upside down' roof construction be carried out only by 'reputable roofing contractors who are members of roofing trade associations' as the processes involved are not of a do-it-yourself nature.

12 Tank and Pipe Insulation

Tanks

If you put insulation on top of the ceiling of the top floor, it follows that the attic will become colder: the amount of heat that rises into the roof from the rooms below will be greatly reduced by the insulation. Any water tanks or pipes in the roof will be much more likely to freeze, and, even if there are no bursts, one freezing winter could lead to at least a loss of water and at worst to a boiler blowing up.

The first way to prevent the cold water tank from freezing is not to put any insulation under-

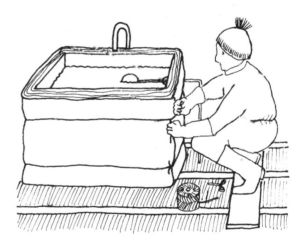

neath it when you are insulating the ceiling. This will allow some heat from the house to rise and keep the tank warm. The next step is to carry the insulation round the outside of the tank. Glass fibre and mineral fibre are relatively easy to use: wrap the fibre round the sides of the tank, to a thickness of about 100mm, and secure it in place with string tied round loosely so as not to compress it. Cover the top of the

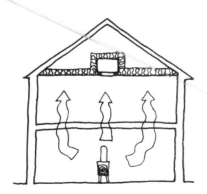

tank with a sheet of plywood, hardboard, or a purpose-bought lid before insulating the sides. You can then also cover the lid with a piece of glass fibre or mineral wool. If the tank has an overflow pipe discharging into it, which is often the case, cut a hole in the lid below the outlet of the pipe and put in a plastic funnel, about 200mm across the wide end, to catch any discharge from the overflow.

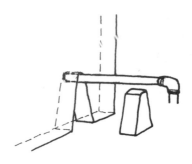

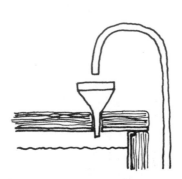

A tank wrapped with glass fibre or any similar floppy insulation will keep warm enough. But you may like to go up into the attic occasionally, to check the tanks; and you do not want to go raking about in a lot of itchy insulation every time you want to have a look at the ball valve. In this case, the best solution is to build a box of 75mm thick expanded polystyrene round the tank. You can cut the pieces of polystyrene to size with a panel saw and hold them together

by pushing 150mm nails through the edges. A coating of PVA glue on the joints will make the thing a bit stronger, but do not be tempted to try other sorts of glue such as contact adhesives, as they may well dissolve the polystyrene. Where pipes pass through the insulation a wedge can be cut out as shown in the diagram and then glued back in place once the insulation is fitted. Make a lid with more expanded polystyrene, held either with nails or an inner block if you want added refinement (see diagram). Do not forget the funnel for the overflow where necessary. This type of tank cover will be easier to open.

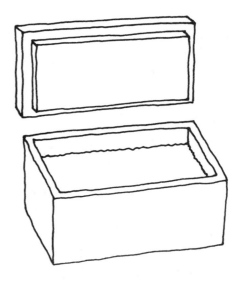

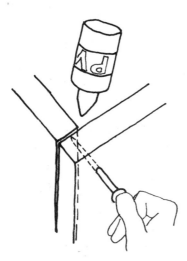

Pipes

All pipes in the attic should be lagged to prevent them freezing, and to avoid heat being wasted from hot pipes. You can buy rolls or lengths of material for insulating pipes, or you can cut

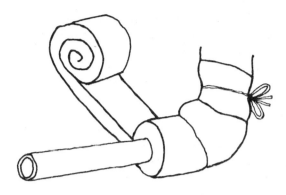

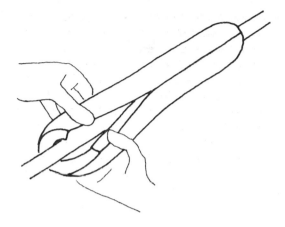

glass fibre or mineral wool into strips to bandage round them. The insulation should be at least 25mm thick, and held on with loosely tied string. Where pipes run at or near ceiling level, lay the roof insulation over them so that the pipe is on the warm side of the building.

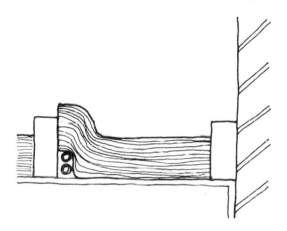

It is also important to lag the hot water pipes in the main part of the house, to prevent heat being lost as the water makes its way from the hot water cylinder to the taps. If the pipes are exposed you may not wish to use bits of glass fibre tied on with string; in this case it is preferable to buy pre-formed pipe insulation in the shape of a tube, with an inside diameter made to fit over the more common pipe sizes. The tube is slit along one edge so that it can be pulled open and fitted over the pipe. You can bend most types round corners but you will have to tape them on at bends to prevent the

slit coming open — you can use electrician's PVC insulation tape. At tees and other complicated junctions all you can do is fit the insulation as neatly as possible.

Hot water cylinders

As far as the hot water system is concerned, the most significant amount of heat is lost from the hot water cylinder, which should therefore have an insulating jacket at least 75mm thick. You can buy jackets ready made to fit all standard cylinder types and sizes, but it is better to buy one too big than too small. Alternatively you can tie glass fibre loosely round the cylinder with string to increase the insulation thickness to 100mm or 150mm. Cover the

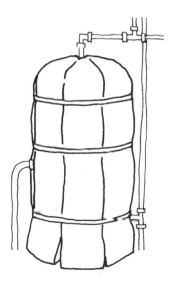

insulation with polythene sheet taped or tied on to reduce the problem of loose fibres causing irritation. You can also box the tank round with hardboard on timber framing, leaving holes for pipes and for access to valves; stuff the gap between tank and casing with offcuts of glass fibre insulation or expanded polystyrene packaging, which you can often get free from shops, broken into bits about 10mm across, or purpose bought granular insulation. Whatever method you choose try to make it at least 75mm and preferably 100mm thick.

As mentioned earlier, savings in the energy used to heat water can also be made by conscious effort rather than by technical means. For example, do not wash dishes, clothes or hands under running hot water, use a bowl or sink instead; mend leaky washers to stop dripping hot water taps; be sure to turn off hot taps properly; and do not rinse clothes in hot water after washing them. These things are all fairly obvious and many other savings will occur to you if you become more conscious of how energy is used.

13 Floor Insulation

The ground floor of a house does not lose as much heat as, say, the walls or roof, but in a thorough insulation scheme the floor should not be forgotten. Ground floors are usually made of concrete laid direct on to the earth or of wooden boards nailed to joists with a ventilated air space beneath (i.e., a suspended floor). Occasionally floor boards are nailed to pieces of wood set into a concrete slab. If you jump on the floor you will be able to tell if it is of boards on joists by its slightly springy feel. Another sign of a suspended floor is the air vents near the ground in the external walls of the building.

Suspended timber floors

Heat losses occur through the structure of a suspended timber floor and through the draughts that it may create. The problem is that the space under the floor must be well ventilated to prevent the build up of moisture and subsequent dry rot, but if it is well ventilated a powerful draught will often come into the house through the gaps beween the floorboards.

The most thorough solution to the draught and insulation problem is to take up the floorboards and insulate between the joists. The best material for the purpose is expanded polystyrene standard duty, with flame retardent additive (Type SD FRA). If you plan to re-use the floorboards you will have to romove them very carefully; and remember to turn the electricity off at the mains before you start.

The first step is to find if the boards are square edged or tongued and grooved. Push a penknife blade between two boards in several

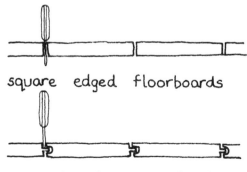

square edged floorboards

tongued and grooved floorboards

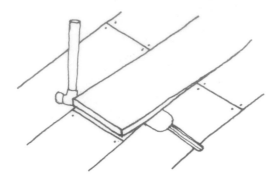

places: if the knife goes through easily the boards are square edged. Lift one end of a square edged board carefully with a bolster until the claw of a hammer can be slid underneath to keep the gap open. Then slide the bolster along the gap, carefully levering up the board. Once you have lifted the first board use the claw hammer to lever the others free of the joists, using the bolster to ease them up as necessary. Do not be tempted to rush in with a crowbar as you will split the boards and they will be useless.

If the boards are tongued and grooved cut the tongue off one board with a padsaw so that you can lever it up with the bolster. This is a long job so try to choose a short piece of board

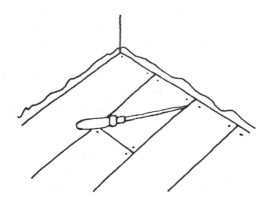

to do it on. Once the cut is started with the saw held vertically, tilt it back to a shallow angle and cut very slowly, using the tip of the saw. After every few strokes of the saw, turn it over and feel about with the back of the blade for pipes, joists and electric cables. Once you have cut off the tongue of the first board the others can be

levered up as before, but you will need extra care to avoid splitting off the tongues. All this assumes that, on inspecting the floor, you have been unable to find a board previously removed and screwed back after some rewiring or some plumbing job.

When the boards are off the insulation can be put in. Clean off the tops of the joists with a scraper, and give them three coats of timber preservative. Next nail 25mm×25mm pieces of Tanalised (or preservative painted) softwood to the sides of the joists, 50mm below the top for 50mm insulation, 75mm below for 75mm insulation and so on. Now cut the expanded

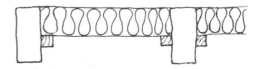

polystyrene to fit between the joists using a normal hand-saw. Make the pieces of polystyrene a fairly tight fit so that there will be no draughts through the floor. When electric cables run across the tops of the joists, use a Stanley knife to cut narrow V-shaped grooves in the top of the insulation, to accommodate them.

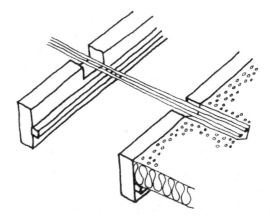

Once the insulation is in place, fitted tightly up to the walls and between the joists, you can replace the boards. To do this properly wedges should be used; they should be cut from wood 25mm thick and should be 500mm long by

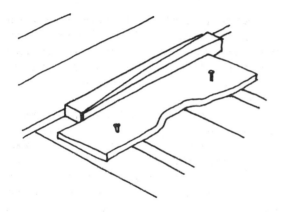

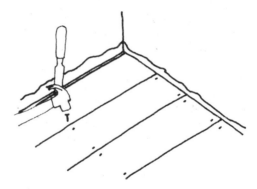

50mm at the wide end. You will need a pair of these wedges to fit every metre. Lay a few floorboards loosely without nailing them to the joists, and place a pair of wedges against the edge of the boards at one metre intervals. Then nail a scrap board against each pair of wedges leaving the nail head protruding so that it can be removed easily. Use two hammers to tap the wedges inwards to force the floorboards together, working on the sets of wedges alternately to keep the floorboards parallel.

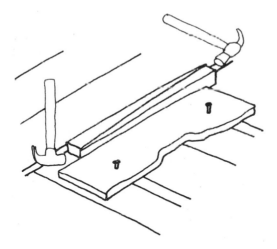

When the boards are good and tight nail them down, starting at the board near the wedges and using floorbrads or oval wire nails about 75mm long. When all the boards are nailed down take up the scrap board and the wedges; lay another five boards and wedge them together. When all the boards have been laid, lever the final board firmly against the others with a chisel and nail it down.

You may feel that taking up and relaying the floorboards is rather a large job. In this case a simpler solution is to seal the gaps in the floor to stop the draughts. The easiest way is to cover the floor with sheets of hardboard: lay it rough side up if you plan to put carpet or tiles on top of it, or smooth side up if it will be visible. The hardboard should be stored in the room where it is to be used for seventy-two hours before fixing it down to prevent it buckling because of changes in its moisture content. Nail the sheets of hardboard (which should measure 1200mm × 1200mm for ease of handling) to the floor at 150mm centres all over and at 100mm centres round the edges, using hardboard pins. Normal floor coverings can be laid on the hardboard if it has been laid rough side up, or the smooth side of the hardboard can be sealed to act as a floor surface itself.

Another way to seal the gaps is to lay a fitted carpet plus underlay or a sheet flooring on top of several layers of old newspapers. However, if you wish to have a floor of exposed timber boarding, you will have to fill the gaps between the boards to cut down the draughts. The filling can be done with stopping, a flexible filler available in a number of colours to match the wood of the floor. The stopping comes ready mixed in a tin and can be pressed into cracks with a scraper. Stopping is preferable to plastic wood as it is more flexible.

An alternative to stopping is to make papier mâché by tearing up scrap paper into pieces about 20mm across and mashing it to a thick pulp with boiling water added a little at a time. When the pulp is cool pour in cellulose wallpaper paste and stir to make a very thick mixture. If the papier mâché is to be visible the paper should be white (newspaper dries to a grey colour). If you want the mixture to match the floor you can colour it with liquid dye before using it. Press it firmly into the gaps with a scraper, and sand it down after about three days.

If the floor is draughty, sealing the cracks will make a considerable difference to the heat lost from the house. However, fitting insulation under the floorboards is more effective since it will cut structural as well as ventilation heat losses.

Concrete floors

Many houses have ground floors which consist of a concrete slab laid either on hardcore or directly on the earth. It is not possible to take up a floor like this and lay insulation underneath it as you can with floorboards, but you can put a layer of insulation on top. First remove the skirting boards from all walls. If the house is old and you suspect there is no damp proof course in the walls and no damp proof membrane (dpm) to stop moisture rising into the concrete from the ground, have a free survey and quote from a damp proofing firm. If the walls need damp proofing it must be done before the floor can be insulated.

If the floor is damp, you should treat it with a waterproofing material to prevent damp rising into the room. The easiest way to do this is to use a liquid such as Synthaprufe, a black bituminous emulsion. Paint it on to the concrete in three coats, using a very old brush which you can throw away afterwards, and wearing rubber gloves and boots. Whatever material is used the manufacturer's instructions must be followed regarding preparation and priming of the floor. Carry the damp proofing material about 300mm up the walls before replastering or insulating them, so that it meets the new damp proof course.

If the concrete floor is not damp, you can omit the black emulsion and the process for damp or dry floors is now the same. Lay sheets of expanded polystyrene, of whatever thickness you think from your calculations will be appropriate, on the floor. The polystyrene should be standard duty grade, preferably with flame retardent additive. The insulation should be laid with as few joints as possible so use 1200mm×2400mm sheets. Butt the polystyrene sheets tightly together so there are no gaps and try to stagger the joints. If you have to walk on the insulation lay pieces of plywood or hardboard as stepping stones to spread the load and prevent crushing the relatively soft foam.

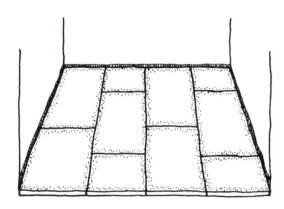

On top of the insulation lay sheets of tongued and grooved flooring grade chipboard, with the joints running the opposite way to the joints in the polystyrene. The chipboard will probably have 'this side down' written on one side and the tongues and grooves will not usually work if one sheet is upside down. Check all

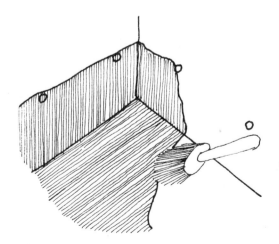

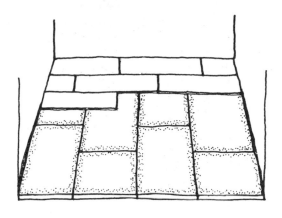

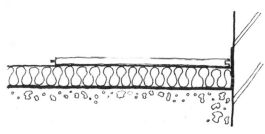

To allow for expansion there should be a gap of about 10mm between the edges of the chipboard and the plastered walls. This gap, which will be covered by the skirting board, also allows a little room in which to manoeuvre the pieces of chipboard to make them fit together. The only bit likely to be difficult is the last piece and if you cannot make it fit by levering against the wall with an old chisel you can nibble off the bottom of the groove with pincers and glue the chipboard down to the tongue of the next sheet.

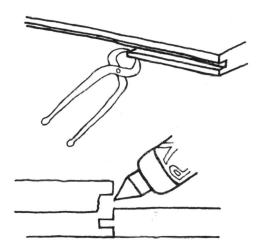

your sheets before laying, as occasionally only some of a batch will have 'this side down' printed on them. Lay the first sheet with its groove against the wall and the tongue protruding into the room. This makes it easier to lay the last sheet. Lay the pieces of chipboard like bricks with staggered joints, and squeeze PVA glue into the groove of the sheet before fitting it on to the tongue of the previous one. The aim is

to build a 'raft' of chipboard which will sit on top of the insulation. If you plan to seal the surface of the chipboard to use it as a floor covering be sure not to leave glue on it as this will affect the colour; spills of PVA glue can be wiped off with a slightly damp cloth before they are dry.

When all the sheets are in place leave them for twenty-four hours for the glue to dry. Then fix a skirting board to cover the expansion gap and hold down the edges of the raft. Finally seal or cover the floor with conventional flooring materials such as cork tiles, carpet, or sheet vinyl.

The new floor will be somewhat higher than the old one, so you will have to cut off the bottoms of doors to suit. This means that the technique is really only suitable for old buildings which have real wood doors. The average modern door, which consists of two sheets of hardboard separated by a paper honeycomb core, has only a thin edging of wood. If you decide to insulate your floor with 50mm of polystyrene plus 19mm of chipboard you will need to cut about 75mm off the bottom of the door and there may well not be any wood left at the bottom. You could cut the door, make a

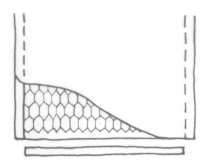

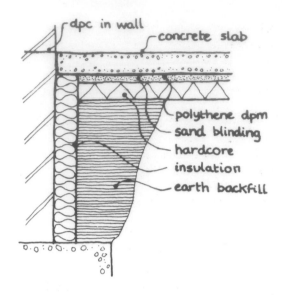

new piece of wood to fit the bottom, and glue it into place.

This method of insulation will also reduce the ceiling height of the room and may therefore upset the building inspector. The relevant regulation, in fact the only really silly one in the building regulations, lays down that a room must be 2300mm high from floor to ceiling, so the inspector may not be anxious to let you remove a precious 69mm from this magic figure. However, most building inspectors are reasonable and practical people so you should be able to reach a working compromise with them. Our experience is that in old buildings they only start to worry if the ceiling heights come down to about 2100mm.

New floors

If the floors of a building, whether concrete, suspended timber or brick on earth, are in really poor condition (dry rot, wet rot, furniture beetle, subsidence) you may decide to replace them. In this case the new floor will inevitably be of concrete and can be insulated when it is being laid. The techniques described below are appropriate if you want the building to have a high thermal mass, as discussed in Chapter 3. If you want a low thermal mass for intermittent heating you would be better advised to lay a floating chipboard floor as described above on top of your new concrete.

Assuming that you decide to benefit from the thermal mass of the concrete, the best way to insulate the floor is to excavate against the external walls to create a narrow trench down to the footings. Place expanded polystyrene 100mm thick next to the wall, resting on top of

the foundations, and fill in behind it with earth to keep the insulation in place. Be sure that you do not dig below the bottom of the foundations or the building will start to move and may collapse. A normal concrete slab on hardcore can then be laid over the floor and over the edge of the insulation. If a polythene sheet dpm is used it can be laid under the concrete on a layer of sand to stop the hardcore from making holes in it. If a painted dpm is preferred it should be applied to the top of the slab with a 50mm screed laid on top of it to take the floor finish.

In some old buildings there are no proper foundations. You may dig down next to the wall and discover that about 150mm below ground level the wall widens out, and then stops. If you find this do not go on digging or you will undermine the building. The solution is to lay the concrete slab on hardcore, put a dpm (either

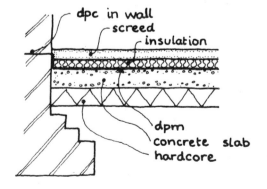

90

painted or a sheet material) on the concrete, and then lay your insulation on top of this. The insulation can be made up of 50mm or 75mm thick expanded polystyrene standard duty type. On top of the insulation lay a 50mm thick screed of one to three or four parts by volume of cement to fine aggregate. The screed can incorporate some galvanised wire mesh reinforcement (chicken wire is suitable) laid near the bottom of the screed to guard against cracking, but this should not be necessary on a domestic scale floor.

We are assuming, perhaps wrongly, that if you are confident enough to lay your own concrete you know how to do it. If not, look at the Reader's Digest book given in the Bibliography. If you have never laid concrete before an insulated floor is perhaps not the best place to start learning. If you do not feel that you can do the concreting yourself, and somehow the 'wet trades' like plastering, concreting and brick laying seem more difficult that the dry ones which involve only hammers, saws and nails, you can still use the ideas above for concrete floors and even carry out the unskilled labouring yourself, but have a builder to lay the concrete and screed.

The problem with work that involves some skill is that you need to do it a few times until you have the hang of it, but on most d-i-y jobs you only want to do it once so you do not get the practice. You could perhaps come together with a group of friends or neighbours to lay each other's insulated concrete floors but you will have to draw lots for who is to have the first unskilled one done on their house!

14 Installing Shutters

Making the frame

It is preferable to fit insulated shutters on the *inside* of windows or glazed doors (which must be draught-sealed first) so you don't have to go outside to close them at night. Also, internal shutters do not have to stand up to the elements and are therefore easier to make. The first step is to fix a frame round the opening to which you want to fit the shutters. This frame provides something for the shutters to close against and allows them to be hinged. It can be of suitably sized planed softwood; a good thickness would be 26mm (32mm before it is planed). The wood must be thick enough to be quite rigid, so that it will not distort when fixed and cause the shutters to stick.

The frame should be as wide as the shutters are thick plus about 25mm to allow for a stop to be nailed on. If the shutters are to fold back against the wall, the frame should be fixed more or less flush with the surface of the wall; if they are to fold against the sides of the opening, the frame can be fixed against the existing window or door frame. If you are fussy about such things the corners of the new frame can be mitred but it is much easier to make butt joints, and they look quite acceptable.

Pack out the frame members with pieces of plywood, hardboard or scraps of wood if the opening is not square. Now check the vertical pieces with a level to ensure that they are upright, or the shutters will not hang properly.

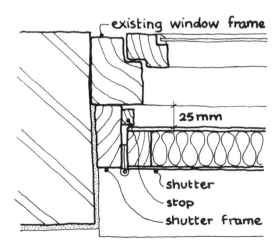

existing window frame

25mm

shutter
stop
shutter frame

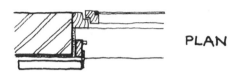

PLAN

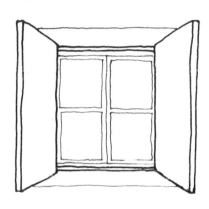

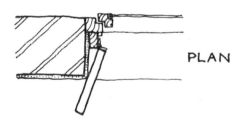

PLAN

Check that the frame is square by measuring across both diagonals – the measurements will be equal if the frame is square. If the frame is out of alignment it will be difficult to make the shutters so it is worth taking some time to get all this right. When you are satisfied that it is square, screw the frame into the opening with no 10 or no 12 screws and make sure that it is rigidly fixed.

Making the shutters

Once the frame is in place the shutters can be made. Their thickness will be governed by various factors such as cost, the space available for them to fold up in and the desired insulation value. As an example, a shutter made of 50mm thick expanded polystyrene covered on both sides with 4mm plywood will reduce the heat loss of a double-glazed window from 3.4 Watts/m^{2}degC to 0.5 Watts/m^{2}deg C (for an explanation of heat losses and how to calculate them see Chapter 4), while a similarly constructed shutter containing 25mm of insulation used on a single-glazed window would result in a reduction from 5 Watts/m^{2}degC to 0.8 Watts/mm^{2}degC. The practical limit to insulation thickness is about 50mm; otherwise the shutters would become very unwieldy.

The simplest way to make the shutters is to use expanded polystyrene which is fairly cheap and very easy to use; glass fibre, expanded polyurethane, mineral wool and similar materials are all suitable. If a rigid material like expanded polystyrene is used it will improve the stiffness of the shutters. Whatever insulation you choose it will need a facing to protect it from damage, and an edging so that hinges and handles can be fixed to the shutter.

To make the shutters, measure the inside dimensions of the frame that you have fixed

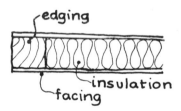

edging

insulation

facing

for use with expanded polystyrene. Cut more pieces of edging to fit on the two short sides, plus internal cross pieces at intervals of about 400mm, and glue and pin all these into place. Keep the panel pins well in from the edges of the shutters so that they will not get in the way when the edges are planed. When all the framing has been fixed to one facing, cut pieces of insulation to fit tightly into the spaces between the wooden members, push the insulation into place, spread glue on the frame, and pin the other facing into position. Let the glue dry and the shutter is complete.

into the opening and then decide how many shutters you wish to use to fill the space. The fewer shutters you need the easier they will be to make and fit but the more space they will take up when open. A larger number of narrow shutters will occupy less space when open but will need more skill to make and more hinges.

The facing of the shutters can be 4mm plywood or hardboard. Divide the measured size of the frame opening into equal parts according to the number of shutters required and cut the facings to these sizes. It is better to make the facings too big than too small as they can always be planed down to fit. The edgings of the shutters can be of 25mm×25mm softwood if you are using 25mm insulation, or 25mm×50mm for 50mm insulation. The wood need not be planed.

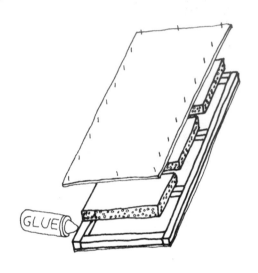

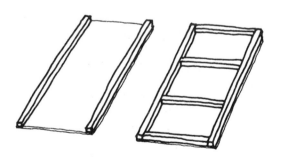

This description shows a simple method of construction but all sorts of refinements are possible. For example, the edgings can be rebated so that the edges of the facings do not show, or the facing could be of pine matchboarding to give a better appearance. The only essential is the insulation, as it is this that makes the shutters energy-conserving rather than purely decorative.

Cut the two edgings for the long sides of a shutter first, making them the full length of the facing, then glue and pin the facing to the softwood edgings. Take care to use a glue that does not damage your insulating material; PVA glue (such as Evostick Resin W) and the traditional hot melted Scotch glue are both suitable

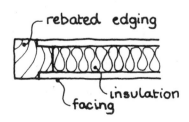

Fitting the shutters

Having been made the shutters must be put in place. First, plane them so that they fit snugly into the new frame. Use the longest plane you can get to plane the long edges; if possible use a jointer plane with the blade set to cut very shallow. The longer the plane and the shallower the cut, the less chance there is that you will end up with two concave-edged shutters that do not meet in the middle. This problem is worse for large numbers of shutters because there are more edges to get right. Check the fit of the shutters frequently to avoid planing off too much. For the short ends, use the plane from the sides to the middle to prevent splitting the end grain of the edgings.

It is possible to nail a stop to the frame, fit handles to the shutters and push them into place; when not in use they could be hung on the wall. However, the shutters are easier to use and therefore more likely to be used, if they are hinged to the frame. A single shutter can be hinged at the side, top or bottom, although if top-hinged it will need a catch to hold it up. A pair of shutters or multiple shutters must be hung from the sides. The best fit is obtained by using ordinary butt hinges recessed into the shutter and frame, but flush hinges which are screwed to the face of the work and do not need a chiselled recess can also be used. The gaps between the shutters from using surface-fixed hinges can be filled with a draught strip, or ignored. For shutters that are to fold against a wall parliament hinges may be useful. These allow the shutters to swing out to clear skirting boards, architraves, picture rails and other obstructions.

Once the shutters are hinged in place, nail a strip of softwood as sold for doorstops (finished size 8mm×19mm is available) to the frame for them to close against. Fix some handles to the shutters so that you can open them. If you find that the shutters do not stay closed you can fit a pair (or possibly more if there are several shutters) of small bolts to hold them shut. The bolts should be screwed to the timber edgings of the shutters, not just to the facings. Finally treat the frame and shutters with a clear finish, a coloured stain such as Sadolins, or ordinary paint as required.

If you want to have conventional curtains with your insulated shutters so that you can, for example, use curtains in the summer rather than shutters, lengthen the curtain rail so that the curtains can be opened enough to allow the

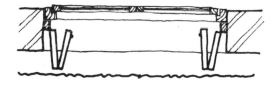

shutters to be folded away. If the shutters fold against the sides of the opening and project into the room use extension brackets to mount the curtain track far enough out from the wall for the curtains to clear the open shutters.

Once the shutters are finished you will only have to remember to close them when night falls in order to gain the benefit of the extra insulation.

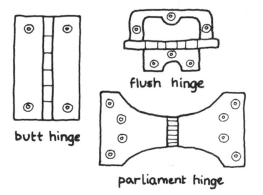

butt hinge

flush hinge

parliament hinge

15 Draught Proofing

Detecting draughts

Sealing up the cracks and holes through which draughts enter your home is a cheap and simple way to save fuel; at least it is a lot simpler than insulating a solid wall or building a solar heating system. Before you rush out to buy great lengths of draught excluder you need to know where the draughts are coming from. Some you will no doubt be aware of, but others may have so far gone unnoticed, so the first job is to find all undetected draughts. Smoke is the most efficient detector; don't trust a candle flame. If you are a smoker, your problem is solved, but if you are not we would hate to encourage you to start, and we suggest you buy a packet of joss sticks. The idea is to go about the house on a windy day with a smoking joss stick clutched in your hand: even though the neighbours may well think that you have begun to seek Enlightenment you will at least find out where there is a draught. If there is no draught the smoke will rise straight up. Your house will smell of incense for a bit but if it is draughty the smell will soon clear.

The simpler solutions

Now that you know where the draughts are coming in you can start to keep them out. We have covered the sealing of floors in Chapter 13, so here we will deal mainly with doors and windows. First we offer some cheap and crude solutions.

You can make a draught excluding bolster from a piece of cloth formed into a cylinder with two ends sewn on, stuffed with kapok or old nylon tights cut up into small pieces. Make it about 75mm in diameter and 150mm longer than the door you are trying to seal. Start with two circles of cloth about 95 or 100mm in diameter and sew one to the end of a long rectangular piece taking a 10mm seam. Pin the pieces of fabric together, right sides facing, and sew them, leaving a gap so that the whole thing can be turned inside out when you have finished. Now put the stuffing in tightly, using a piece of dowel or the wrong end of a knitting needle to pack it in place; then oversew the gap to hold the stuffing in. The result can be quite attractive if you use the right fabric.

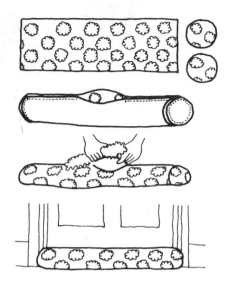

An even simpler draught sealer could be made from an old trouser leg gathered at one end, stuffed and then gathered at the other end. If you feel you cannot sew you could tie the ends with a piece of string. If you can knit you can also buy knitting patterns for draught excluders which are usually shaped like dogs, caterpillars or snakes.

There is an even cheaper way to seal doors or windows that you will not want to open until the warm weather comes. Take a sheet of newspaper and fold it over and over from one end to make a strip about 15mm wide and as thick as required to fill the gap. Ease the piece of newspaper into the opening and you will find

that you have successfully reduced or even eliminated the draught. This method works very well for sash windows. On casement windows and doors the strips can be stapled to the wood of the opening part (not the frame) to hold them in place.

If you can find a piece of heavy plush or velvet in a jumble sale you could use it to make a draught excluding curtain for an external door. The curtain should fit closely against the door and must touch the floor at the bottom to make a seal; ideally it should brush against the ceiling as well. Hang it from a curtain track or one of those brass rods with rings, so that it can be drawn back in the summer. You will find that it will become a popular hiding place with the kids.

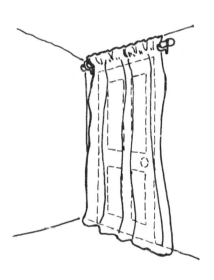

Fireplaces

If you have an unused fireplace in your house it will be a major source of draughts. Here there are three choices open to you. The first is to install an efficient stove in the fireplace as described in Chapter 18. The second is to brick up the fireplace, remembering to incorporate an air vent, to the outside if possible (see Chapter 10). Finally you can make a frame of 50mm×50mm timber with a piece of hardboard or plywood nailed over it which can be wedged into the fireplace opening. If the chimney is on an external wall and you do this

be sure to make a row of holes in the cover so that air can circulate up the chimney and so prevent condensation. This ventilation is unavoidable but at least it will be a lot less than the draught through the open fireplace.

When draught sealing do not forget the hatch into the loft. If the roof space is properly ventilated there may well be a flow of air round the hatch, and one of the techniques described later for the edges of doors should be used to seal it.

Doors

There are two different types of draught seal for doors, those used at the bottom of the door and those for the sides and top. Bottom or 'threshold' seals must be durable, particularly if you use the type which fits on the floor, because people will tread on it. All draught seals are a compromise between cost and durability, but perhaps one of the best threshold seals is the brush seal which is suit-

able for internal or external doors. This consists of a thin brush made of closely packed bristles usually of nylon, held in a plastic or aluminium frame which is screwed to the bottom edge of the door. You fit the brush to the inside edge of the door so that the bristles rest firmly against the floor or doorstep. The bristles will deform to cope with uneven floors and will pass over carpets or other obstructions.

It is a good idea to fit a weatherboard to the bottom of the door, if it opens inwards, to help throw off rainwater. You can buy the weatherboard moulding from a wood merchant; paint it

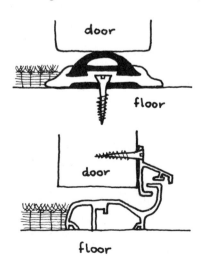

with timber preservative and prime it before fixing it to the bottom of the door with zinc-plated screws. Cut the door stop (as shown) with a narrow chisel to accommodate the weatherboard. The illustration shows some other types of seals for the bottom of doors; many varieties are available and the choice will probably depend on what you can find in the local shops.

The seals for the sides and top of doors range from the very cheap ones which have a short life to those that may last as long as the door itself. The cheapest type is the self-adhesive foam plastic strip which comes on a roll. You open the door, unroll a piece of strip and cut it to roughly the right length. Peel off the backing paper at the top of the strip and stick the foam to the top of the door frame against the stop. If the stop is not clean it should be wiped with a damp cloth and allowed to dry before you do the draught sealing, as the strip will not adhere if the door frame is greasy or dirty. When the top of the strip is stuck peel off some more of the backing and stick the strip down again.

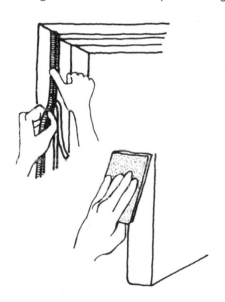

When you reach the bottom of the door cut the strip to the correct length before you peel off the last of the backing. When you have fixed all the draught strip it is a good idea to round off the edges of the door where they will touch the strip. This will help to prevent damage to the

foam when the door is opened. Even if you do this the seal is not likely to last more than a year or two if the door is often in use. There is a slightly more expensive foam strip which is encased in a PVC cover and has a reinforcing cord running down the middle. The cover protects the foam from damage and it is worth using this type in preference to the cheaper plain foam.

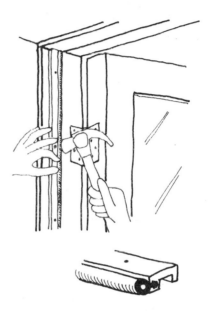

The next step up in the search for a long-lasting cheap draught seal is the type which has a hollow flexible plastic strip against which the door closes, held in a rigid plastic holder which is nailed to the door frame. This type is cut to length and fixed with the pins provided. When you fix the strip the flexible sealing part should be pressed reasonably firmly against the door before nailing. Check that the door closes easily without crushing the plastic after you have fixed the strip with a few pins. Do not drive the pins right in until you have finished adjusting it if you need to. A variation on this type of draught excluder has a neoprene rubber seal held in an aluminium edge section but this is, as you would expect, more expensive than a plastic one.

An old fashioned but effective and long-lasting draught seal consists of a strip of springy metal made of phosphor bronze, a

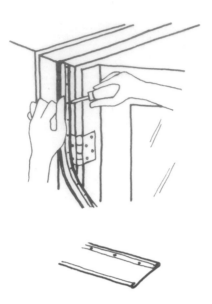

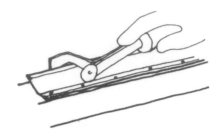

first. At hinges and lock plates, cut the strip with tin snips and fold it back as shown to clear the obstructions before pinning it in place. When both side pieces are fixed, run the Atomic springing tool along the line marked on the strip to raise the free edge slightly so that it presses against the door when it is closed. The

height that the strip is raised depends on how hard you press: go carefully and press lightly to start with because if you raise it too much it will be very hard to close the door. When the sides are sprung out enough to seal the door you can cut a piece of strip for the top, cutting the ends at an angle to match the angle made by the edge of the strip on the sides of the door frame. Finally pin the top piece in place and spring it with the springing tool to touch the top of the door.

copper alloy, so that it will not rust. The most familiar type rejoices in the name 'Atomic Strip', but do not let this put you off! The strip should be pinned to the door frame with the pins provided, positioned so that the fixed edge is towards the outside of the frame and the free edge is about 3mm from the door stop.

If it is an external door you should buy the solid brass fixing pins as the pins included with the strip are brassed steel and may rust. The easiest way to put the pins in is to use a tool called a pin push, which consists of a thin tube which retracts into a handle. You put a pin in the tube, place the tool on the spot where the pin is to be fixed, and push the handle or tap it with a mallet to drive the pin home. The strip has small indentations in it about 30mm apart and the pins must be put in at each mark.

It is very important that the strip lies flat and does not buckle at all. Nail on the side pieces

Before you leave the door it is worth sealing the letter-box. You can buy a device for this purpose which consists of two pieces of brush type seal which mesh together and are soft enough to bend out of the way when a letter is pushed through. This is screwed over the letter-box opening on the inside of the door.

Casement windows can be sealed in the same way as doors but you can use the techniques for the top and sides of doors all the way round windows because no one walks on the sills. Sash windows can be sealed as described, with newpaper or by double-glazing right across the whole frame (see Chapter 16).

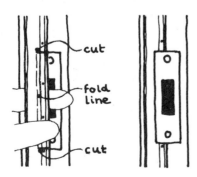

Building a porch

However well you manage to draught seal your house with those little bits of nailed-on plastic, cold air is still going to come through the front door whenever it is opened. The only way to solve this is to build a porch large enough to allow you to shut the outside door before opening the inside one, thus preventing gusts of cold air blowing straight into the house. Before considering the design of a porch it is worth looking at the way you use the building. Typically houses have always been provided with a front door and a back door and in a terraced house both of these are usually necessary. In a semi-detached or detached house it would be possible to use only one door: this would be best covered with a generous porch, then you could brick up the unused door. Apart from dealing with the draught problem of an opening door once and for all, you may also find that you can gain extra usable space inside the house by eliminating the hall.

Having removed the door, and its frame and sill, you will be left with a hole surrounded by bricks. You will have to obtain a brick to match that of the wall and here your builders' merchant should be able to help if you take a brick along with you. If there are no old bricks around the building left over from other alterations such as a new window being fitted, you could remove a sample from the doorway when you have removed the door — you will in any case have to remove bricks in order to key in your new brickwork to the existing opening. Alternatively, and also if you fail to buy matching brick, find as good a match as possible and plan a concealing creeper or a bush where there used to be a door.

If your wall has a cavity the inner leaf can be of common brick or block to match the existing inner leaf. Knock out a brick either side every four courses, to provide a key (use a cold chisel and lump hammer to do this job), and start by building up your brick work from where the old sill rested to damp proof course level. This will be seen as a black line along the mortar joint about 150 or 225mm above ground level. If your house is old and has solid brick walls the

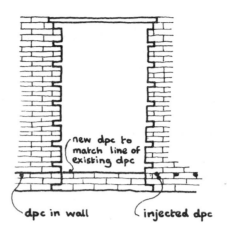

new dpc to match line of existing dpc

dpc in wall   injected dpc

damp proof course may have been injected, in which case you will see a line of mortar-filled holes about the same distance above ground level. In the new brickwork put a length of black plastic damp proof course, either over the whole solid wall or on each leaf of the cavity wall, and bed it in mortar. Continue building up the brickwork above the damp proof course but, if you are forming a cavity, put a couple of butterfly type galvanised wall ties, one at either side of the opening, starting at the level of the damp proof course and then at 450mm intervals above this.

If you have gone to the trouble of having the cavity filled with foam then you will have to build insulation into your new cavity. Glass fibre

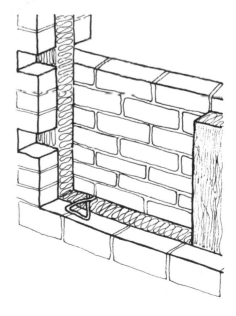

batts, sold for this purpose, are easy to use and should be supported off the wall ties at the level of the damp proof course so there is no chance of them becoming wet. Put the batts in place as the wall is built up.

A window can be built into the door opening with its head up against the lintel that was above the old door, with further lengths of damp proof course all round the window frame and behind the bricks that close off the cavity (as shown in the drawings). The window

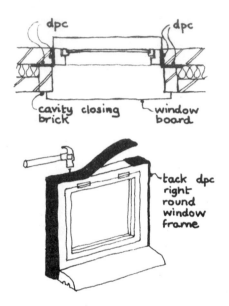

should sit on the outer leaf of the cavity with a timber window board fixed over the cavity and the inner leaf on the inside. If you have chosen to brick up the front door you may have to find an alternative site for the letter-box. The new porch door would be the obvious place and our postman has been very understanding about the increased distance he has to walk round to the back of the house. Elsewhere we have seen bricked up front doors with the letter-box left in its old place and incorporated in the new brick wall.

If you do not go to the length of bricking up the front (or back) door, you may be able to put an extra door in your existing hall to create an airlock. This solution is often very easily adopted in a terraced house. The inner door need not be waterproof so you can buy an

interior grade door and frame which will be cheaper than an external one. The new door should ideally be draught sealed along with the outer door. If the hall is wider than the door block the frame out with some lengths of 50mm×100mm softwood or even with a short length of stud partition faced with plasterboard. When the airlock is complete just remember to shut one door before you open the other or the whole thing will be a waste of time. Perhaps it would help if you imagined you lived on board a starship!

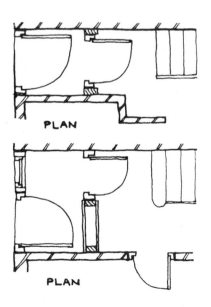

102

If you have room for it outside the house, a fully enclosed porch makes a very good airlock, and a conservatory (see Chapter 21) makes a very good porch, as well as being a source of solar heat. Off-the-peg conservatories are an excellent solution as these are cheap, reasonable in appearance and easy to erect. They usually sit on a simple brick or precast concrete base on very small foundations, so there is not a lot of digging and concreting to be done. Check with your local authority before you start designing a porch: it should not need planning permission but it will need to comply with the building regulations, and you may have to have proper foundations and so on. Given this fact it is probably worth building quite a large porch because it is hardly worth the trouble of digging the footings for a small one.

The drawings show some examples of houses with porches added on.

16 Double-Glazing

The heat loss through windows makes up only 10 per cent of the total heat loss from a typical 1930s semi, so even if you could completely stop the heat loss from the windows you would still have most of the heat loss of the house to deal with. If the windows are double-glazed their heat loss will be halved: if a house needs 10kW to keep it at 20°C when freezing outside, it will need 9.5kW if the windows are double glazed. These comments only represent the conventional views about the effectiveness of double-glazing, but if the double-glazing is used to draught seal the windows, it will reduce the heat loss more effectively by cutting down draughts.

The decision whether or not to double-glaze will depend on the individual house, and you will have to make heat loss calculations to find out how much heat is being lost through the windows and how much less heat would be lost if they were double-glazed. The effect of double-glazing on ventilation heat loss is less easily estimated: draughts should be sealed up by all possible methods as described in Chapter 15 and the individual contribution of double-glazing cannot be separately worked out.

Fitting new windows

If you have very old and rotten windows it may be worth thinking about replacing them with new ones rather than double-glazing. This is a difficult question because there are matters of planning to consider so the choice of windows is complicated. Many Victorian terraced houses, which depend for their architectural effect on the fact that the houses are more or less identical, are spoiled by unthinking

individualists who replace old sash windows with new windows of unsympathetic design. Small building firms and the companies that sell 'replacement windows' are often to blame, as they do not offer their clients any advice or choice of windows. The overall effect is like that of sawing the legs off a Chippendale chair and replacing them with chromium plated steel, but a little thought and attention to detail can allow old windows to be replaced without spoiling the whole street.

If you are replacing wooden sash windows the best plan is to ask for a quote from a small joinery manufacturer to make a replacement to match the existing window. The new window should be made to the specifications of BS 644 but should have weather stripping added to make it draught tight. If you do this the fact that the window is not double-glazed will make little difference to the heat loss, especially if you make insulated shutters for the window as described in Chapter 14. It is surprisingly cheap to have windows made to measure and they often cost less than ready-made mass-produced windows.

Sealed pane double-glazing

If you really want double-glazing in your replacement windows you have two choices. The first is to use sealed pane double-glazing units in the timber replacement windows as described above. These units consist of two pieces of glass sealed together with a spacing strip round the edge. The air in the cavity between the two sheets of glass is specially dried before the unit is sealed so that there will be no condensation inside the unit. These sealed units are expensive to buy and the seal can fail, leading to the formation of condensation between the panes. If this happens the only solution is to buy a new unit.

Some of these units are available in a 'stepped' form so that they can be put in to a window with putty in the same way as a normal pane. If you decide to use them in a replacement sash window be sure to tell the person who is making the window so that the sash balance weights can be made heavier to compensate for the extra weight of the two

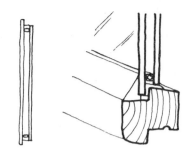

panes of glass. If you do not do this the window will drop down every time you attempt to open it.

Aluminium windows

The alternative to a timber sash window if you want to spend a lot of money is an aluminium replacement window. Until recently these have been poorly designed and have almost universally spoiled the appearance of old buildings, but if you want to use them there are now aluminium sash windows which will give a reasonable match to the existing ones. Take great care when choosing the window that it suits the style of the house. One drawback to aluminium windows is that condensation forms on the metal frames because they have a high thermal conductivity and are consequently very cold. Timber window frames give a degree of insulation and do not become cold enough for condensation to form on them. A recent development is the use of aluminium frames with a core of insulating material to form a thermal break between the inside and the outside of the window frame.

Aluminium replacement windows are more expensive than timber, and are almost always supplied fitted with double-glazed units. They are usually very well draught sealed and have the advantage that, provided you choose aluminium coloured ones, they do not need painting. Some more recent types offer an acrylic finish which is supposed to last ten or fifteen years, but no one is sure what you do when the finish starts to wear out as it surely must. Your safest choice is natural aluminium frames: although in time they will become grey and pitted, they will still work.

Double-glazing existing windows

Most people do not plan to take out their old windows; most can be repaired rather than replaced. A joiner can make new sashes, new casements, fit new hardwood sills and generally rebuild an existing window at less cost than making a replacement. If you are in doubt, ask several joiners for quotes for necessary repairs and for the cost of replacing the window with a copy. The best way to double-glaze an existing window is to fit glass right across the window and its frame, as this draught proofs the window as well as providing double-glazing. If you try to fit glass over the glass part of the window only, you will still have to draught seal the frame (see Chapter 15).

Using cling film

Before discussing double-glazing with glass you might consider a very cheap method which was devised by Geoffrey Horsley, a scientist at the Harwell atomic energy establishment.

This uses 'cling film' kitchen wrapping material instead of glass as the inner pane. Double-glazing works partly by trapping a layer of still air against the window and it is this layer of air that insulates: the insulating effect of the glass or other material is not great by comparison. Tests have shown that cling film double-glazing is at least 80 per cent as good as proper double-glazing and, of course, it is extremely cheap.

The glazing works because the film sticks to clean paint, so the first step is to clean the window surround with washing-up liquid and water to remove any grease, and to clean your hands as well. The film is available in rolls either 300mm or 450mm wide which means that it cannot be used for windows wider than this. If you have wide windows you could consider making up a frame of 25mm×50mm planed softwood to fit into the window surround and support the film. If you do this the frame should be sanded carefully to remove any rough spots on the side that will face into the room and then given a coat of primer, a coat of undercoat and two coats of gloss paint. Similarly, if the paint of the window surround is in poor condition it

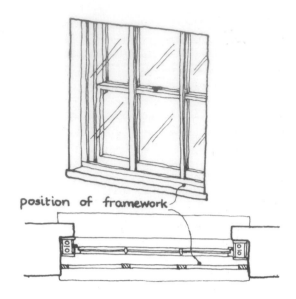

position of framework

should be sanded down and repainted to give a smooth surface. Allow the paint to dry for at least twenty-four hours before trying to apply the film.

When the paint is ready take the roll of film out of its box and allow about 50mm to unwind from the end. Put one of your little fingers inside each end of the cardboard roll on which the film is wound and hold the corners of the piece that you have unrolled between thumb and forefinger. Take the roll to the window and make sure that the film is unwinding from the side of the roll nearest the glass. Press the film that you are holding in thumb and forefinger against the top of the window frame or sur-

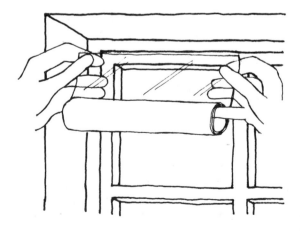

round, making sure that the side edge of the film always overlaps the sides of the window frame. Using your thumbs, press the film against the painted window frame and smooth it down to exclude air bubbles.

When the film has stuck down firmly use one hand to hold the roll while you smooth down the rest of the film at the top of the window. Then let the film unroll slowly down the window and press it against the sides of the frame, doing about 100mm at a time. When you reach the bottom of the window press the film firmly against the frame and trim it off with a single-edged razorblade (to prevent cutting your fingers with a conventional blade), or a Stanley knife.

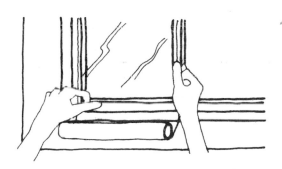

At this stage the window will not look very impressive as the film will be rather wrinkled, so the next step will be to remove the wrinkles. To do this peel back one of the top corners of the film for a distance of about 100mm. Pull the film gently so that it is taut and press it back again. Then gradually go round the window unpeeling the film, pulling it tight without splitting it, and pressing it back into place. With any luck this process will remove the wrinkles and you will be left with a clear taut film covering the window.

If you have added a wooden frame to the window to make it narrow enough to take the film, make sure that the film does not come more than halfway across the width of each vertical framing piece. Use the razorblade to trim it if necessary. If you do not do this you may find that the previously tightened film will be loosened by the removing and refixing of the subsequent piece of film. The film should last

for at least a year if you are careful with it, and can then be replaced with a new roll.

Because of the problem of width limitations the film is best suited to windows that are divided into small panes. On Victorian windows these dividing bars are too narrow for the film to stick to them; but modern mass produced 'Georgian' windows use a wide flat bar which is ideal for sticking on the film. If you need to use a wooden frame to divide up the window area into smaller widths the cost will be increased, but this method will still be much cheaper than any other double-glazing techniques.

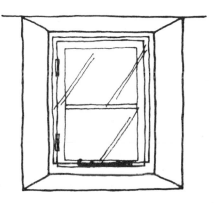

If the film extends across the whole window area it will help to reduce ventilation heat loss by acting as a draught seal, but if you use a non-flued combustion heater such as a paraffin stove or portable gas heater or if you have a gas fire be sure enough air for combustion can enter the room, otherwise you will run the serious risk of being overcome by fumes. If you use a coal fire with a chimney you will know if there is not enough draught because the chimney will not draw.

Temporary double-glazing
If you do not want to replace cling film every year, the next stage up in double-glazing is to use real glass with a simple edging to hold it in place. This type of glazing is not openable so you will have to take it down in the spring and store it somewhere until the autumn, hoping you do not break it in the meantime. The simplest type uses a plastic edging strip which you press on to the edges of the glass, cutting 45°

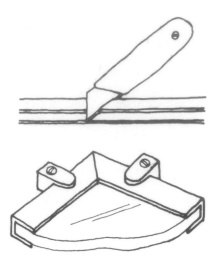

enter the cavity to evaporate any moisture that forms in there as a result of condensation. ·

If you are adding a fixed pane of glass to a window, remember that building regulation K4 stipulates that, in any room, there must be a ventilation opening with an area at least a twentieth of that of the floor area. You will need the ventilation anyway if you are using a paraffin stove, calor gas heater, or gas stove. If you plan to use any of these do not seal up the windows or you may fail to wake up one morning.

D-i-y glazing

It is easier if you can open your double-glazing so that you can open the existing window for ventilation, and it is very helpful not to have to take down the double-glazing and store it each summer when you want the windows open. There are various do-it-yourself systems of permanent hinged and sliding double-glazing. Points to look for when choosing one of these systems are that it should be made of long-lasting materials and that it should be easy to assemble. Most types of hinged double-

angles at the corners with a sharp Stanley knife to make it fit neatly. Small plastic clips are then fixed to the window surround and they are used to grip the edging strip that you fixed to the glass. The edging cushions the glass and provides a seal to keep out draughts and noise.

The cavity between the existing window and the new sheet of glass should be ventilated to the exterior. If the old window is loose fitting you need take no further action, but if it is fairly tight you should drill 6mm holes through the top and bottom of the window at 300mm centres. Slope the holes downwards to reduce the chance of rain coming through them and plug them with small bits of glass fibre to keep out insects but allow the air to permeate. The purpose of the holes is to allow sufficient air to

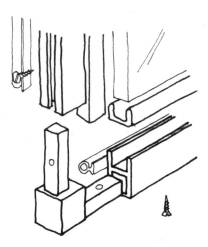

glazing are made of aluminium sections with plastic gaskets to hold the glass and plastic or longer lasting neoprene rubber seals to fit against the window frame. The hinges and fasteners are usually nylon.

The types that are easiest to assemble use moulded corner pieces which eliminate the need to cut 45° mitres at the corners of the

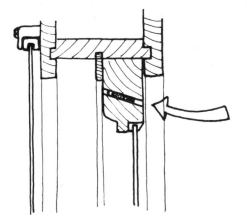

frame sections: it is much easier to cut a piece of frame to length at right angles rather than trying to cut to length at a mitred corner. The sliding systems are more expensive because there is a separate frame in which the framed pieces of glass slide. The seal between the sliding part and the fixed frame is maintained by pile seals which are like small brushes that brush along the sliding section. The sliding frames themselves are made like the hinged frames described above. Most of these systems have clear instructions and it is best to follow these carefully, reading them at least twice before starting to cut into the pieces of framing. The instructions will also tell you what size to have the glass cut to fit the chosen glazing system.

Frames

For many of these systems you will have to fit a simple wooden frame into the existing window opening. If you have sliding sash windows you will probably be able to screw the double-glazing directly to the surround of the window but many more recent houses have metal windows and the sides of the window openings are of plastered brick. In this case a frame of ex 50mm×50mm planed softwood should be

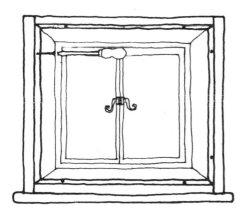

screwed to the window opening using 75mm no 12 screws, preferably zinc-plated, and plastic plugs. At the top of the opening there will be a lintel to carry the wall above; if it is made of concrete you will have great trouble drilling into it. The easiest solution is to hire a

percussion drill which delivers hammer blows to the drill bit while it rotates; this used with a masonry bit should make suitable holes. Try to make the surface of the frame level all the way round so that the glazing will fit flat against it. Before fixing the glazing, the timber frame should be primed and painted or else treated with a preservative stain.

Alternative solutions

Curtains

Before deciding to build double-glazing you should think whether it is really necessary. If your windows are fairly small (10–15 per cent of the total external wall area of your building), and if you can draught seal them effectively, you may not need double-glazing at all. Other ways to prevent more heat being lost through windows than absolutely unavoidable include the use of thick lined curtains which touch the ceiling or else have a pelmet to reduce the chance of air circulation at the top. Ideally the curtains should be long enough to brush along the floor so as to form a draught seal against the cold air that will tend to flow down the window. If you shut the curtains as soon as it becomes dark you will save a worthwhile amount of energy.

Radiators

Another saving is to contradict the universal practice of putting radiators under the windows if you install central heating. The idea is to use the heat from the radiators to counteract the down draughts of cold air from the surface of the glass and try to warm up the draughts before they enter the room. What happens is that the heat from the radiator is almost immediately lost through the windows and you receive little benefit from it. The best place to put radiators is on internal walls, so that they heat the fabric of the house, rather than on the colder outside walls.

If you already have radiators under your windows and do not want to move them you can fit a shelf above them to deflect the hot air from the window; arrange the curtains so that they touch this shelf. You can also fit shiny foil

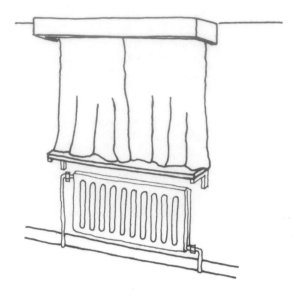

insulation behind the radiators to reflect heat into the room and away from the outside wall. Finally, do not sleep with your window open in a heated bedroom, either leave the heating on and open your door, or turn off the heat and have the window open. When you do want to ventilate the house choose a warm day when the heating is not operating at full blast and remember to close the windows when the air has cleared.

U values

To help you decide whether double-glazing is worthwhile or whether you might do better just to have insulated shutters or a draught sealed single-glazed window, here are some comparative U values, assuming a normal degree of exposure in all cases.

Glazing	W/m²deg C
single	5.6
double 6mm gap	3.4
12mm gap	3.0
20mm or more gap	2.9

Shutters (closed)		W/m²deg C
single-glazing,	12.5mm shutter	1.14
	25mm	0.82
	50mm	0.53
double-glazing,	12.5mm	0.96
	25mm	0.72
	50mm	0.49

Average U values for shuttered windows are shown below. The first table shows the average value if the shutters are open for eight hours a day and the second assumes they are open for twelve hours. In all cases the windows are assumed to be draught sealed.

Open eight hours, closed sixteen hours

single-glazing,	12.5mm shutter	2.6
	25mm	2.4
	50mm	2.2
double-glazing,	12.5mm	1.6
	25mm	1.4
	50mm	1.3
	100mm	1.2

Open twelve hours, shut twelve hours

single-glazing,	12.5mm shutter	3.4
	25mm	3.2
	50mm	3.1
double-glazing,	12.5mm	1.9
	25mm	1.8
	50mm	1.7

The average values over twenty-four hours may be slightly different than shown in these figures because it is colder at night than in the daytime and these averages make no allowance for this.

The final choice will depend on you and how much money you want to spend. The important thing is not to have double-glazing just because it is the thing to do, as it may not be the best thing to do if you are really trying to save energy. The costs you will have to work out for yourself.

17 Dealing with Condensation

The formation of condensation is discussed in Chapter 3; the aim of this chapter is to describe the methods for preventing and controlling condensation. Briefly, the moisture vapour in the air forms condensation when it comes into contact with cold surfaces, because cold air can hold less water vapour than warm air; as the air cools it reaches a dew point temperature where the water vapour it contains can no longer remain as a gas, so it condenses. This is frequently seen on windows, and in some cases the condensation forms on walls, leading to mould growth.

The presence of water vapour in the air depends on what you are doing in the house, so one way of reducing condensation is to change your habits. For example, if you are in the habit of boiling nappies on the stove, or if you frequently wash down the floor with a lot of water you are adding to the water vapour in the air. Some activities are unavoidable, but others can be managed to reduce the vapour content of the air. The vapour emitted around the house is shown in the table below, measured in kilogrammes per day.

two adults asleep for eight hours	0.6
gas cooking: breakfast	0.4
lunch	0.5
dinner	1.2
washing up: breakfast	0.1
lunch	0.1
dinner	0.3
floor mopping	1.1
washing clothes	2.0
drying clothes	12.0
bathing	0.05
showering	0.23
house plant	0.84
paraffin stove	0.35/hour
portable gas heater	0.13/kWh

You can see from the table that it is a good idea not to hang damp washing round the house to dry it; try to hang it outside or use a spin drier before you put it on an indoor line. If you must hang washing indoors because it is raining or there is nowhere else to hang it, put it in the bathroom and open the window to let the extra ventilation remove some of the moisture vapour.

111

Another way to reduce the effects of condensation is to use natural materials and furnishings. Materials such as wood, cotton, linen and wool absorb moisture; provided that the periods of excess moisture are limited these materials can absorb the excess and give it out later. Try to use cotton or linen curtains, wooden furniture with linen upholstery, cotton sheets, sisal or wool carpets and other natural materials in preference to man-made fibres and you may reduce the condensation. However, these materials will not solve the more serious cases which will require more drastic remedies.

The usual ways to deal with condensation are ventilation, insulation and heating. If you seal your house to reduce its ventilation heat loss rate you will prevent air from circulating and removing water vapour, and the result may be an increase in condensation. Condensation mainly occurs in kitchens, bathrooms and, to a lesser extent, bedrooms. One simple solution is to open a window if condensation starts to form; but be sure to shut the door of the room so that the draught does not blow through the whole house. This is an advantage of old fashioned houses with separate rooms, but if you have an open-plan house you will just have to put up with the draught.

If the building is well insulated the walls and windows will be warmer and there will be less condensation. In properly insulated houses you can heat all the rooms constantly fairly cheaply and doing so will help to keep surfaces above the dew point temperature.

If a combination of changed habits, insulation and heating do not reduce condensation to manageable levels that can be controlled by occasionally opening a window, you can also try using an extractor fan. To prevent excessive ventilation, wire the fan to a dewstat, a device that turns the fan on when there is a risk of condensation and turns it off when the risk is passed. This ensures that the fan operates for the least possible time to remove the water vapour.

If you use insulation in a building be sure that you follow the instructions concerning vapour barriers and ventilation of air spaces given in Chapter 10, because condensation in insulation can cause a lot of damage. On walls and windows, it is a nuisance and it may stain paint or wallpaper; but within insulated walls and roofs it can lead to dry rot and to very expensive repairs, if not the complete deterioration of the house.

18 Wood-Burning Stoves and Chimneys

When and why to choose a woodstove

In the UK, in 1973, you could only buy four different models of woodstove; now there are well over fifty (foreign and home produced) models to choose from. Which one you select will remain largely a matter of personal preference: but do check that the manufacturers' suggested rates of heat output are compatible with the heat required in your house. Also, a cast iron stove will last longer than one of thin sheet steel; 6mm steel plate should, however, last as long as cast iron. As with all equipment, the simpler the stove, the less chance there is of a breakdown. A simple pivot draught control should last as long as the stove (fifty to a hundred years for cast iron); but electric fan assisted heat transfer may be an unnecessary and complicated addition.

It must be emphasised that by replacing part of your central heating system with a woodstove you will not be helping to reduce the national domestic consumption of energy. All you will be doing is hastening the day when the meagre wood resources of this country are finally exhausted. The only way to reduce energy consumption is to insulate the building, for example by lining walls and sealing off draughts, as described in earlier chapters.

Once you have insulated your house you can consider the best way to heat it. A woodstove will save energy if it replaces an open fire: when coal or wood is burned in a grate, 80 per cent of the energy contained in the fuel is lost up the chimney. In a closed wood-burning stove only 40 to 50 per cent of the available energy is lost up the chimney. This also compares well with a central heating system where maybe 40 per cent of the energy is lost.

Demolition sites are good sources of waste wood, which would otherwise be burnt without doing more than warm the hands of a few building workers. In managed forests you can find trimmings and slab wood (the bits with bark on one side which are cut off to square the log prior to sawing). Slab wood is often burnt on site at sawmills as it would be a fire risk if stored in large quantities. The estimated two million tonnes of waste wood produced each

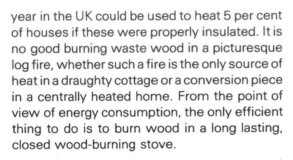

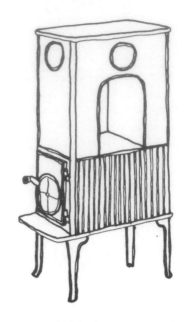

year in the UK could be used to heat 5 per cent of houses if these were properly insulated. It is no good burning waste wood in a picturesque log fire, whether such a fire is the only source of heat in a draughty cottage or a conversion piece in a centrally heated home. From the point of view of energy consumption, the only efficient thing to do is to burn wood in a long lasting, closed wood-burning stove.

Selecting the right model
Some of the most efficient stoves available in

the UK are the airtight box stoves: these consist of a sealed container to hold the wood with an adjustable air inlet to control the rate of burning. Copies of the original Scandinavian designs are also now being manufactured. Of these, the taller models with extra baffles provide longer pathways for the hot flue gases before they go up the chimney. This both ensures more complete combustion of the wood and gives a greater area of hot metal to radiate heat to the room. A stove run with the

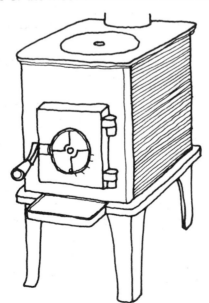

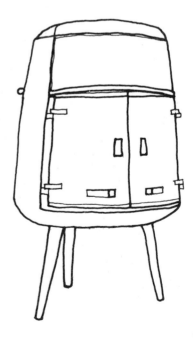

door open, and there are combination stoves which can be either open or airtight, will consume more wood per kWh of heat emitted into the room than an airtight stove; running a stove with the door open so that you can see the flames is not going to save energy. The only thing to be said against the more efficient airtight stove is that when it is burning on its lowest setting creosote forms on the inside of the flue, and this could lead to a chimney fire; so the chimney should be swept regularly.

Installation

Dealing with the risk of fire

The installation of a stove should aim to be as long-lasting as the stove itself. The picture of long runs of metal stovepipe, glowing a cosy red across the classroom ceiling of an American midwest schoolroom at the turn of the century is not on. Apart from being unacceptable to fire officers and building inspectors, the metal pipes will inevitably become a hazard as they corrode unless frequently checked. If such stovepipe is used for a chimney outside it will need replacing every one or two years. Today, the stove should be linked to some type of permanent chimney stack.

The building regulations set out various minimum distances between a combustion

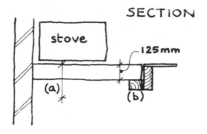

SECTION

Hearth must be 125mm thick.
Underneath no combustible material is allowed within 250mm of top of hearth (a).
A timber support at (b) is allowed.

'appliance' and the walls and floor surrounding it where these are of combustible material (such as a timber floor); these distances are shown in the diagrams. What this really means is that the stove should be placed on a stone or concrete hearth, and that the wall behind it (or walls surrounding it if it is placed in a recess) should be of brick or plastered brick. Houses are traditionally built of brick in the UK; it is in the USA where wood is burned in houses built of timber that stringent safety precautions are needed. Nevertheless, any fire is dangerous, so bear this in mind when you are installing or using a wood-burning stove; and when you buy the stove get a fire extinguisher as well. Put it in an easily accessible place in the house, say at the bottom of the stairs, near the door of the room containing the stove; and don't neglect its maintenance for most types need replacing every few years.

In a typical house with plastered brick walls and a concrete floor, fire prevention is not too difficult. Having a mass of masonry around a stove will also help to even out the heat flow. When the stove is burning hot the walls and hearth will heat up; as the stove cools, before refuelling or at night, the walls and hearth will radiate heat into the room. However, do note that wallpaper on a plastered wall is combustible and is not acceptable within the minimum distance between stove and combustible material, the same applies to carpet laid over a concrete floor. In the latter case, not only is there a possibility of the carpet becoming too

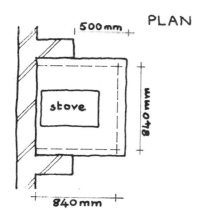

PLAN

Hearth must contain a square of 840mm and must project 500mm in front of any piers.

115

hot and catching fire, but whenever the stove door is opened for refuelling there is a high chance of hot ash falling to the floor as the bed of ashes within the stove is raked over.

A generous hearth is always an asset rather than an inconvenience; not only does it lessen the chance of smouldering carpets but, especially if it is only slightly raised above floor level, it provides a 'stove area' which can be prohibited to children (for even fireguards around a stove can become hot enough to burn fingers), a useful place to keep the ash bucket and stove tools and somewhere for the bread to rise. However careful you are, the day will inevitably come when the draught is carelessly left open too long and you walk in to find the hot plate on top of the stove glowing a dull cherry red; at such times a properly planned installation surrounded by non-combustible materials is very comforting.

Fireplaces

Adapting existing ones
Many houses in the UK, especially those built in Victorian and Edwardian times which relied on coal fires for heating, often have fireplaces in bedrooms as well as downstairs. These houses also have timber floors and you should find that the old stone hearth extends some 600mm into the room, supported underneath by a short arch of brickwork. This would have been adequate for the old type of register grate fireplace, which had a plate to blank off the

chimney when not in use, and there are no regulations to stop you from using the old hearth for a new woodstove installation. It would be best to choose an upright stove so that some of the old hearth projects in front of the door to catch any spilt ashes.

However, if you feel the old hearth is inadequate, it will have to be removed and replaced with a new cast concrete hearth. The regulations will not allow you simply to extend the existing hearth over the timber floor: the worry is that wood in contact with a hot hearth stone will itself become hot, dry out and eventually char, until at some point it will ignite. You will also have to make a concrete hearth if you wish to install a woodstove in a building with timber floors where there is not already a hearth.

Building a suitable base
When you have removed the old hearth stone, you should find a trimmer already in position carrying the floor joists. If you are making the hearth new, you will have to put in a trimmer extending the desired width of the hearth. The trimmer should be made with two pieces of wood, each the same size as the floor joists (two pieces 50mm×125mm if the joists are 50mm×125mm). Before you saw through them, prop the floor joists up. This can be done with bricks off the earth for a timber ground floor (use bits of slate as packing to make up the required height), or, if the hearth is being formed in an upper timber floor, the joists will have to be supported off the floor below with Acrow props.

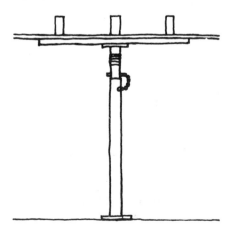

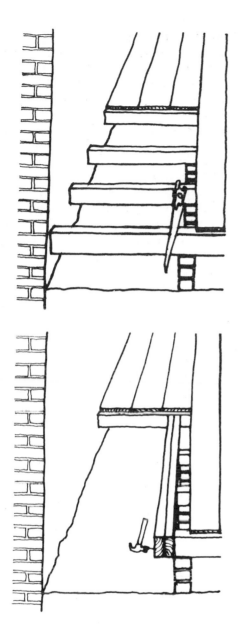

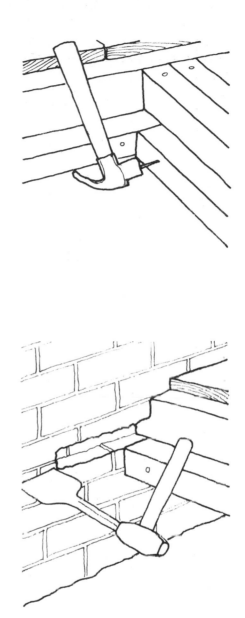

Before you cut the joists turn off the electricity at the mains in case you meet a cable. Saw through the joists and nail the trimmers in place, making sure that the top of the trimmers is level with the top of the joists. Once the trimmers are fixed in place you can remove the supports. Nail a 50mm×50mm length of wood to the bottom of the trimmer to form a support for the hearth. To support the opposite edge you will have to chip out enough brickwork to give a 50mm bearing. Nail two more 50mm×50mm lengths to each joist at the side of the opening. Set in place a piece of 16 gauge galvanised mild steel sheet to form the base of the hearth, packing up the brick side with bits of slate until the sheet is level. Form a tray of heavy-duty polythene sheet covering the steel; take it up the cut away brickwork and over the joists and trimmer.

Provide some kind of reinforcement to the concrete using 6mm diameter mild steel rods at 300–400mm centres (lengths of old bed-

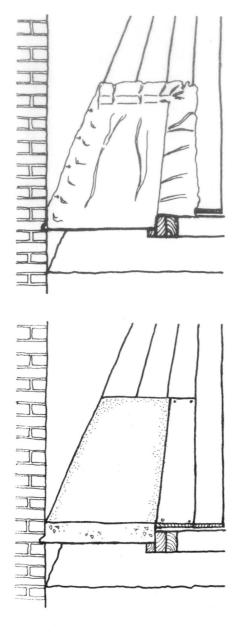

The flue and soot door

Having found or made a suitably fireproof base for the stove to stand on, the stove will have to be connected to the flue. The outlet, which is usually a circular metal flange, will be on the top, at the back, or even through the side of the stove, so select a model that is compatible with the chimney. For a typical small fireplace chimney opening, the type that usually comes with a tiled surround, the stove outlet will have to be at the back. Blank off the chimney, leaving a hole the size of the external diameter of the piece of stovepipe that fits over the outlet flange of the stove. This is best done by bricking up the opening and mortaring in the length of stovepipe. Use vitreous enamelled cast iron stovepipe or plain cast iron pipe.

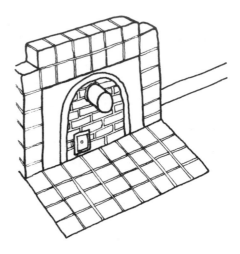

stead will do) propped up approximately 25mm above the sheet on small wooden blocks. Make a mix of one to three or four parts by volume of cement to fine aggregate and fill until level with the top of the floorboards. Alternatively a raised hearth can be created if you fix extra shuttering around the formed opening and fill to the top of the shuttering with the concrete mix. This shuttering can be of hardwood to form a permanent lipping to the hearth.

Asbestos cement, apart from being a health hazard to the people who make it, can crack if the stove accidently runs too hot, and if it is cracked flue gases could seep into the room without your knowledge, and these are dangerous. Pressed metal or enamelled steel stovepipe could be used, but its life will be nowhere near that of cast iron, and if you have a stove that looks as if it will last for a hundred years you might as well use stovepipe to match.

When bricking up, incorporate a cast iron soot door (a standard item at a builders' merchants): this is best placed at the bottom and to

the side of the opening. It will provide somewhere for the sweep to put the brush and the
flexible vacuum hose to clear away the soot
when the chimney is swept.

If your chimney opening is larger, up to the
full ingle nook, you may not wish to brick it up
but prefer to stand the stove within the fireplace opening. In this case it is best to have the
outlet on the top of the stove and to take the
stovepipe vertically up through a register plate
blocking off the chimney. An outlet from the
back of the stove would require a bend in the
stovepipe and bends are always best avoided if
possible because they reduce the velocity of
the flue gases. The only time you might need to
use a side outlet to the stove is to prevent a
large stove sticking out too far into the room
where there is no chimney opening to stand
the stove in.

Fitting the register plate

The register plate will have to be fitted in the
brickwork of the fireplace opening before the
brickwork starts to narrow to form the restric-
tions for the chimney. Measure the opening at
this point, including the diagonals as it is most
unlikely that the opening will be a true
rectangle, and mark these measurements on a
piece of 16 gauge galvanised mild steel sheet.
Cut the steel sheet out 12mm beyond the
marked lines at back and sides and cut to the
line at the front edge. Cut a hole in the register

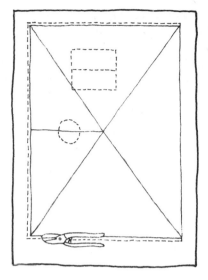

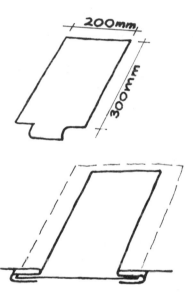

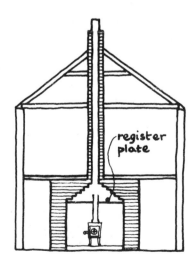

register plate

plate to fit tightly round the cast iron flue pipe
from the stove. You could also cut a hole for a
soot door. The edges of the soot door opening
must be bent back as shown in the diagram and
a door to fit the opening cut from a further piece
of galvanised steel sheet with a projection bent
to form a handle. The soot door can then be slid
open as required.

In the chimney, rake out a mortar joint right
the way around the back and sides of the
opening. Bend the steel sheet so that it can be

119

eased into the raked recess at the sides of the opening and then pushed up to fit into the recess at the rear. At the front of the opening use a piece of 25mm×6mm mild steel strip or 25mm×25mm angle (angle can only be used if the top of the fireplace opening is horizontal) cut to be 25mm longer than the opening. Fit this as shown in the diagram to provide a support for the front of the register plate, which should be sealed to it with fire cement. Pack the plate up to the top of the recesses with small strips of slate and then mortar it in place.

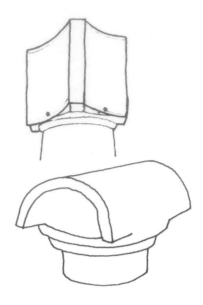

The short length of cast iron stovepipe should be sealed to the stove outlet with fire cement and similarly sealed where it passes through the register plate. The stovepipe should project 100–150mm beyond the register plate up into the flue.

Fitting the cowl
With the register plate installed some type of cowl must be fitted to the chimney to stop the rain coming down and rusting the plate. There is nothing worse than sitting in a room listening to the steady dripping of rain on to thinly galvanised steel. On round chimney pots the adjustable metal cowl is easy to fit by tightening four bolts but may be knocked off by the sweep's brush. A clay bonnet cowl must be mortared in

to the top of the chimney pot but will make a good job. With square or other fancy pots some kind of cowl will have to be devised from sheet metal.

Chimneys

Choosing the best position
To make the most of any stove installation it is best to use a chimney placed in the middle of your house. Any brick or stone chimney will become warm as the hot flue gases pass up it, especially if the stove is run continuously throughout the winter. The warmed bricks will then radiate heat to the upper rooms through which they pass and this contributes considerably to the distribution of heat around the house. Such a chimney might increase the 50 per cent stove efficiency by between 5 and 15 per cent. If your existing chimney is on an external wall most of the heat of the flue gases will be lost and you may therefore decide to put in a new chimney somewhere in the middle of the building.

Prefabricated chimneys
Building a chimney is not the best thing to start on if you have not yet put trowel to mortar, as a chimney must be airtight to prevent poisonous flue gases leaking through into the rooms.

However, there are prefabricated chimneys available on the market which will take two people an afternoon to install. These chimneys are in fact elaborate versions of the old American midwest stovepipe chimney. An inner ceramic or metal circular stovepipe is surrounded by mineral fibre insulation and the whole is covered with an outer metal casing. The inner stovepipe must be insulated in this way to prevent it becoming too hot and therefore a fire hazard.

The firms who make prefabricated chimneys will advise you what parts you will need. You should supply them with a sketch of the position of the chimney, showing floor to ceiling heights of the rooms it is to pass through, the pitch of the roof, the presence of other roofs nearby (which will affect how far the chimney should stick up above the roof to work properly), and the size of the outlet of the appliance to be connected.

The materials

You will be able to buy all the parts necessary to make up the chimney including sufficient lengths of the insulated flue; a loadbearing plate to fix to the top of the first floor joists to carry the weight of the chimney (this can be covered with the floorboards of the room afterwards); firestop plates which are fixed to the top of the upper floor ceiling joists and the underside of the rafters; dust stop plates which are fixed to the underside of the first floor and ceiling joists (these will be covered with plaster afterwards); a flashing to weatherproof where the chimney comes through the roof; an outer weathersleeve to protect the part of the insulated chimney that projects beyond the roof; and some type of coping cap that fits over this. The type with the ceramic liner has to have this liner fixed together with fire-cement whilst the all-metal insulated chimneys simply twist-lock together.

Assembly

Start putting the sections together, beginning with the support plate, until you reach a point below the roof. Remove the tiles and slates directly above the chimney and, if necessary,

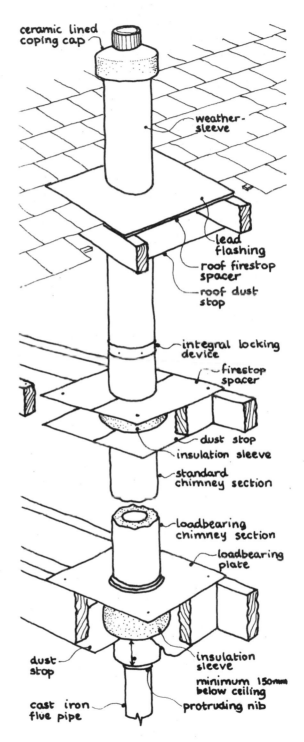

Parkaflue prefabricated chimney system

121

make a hole in the roofing felt. Do not come directly underneath a rafter; if during the installation you come out directly under a tiling batten, this can be cut out between the rafters. Now drop in the last section of the chimney from above and fix it into place; then fit the flashing, the weathersleeve, and lastly the terminating cap.

The most difficult part of putting up the prefabricated chimney is making and flashing the hole in the roof. In our own case we had to deal only with a flat roof covered with white rubber material. The hole was made in the chipboard roof with a padsaw and after the chimney had been fixed extra white rubber flashing pieces were heat-welded to the chimney and the roof covering. If you are happy on ladders and have an idea of what is involved in repairing a slate roof have a go at making and flashing the hole. If you have any doubts, however, it would be wise to employ builders to do this part of the work for you as they will have both the equipment and the experience necessary.

We have always found that sharing the work with builders has been a great help when it comes to jobs where you do not want to make any mistakes. It is easy enough to take over the labouring jobs and save yourself money, employing people to do skilled work only when it is really necessary. We have also found it instructive to practise increasing our building skills by altering and constructing barns and sheds where the success or failure of the work is not so critical. Perhaps you know of a cow that would appreciate a woodstove connected to a prefabricated chimney?

Selecting the appropriate model

The choice of a particular prefabricated chimney depends on the external appearance, stainless steel or painted metal, but the type with a ceramic flue liner will have a longer life than that with a stainless steel liner. There is one other type of prefabricated chimney which consists of a special building block with a ceramic flue liner moulded in. Although these would be a quick way of installing a chimney in a new building or an extension they would be difficult to install in an existing building. The metal prefabricated chimney, although it will be warm to the touch, will not radiate as much heat as an existing internal masonry chimney just because it is insulated. However, the type with a ceramic liner will have some heat storage if the stove is used intermittently, and any internal chimney will put more heat into the house than a chimney on an external wall.

Checking existing chimneys

If there is a suitable chimney in the building, before installing a stove it would be wise to check it over first, especially if you do not know when it was last in use. From the ground it is possible to see if the stack protruding through the roof is sound or crumbling and this will be an indication of the state of the whole chimney. Inside, damp patches around chimney stacks indicate that the flashings are either faulty or missing, and these should be repaired either by yourself or a builder. To test the whole chimney temporarily seal the pot at the top, perhaps with a large plug of glass fibre, and light a smoky fire with corrugated cardboard or real sacking in the fireplace. Now spend a few happy minutes, felt tip pen in hand, inspecting the stack in all the rooms it passes through including the attic, looking for leaking smoke and marking the holes.

If there are no leaks and you are satisfied with the exterior of the chimney, have it swept and put your stove in. If there are one or two leaks these can be mortared up although it would be wise to check the repairs with a second smoky fire. It may not be possible to detect all the leaks by this method, if for example the stack leaks within the thickness of the floor, but it will give an indication of the relative soundness of the construction.

If the chimney stack is badly cracked or full of tiny leaks then you have two choices. If the old chimney is on an exterior wall forget it and connect your stove up to a new prefabricated chimney in the centre of the house. Alternatively, Rentokil have a method of providing a new chimney within an old stack. An inflated rubber bag is put down the chimney and vermiculite concrete is poured round it. The bag is removed after the concrete has set, leaving a smooth-walled insulated flue, ideal for solid fuel appliances. This is not, however, a d-i-y technique. Metal stove liners, such as are used in old chimneys for central heating boilers, are not robust enough to stand the higher temperature and more corrosive flue gases of a woodstove.

It is important to check the condition of the chimney as without it the stove cannot function. As a safeguard the chimney should be capable of withstanding a chimney fire. Any leaks in the flue could bring fire into the house with tragic consequences. The exterior of the chimney should be well pointed and the mortar cap around the chimney pot should not be cracked so that rain cannot penetrate the stack. This should be seen to when the stove is installed. In the UK, where coal fires are traditional in brick buildings, many houses come provided with chimneys suitable for woodstoves. Providing these are kept structurally sound and swept at yearly intervals to remove the potentially dangerous creosote, then the stack and stove together should provide a robust method of heating the building, which will require relatively little maintenance.

The wood

Building a sawing horse

Your wood may arrive by the ton, already cut and split, and then it will only remain for you to hand over your money and cart the wood to some place where it can be stored, preferably under cover. If you have to cut slab wood or timber from a demolition site, you would do well to use some of your first lengths of timber to build a sawing horse.

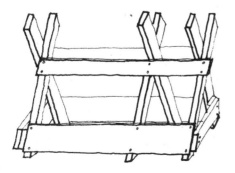

First cut six equal 1100mm lengths of 75mm×50mm or similar sized wood. Nail these in three equal cross shapes as shown, the crossover coming one third of the way along the length of the wood. Cut two short 100mm pieces of the same thickness of wood and nail these on to the feet of two of the crosses as blocking pieces. Measure the width of the foot of the cross and cut a piece of 25mm×150mm plank to brace this lower end, shaping the ends to fit the cross. Nail the braces into place. Cut four pieces of plank, again about 25mm×150mm, the length of the required sawing horse; 1100mm, the same dimension as the basic cross pieces, is elegant and satisfactory.

You will now need a measure of the length of wood to fit inside your chosen stove. Cut off a measured piece of wood, mark it and keep it by your sawing horse as a useful guide when cutting up long lengths of wood. Set the first crosses slightly closer together than your measured length. This is so that when cutting short lengths the piece remaining on the sawing horse will fit the stove. Nail two long planks on to one side of one of the braced crosses, set the unbraced cross in place and nail this on; finally fix the other braced cross at the other end. Nail the other two planks on the other side. This type of sawing horse is ideal for holding the classic log but it will also be useful when sawing up slab wood and demolition timber.

Saws

The bow saw with a replaceable blade (have one 750mm or 900mm long) is easy to use but if you are cutting up at least a ton of wood over

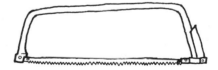

the winter you may find that you use two blades, depending on how many nails you saw into accidentally. Chain saws are expensive but with them you can go out and saw up fallen trees—with the owner's permission of course.

Chain saws are also dangerous and noisy. They will cope well with slab wood, which can be sawn up in bundles, but are best not used with old house timbers because of the danger of hitting a hidden nail. There is something to be said for the old adage that 'fuel wood warms you twice' and we have found that two hours hand sawing on a frosty afternoon leaves you both glowing inside, and with enough wood to fuel a small airtight stove for a week.

The wedges

If your wood comes in the form of large logs you will need a pair of steel wedges to split it into usable pieces. The wedges should be used once the logs have been cut to the right length to fit the stove. Drive them into the wood with a sledgehammer, using the second wedge to

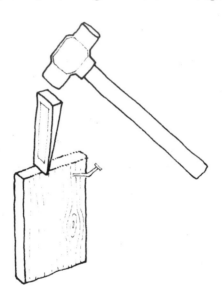

widen the gap when the first is driven in as far as it will go. You will find that some kinds of wood split more easily than others.

Carrying and stacking

Having cut the wood and stacked it under cover for as long as possible to allow it to dry out properly, it only remains to carry it to the stove and store it nearby. Keep a woodbasket near the stove but not next to it to avoid burning the wood before you intended to. We tried carrying

wood in both basket and bucket but have found a log carrier the easiest. You can make one with a sack; nail two bits of 25mm×50mm timber across the shorter ends with clout nails. Fix two screw eyes into each of these pieces of wood; thread a rope through and fix it with knots at the ends. The length of the rope handles will depend on the amount of wood you wish to carry each time but 500mm of rope will be about right, and you can always put in less wood.

19 Building Solar Panels

One way of making a solar water heating system is to use solar panels: these are small solar collectors, each in a waterproof, well insulated box which can be mounted anywhere convenient and connected to a hot water cylinder. Commercial solar panels have cases made of aluminium or glass fibre which will not rot or weaken when continuously exposed to the effects of sunshine and rain. Any homemade collector must be as weatherproof as possible otherwise it will fall apart before it has a chance to provide you with any appreciable quantities of hot water. However, the only possible material for a homemade collector casing is wood because other materials are not easy to handle without a proper workshop.

The materials

The size of your solar panel will be governed by various factors: the total weight — it is no good building a beautiful solar panel and then finding that you cannot lift it into place; the size of glass that can safely be used; and the size of the heat absorbing plate.

The radiator

The best choice for the plate on a homemade installation is a steel central heating radiator. Be sure to use the modern steel rather than old fashioned cast iron radiators. Modern radiators contain only a small amount of water so when they are used as solar collectors the sun does not have to heat up a large volume of cold water

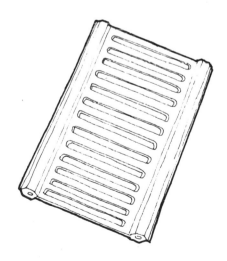

before the collector can begin working. This means that it will respond quickly to short periods of sunshine and will collect more heat.

The glass

The glass should be 4mm thick horticultural glass if you can obtain it: it is cheaper than window glass because it tends to give a slightly distorted view like the glass in Victorian windows. Horticultural glass comes in standard sized panes made for conventional and Dutch light greenhouses, the Dutch light being the sort which uses large panes of glass in wooden frames. Dutch light glass 4mm thick is available in the following standard sizes:

1410mm x 730mm	1651mm x 730mm
1422mm x 730mm	1676mm x 730mm
1613mm x 730mm	1778mm x 730mm

Try to make your collector the right size to fit one of these standard panes.

You can buy the glass from a major outlet (ask the merchant for horticultural glass) or perhaps from a plant nursery which uses Dutch light greenhouses. If all else fails you will have to buy ordinary 4mm glass and have it cut to size by your local glass merchant. Do not use glass larger than 1410mm×730mm: you will not be able to manage a panel bigger than this as it will be too heavy and unwieldy to lift and fit into place.

The dimensions

The size of the glass determines the overall size of your solar panel, and this will then give you the dimensions of the radiator for the absorber plate. The most important thing to look for when buying a radiator is that it should have ¾ inch iron tappings (to accept pipe connections) at all four corners. To fit the size of the glass described above you will need a radiator no bigger than 650mm×1200mm, otherwise you will not have enough room in the casing for the connections to the radiator.

Durability

If your solar collector is to be cost effective in its saving of the cost of heating water by conventional means it must last for a long time, say fifteen to twenty years. If it falls apart or corrodes after only a couple of years it will have been nothing but an expensive toy. For this reason it is worth using the best materials and taking care to make a very good job of the construction. We would also recommend that you do not mount the collectors on a roof, because once they are up there you will not be able to check them and maintain them easily. To climb a roof you need ladders, roof ladders and in some cases scaffolding, all of which tempts one to leave the collectors to look after themselves and not bother to climb up to look at them. If you do not check them and repair any leaks of rainwater or damage to the casing they will deteriorate very quickly and will become useless. We suggest that you mount the solar panels near the ground so that you can see them easily and check whether they need any repairs.

Assembly

The box

Start building your solar panel by making the box. The sides should be made with 32mm×175mm wood planed all round, and this will bring the finished dimensions to 26mm×169mm. You can order the wood planed all round instead of doing it yourself; the planing machine at the timber yard will do it quickly and efficiently.

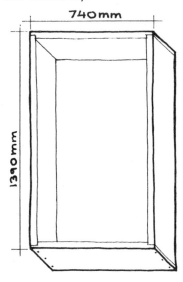

The collector will be exposed to the worst possible weather, stuck outside in frost, rain and bright sunshine, so buy the wood Tanalised; and, when you cut out the parts for the solar panel from the bought timber, give all cut edges three coats of wood preservative before assembly. If you cannot obtain Tanalised wood you will have to give the wood three coats of preservative. Do this when the box is assembled, having treated all the joints before assembly as described below. Wear rubber gloves when putting on the preservative, use an old brush and take a bit of time over the job. This may sound like a lot of work, but if you omit all this preservative treatment the panel will start to deteriorate quite quickly.

The box should be 740mm wide and 1390mm long. Make the top and bottom first,

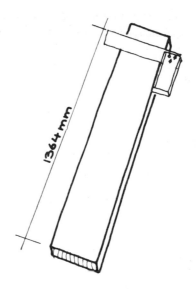

cutting them down to the correct width or slightly over so that they can be sanded down. Mark out the rebates as shown in the drawing, making sure that the inner faces are 688mm apart, and that the projecting piece of the joint is 13mm thick. Use a marking gauge for accuracy, and to ensure that all the joints are the same size. Cut out the waste with a tenon saw.

The sides can now be cut out, and should be 1364mm long. Take some time with the marking out and sawing to length to make sure that the edges are at right angles. Now give the cut ends of the sides and top and bottom three generous coats of wood preservative. Cut out a base for the panel from 6mm WBP plywood

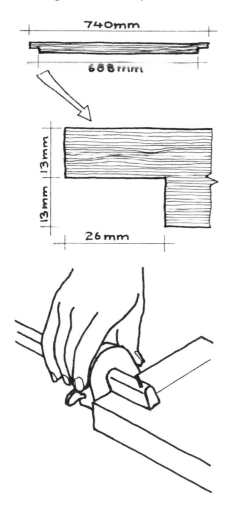

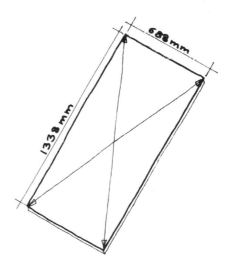

(WBP is the external grade). It should measure 688mm×1338mm: when you mark it out check that the diagonal measurements are equal as this will ensure that the piece of plywood is truly square. Paint it thoroughly with preservative.

Now make the supports for the base from Tanalised 25mm×25mm wood. Cut two of these 1338mm long for the sides and two 638mm long for the top and bottom. Again give the cut edges three coats of preservative.

When all the preservative is dry, ideally a week after the last coat was applied, you can start to assemble the collector. Begin with the sides by marking a line 13mm in from each end, then nail and glue a piece of 25mm×25mm wood to the bottom inside edge of each side,

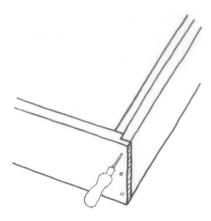

2mm drill. When all the ends have been marked out and drilled and the pilot holes are drilled (mark the ends and sides so that you know which side goes with which end), apply waterproof glue liberally to the joint and screw in the screws.

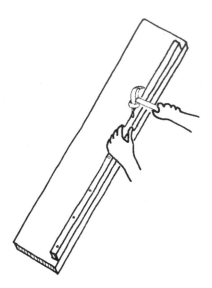

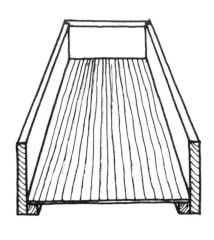

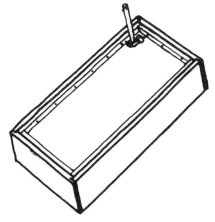

lining it up with the mark you have just made at each end. The nails should be galvanised or sherardised lost head, 38mm long, and the glue must be Cascamite or a similar *waterproof* wood glue.

Next, in each end, mark the positions for three 63mm no 12 screws. The screws should be galvanised or otherwise treated against corrosion. Drill the holes, countersink them, and place one end in position on one side. Mark the location of the holes in the end of the side pieces by pushing a bradawl through the hole, and drill pilot holes at the marked spots with a

When the sides and ends are joined together apply more glue to the top of the strips that are nailed to the bottom of the sides, and nail on the plywood base with galvanised or sherardised 19mm lost head nails. This will hold the box square. When the glue is quite dry nail on the other strips of 25mm×25mm wood using plenty of glue, so as to support the plywood.

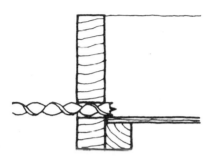

When the glue has dried drill three 10mm holes as shown, in the bottom edge of the box positioned so that the lower edge of each hole is in line with the top surface of the plywood. Use a small triangular file to shape the lower edge of each hole as in the drawing. These holes allow any condensation that occurs inside the collector to drain away.

Finally, give the box four coats of water-repellent preservative wood stain inside and out, making sure that you cover every surface and the inside of the holes. Black would be an appropriate colour, but the choice is yours. The stain is preferable to paint because paint forms a film on the surface of the wood and will eventually crack and peel, so you will have to scrape it off and rub down before repainting. The stain soaks into the wood without forming a film and you can add new coats as required without any further preparation.

Cut two pieces of 50mm×50mm Tanalised softwood each 688mm long and nail two spacers of 25mm×50mm to the bottom of

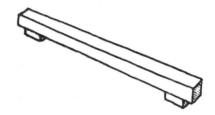

each. The spacers allow any condensation in the solar collector to run out under the 50mm×50mm members, which are the supports for the absorber panel. Give the supports and spacers four coats of the stain you used for the rest of the box. When dry the supports should be screwed into the box through the plywood base, using galvanised or sherardised screws 63mm no 12 countersunk into the plywood.

Finally cut four pieces of 25mm×25mm aluminium angle 169mm long. These are to

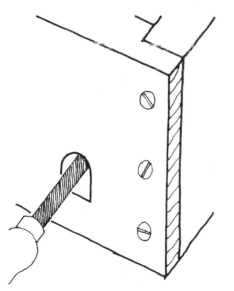

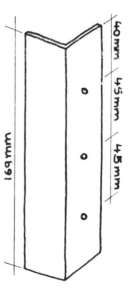

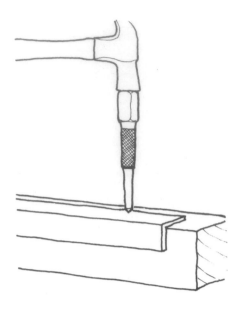

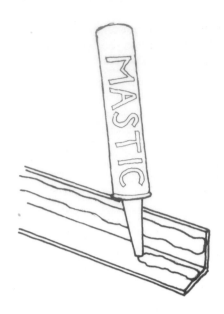

protect the exposed grain of the timber case. Mark positions for holes on the angles as shown in the drawings, making sure that the upper holes are at least 35mm from the end of the angle. The holes have a diameter of 5mm to take 38mm no 8 round head screws. To make it easier to drill the holes, because the drill point will slide on the aluminium, first mark the positions of each hole, then take a centre punch, put it on the mark and hit it with a hammer. This will leave a small dent in the metal which will hold the point of the drill and prevent it from slipping about.

When the angles are drilled hold them in place on the collector box, mark the positions

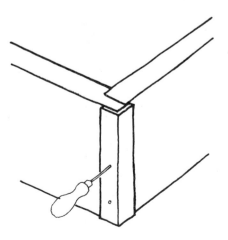

of the holes and make pilot holes for the screws in the wood with a bradawl. Before you screw the angles in place coat the back of each with a layer of mastic, a sticky sealing material. This can be bought in two forms, either as a cardboard cartridge which fits into a mastic gun, or as a 'self-propelling' cartridge. The cartridges for the gun are cheaper but you also have to buy the gun. You can use a mastic gun one-handed which is sometimes an advantage, and it tends to make a neater job because it is easier to control the flow of mastic. At the end of the self-propelling cartridges there is a plastic wheel which you turn to force the mastic out.

The best and most expensive mastic is silicone, which should last over twenty years. Before using any mastic check with the manufacturers that it can be used with aluminium. Some types may require that you degrease the metal or use a special primer before applying the mastic itself. When you have put mastic on the angles screw them into place, and be sure to use stainless steel, aluminium alloy, galvanised, sherardised or cadmium-plated screws to prevent rust. Some mastic will squeeze out round the edges of the angles and this should be cleaned off with a razorblade or Stanley knife after it has had a few hours to set.

When you have put on the corner angles the box is finished and you can put it aside and turn to the solar collector itself.

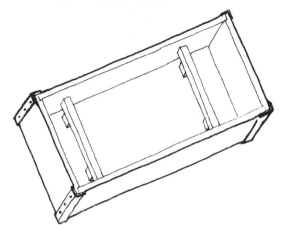

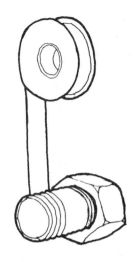

The radiator

The collector is a single panel steel radiator no larger than 650mm×1200mm. The exact dimensions will depend on the manufacturer, but the important thing is to get a radiator with ¾ inch iron tappings at all four corners. When you buy the radiator make sure you buy two plugs to block up two of the holes. Buy two fittings, each with a ¾ inch male iron at one end and a 22mm copper compression fitting at the other (This strange mixture of metric and imperial measurements is unavoidable since radiator connections have not yet gone metric.)

Wrap PTFE tape round the thread of the two plugs and screw them into diagonally opposite holes one at each end of the radiator. Wrap the tape in the direction shown on the diagram – if you do not do this the tape will tend to unwind as you screw the fitting into the radiator. Next screw the male iron/compression fittings into the remaining two holes in the radiator again using PTFE tape to prevent leaks. Tighten all the fittings and plugs with a spanner.

Block off one of the compression fittings with a blanking-off disc, using PTFE tape to seal the screw thread. Fill the radiator with water through the other fitting and stand it over a sheet of dry newspaper. If you find no spots of

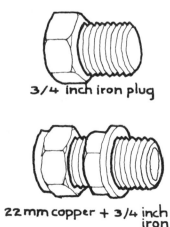

3/4 inch iron plug

22mm copper + 3/4 inch iron

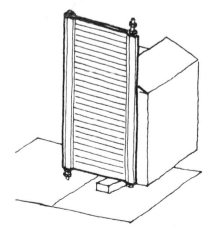

water on the newspaper after an hour you can assume that you have made all the connections tight enough. Remove the blanking-off disc and fit it to the compression fitting through which you filled the radiator, turn the radiator the other way up and repeat the test. It is better to do this than to assemble the collector panel and then find a leak.

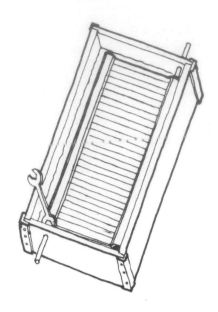

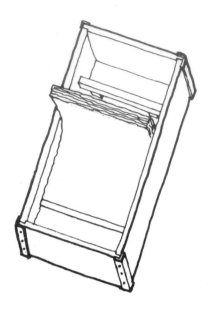

When you have finished the leak test, empty the radiator, remove the blanking-off disc, and give the upper surface of the radiator a coat of matt black blackboard paint. Cut some glass fibre or mineral wool insulation 75mm thick and lay it in the bottom of the box that you made earlier. Do not be tempted to use expanded polystyrene insulation because, although it looks neater than glass fibre, if the collector stands in the sun with no water flowing through it will reach a high enough temperature to melt the polystyrene. If you want to you can paint the surface of the insulation with matt black paint to make it look neater, but painting glass fibre is a thankless task and best avoided.

Assembling box, radiator and pipes
You can now lay the radiator in the case and mark on the top and bottom edges the positions for the holes through which the pipes to the radiator will pass. Drill the holes carefully

with a brace and a 25mm bit, and paint the inside of the holes thoroughly with more preservative stain. Put the radiator in the box and connect two short lengths of 22mm copper pipe to the compression fittings. Give the nut on the fitting one full turn with a spanner after hand tightening it, to give a watertight connection. The pipe should protrude about 150mm from the ends of the case; where it passes through the holes, it should be thoroughly sealed with silicone mastic.

It is important to make sure that the sealing of the pipe to the casing is done well so that

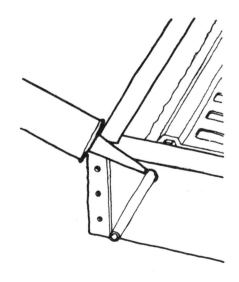

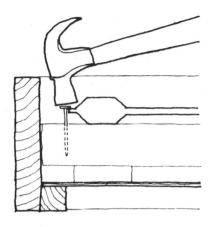

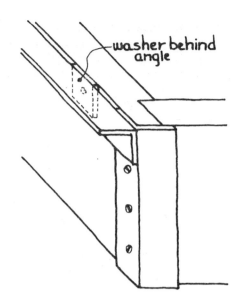

rainwater will not seep inside the solar panel and cause damage. Complete this part of the job by hammering a 50mm galvanised clout nail into the collector support at each side of the radiator to keep it in position.

Glazing

The final step is the glazing. Lay the solar panel on a flat surface and measure the width of the bottom edge, which should be 740mm. Cut a piece of 25mm × 25mm aluminium angle to this dimension, drill it with four holes 5mm in diameter to take 19mm no 8 round head screws. You will find that if you try to fit this angle in place it will bend inwards slightly because it overlaps the two corner angles. To overcome this slight problem make some washers by drilling holes in a piece of 25mm × 25mm angle and then cutting it up as

shown with a hacksaw to give you a number of small square pieces of metal with holes in. If you put one of these washers under the angle at each screw hole they will pack it out level. This angle should be bedded on mastic like those at the corners.

Now lay the glass, which should be clean and dry on both sides, on top of the casing: leave an equal gap on both sides, and put the glass flush with the edge of the angle you have just fixed at the bottom of the collector. Cut two more

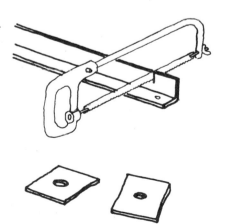

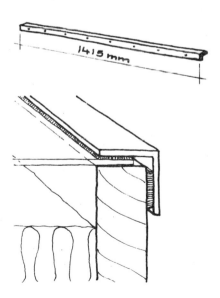

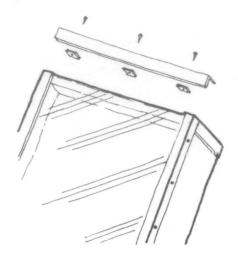

control the pump. When the sensor is fixed in place, as described below, the panel can be completed like the others.

Mounting the completed collector

Before turning to the problem of plumbing you must somehow mount the collector. The angle between the panels and the horizontal is not

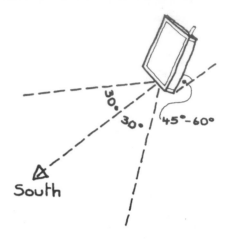

too critical and can be anything from 30° to 60° without having much effect on performance, but an angle of 45° to 60° will allow the rain to run off the panels better than if they are at a shallow angle. Ideally, your solar collector should face south, but it can face 30° either side of south without suffering a noticeable reduction in efficiency. What is more important is to see that there are no obstructions that will cast shadows on your solar panels which should if possible have a clear field of view 45° either side (see diagram). It is quite a good idea to see where any shadows will fall, particularly in spring and autumn, before finally siting and installing your panels.

The supporting framework
Most solar panels are mounted on roofs but we would not recommend this for homemade ones because it is so difficult to maintain them when they are up on a roof. A better solution is to build a framework to support the collectors and fix it to the side of the building. The supporting frame should be made of Tanalised

pieces of angle, each 1415mm long, and drill them for no 8 screws as shown. Run a bead of mastic along the edge of each angle where it will meet the glass, and coat the side of the angle that will touch the wooden side of the collector box with mastic (try to ensure that the mastic does not stick the glass to the wood).

Using spacing washers cut from bits of angle as described above, screw the angle to the side of the box making sure that it is well pressed down on to the glass. Do the other side and then cut a further piece for the top of the collector, long enough to cover the two side pieces as shown. This should be drilled and fixed just as the side pieces were, but you may need more mastic where it meets the glass because it will be raised by the thickness of the side angles above the surface of the glass.

Your solar panel is now finished but the work has only just begun. The panel described has an absorbing area of about $0.7m^2$, which is the area of the radiator. To achieve the $4m^2$ recommended by the Building Research Establishment you will need six of these panels. If you estimate that each square metre of solar collector will heat fifty litres of water you could say that a household would need two of these $0.7m^2$ panels for each person. If a lot of people live in your house you will have to spend a long time building panels. Leave one of your panels unglazed, with the radiator not fixed in, if you are building a pumped circulation system. This will allow you to fit in a temperature sensor to

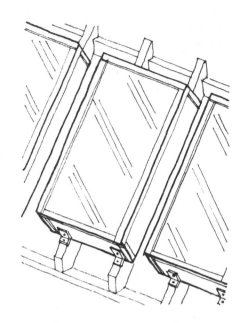

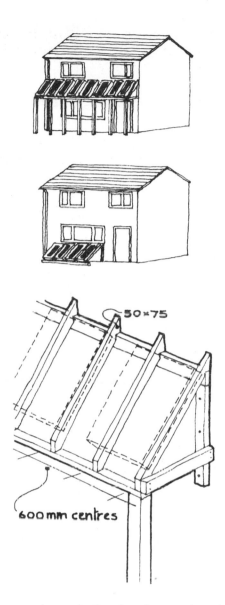

50×75

600 mm centres

centres so that you can leave a sufficient gap between adjacent solar panels to reach the screws if you need to reglaze them. To fasten the collectors to the supporting structure use 50mm lengths of 50mm×50mm aluminium angle, fastened to the solar panel with 25mm no 8 round head screws, and to the wooden supports with 50mm no 10 round head screws. All screws should be zinc-plated or sherardised.

Finally, connect the collector panels as shown in the diagrams — one method is for

timber as shown in the drawings, using plenty of waterproof glue on the joints. If you make the legs long enough the collectors will form a south-facing verandah or pergola, or could be used to shade a window.

The part that is fixed to the building should be bolted to the wall with 10mm Fischerbolts about 100mm long; alternatively, it can be screwed with zinc-plated no 12 screws 88mm long, and plastic plugs. It is easiest to fix this piece first and then build the frame on to it, taking care to have all the frames in line with one another. The supports should be at 600mm

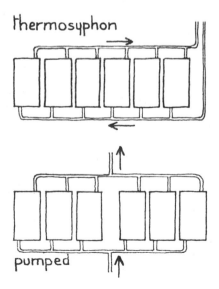

Thermosyphon

pumped

pumped systems and the other for gravity circulation or thermosyphoning systems. The connecting pipes must be lagged with waterproof insulation. To run the pipes into the building you will have either to use a large diameter masonry drill at least 300mm long to go through a normal brick cavity wall, or else to remove a brick and then mortar the hole up. The drill will make a neater job and if you hire a percussion drill for a day it won't take long to make the necessary holes. Pack round the pipes with silicone mastic once they are in place to keep out the rainwater.

The storage tank

The pipes are now inside the building but there is still a whole lot of plumbing to sort out. You will now have to buy a hot water storage tank for your solar heated hot water. The system which makes the best use of the collected solar energy is the one in which the solar heated water forms the cold feed to your existing hot

water cylinder. This system means that when it is not very sunny the collector will be able to supply warm water to the solar tank, and when this warmed water enters the existing cylinder it will need less energy to heat it to a usable temperature than if the feed to the cylinder were cold mains water. The solar hot water tank should have a volume of 50–60 litres for every square metre of collector area. The table below lists the sizes of indirect copper cylinders made to BS 1566. This type of cylinder with a coiled pipe heat exchanger in it is the correct one to use for a solar water tank. Look for the code BS 1566 and the British Standards 'kitemark' stamped on the side.

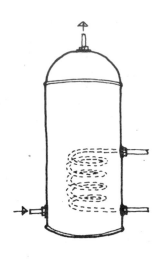

diameter in mm	height in mm	capacity in litres
300	1600	96
350	900	72
400	900	96
400	1050	114
450	675	84
450	750	95
450	825	106
450	900	117
450	1050	140
450	1200	162
500	1200	190
500	1500	245
600	1200	280
600	1500	360
600	1800	440

overflow

boiler

mains supply of water

conventional hot water system

When you have selected a size it is worth checking with the plumbers' merchant to see if a slightly smaller tank would be a lot cheaper: the thickness of metal used changes from one tank size to another, making one size up to twice the price of the size below it. Ask the merchant if you will need a cylinder with a protective anode in it. This may be needed if you live in an area which has what the water people call 'aggressive' water, to prevent corrosion of the cylinder. If in doubt, buy a cylinder with an anode and play safe.

The cylinder will have four connections on it, two for the indirect circuit to the heat exchanger in the cylinder, one for the cold feed and one for the hot water outlet. When you buy the cylinder you will need two connections for 22mm copper pipe to fit the cold feed and hot water outlet, and two connections for the solar circuit, measuring 28mm in diameter if it is a thermosyphoning system and 22mm if it is a pumped system. The plumbers' merchant will supply the necessary bits to enable you to fit these pipe sizes to the tappings on the cylinder if you explain what pipe diameters you want to use. You will not need a boss on the cylinder for an immersion heater, and if there is one you will have to buy a plate to blank it off.

Plumbing

Thermosyphoning

The final problem is how to connect the solar collectors to the solar hot water cylinder. You can connect the whole thing up so that the heated water flows round the circuit under its own power, relying on the fact that heated water is less dense than cold water. If you use this thermosyphoning system the pipes between the collector and the heat exchanger in the cylinder should be at least 28mm in diameter (which is very expensive in copper pipe) and there should be, if possible, a continuous slight upward slope in the pipes from collector to tank; if this cannot be arranged it is essential that the pipes are at least horizontal.

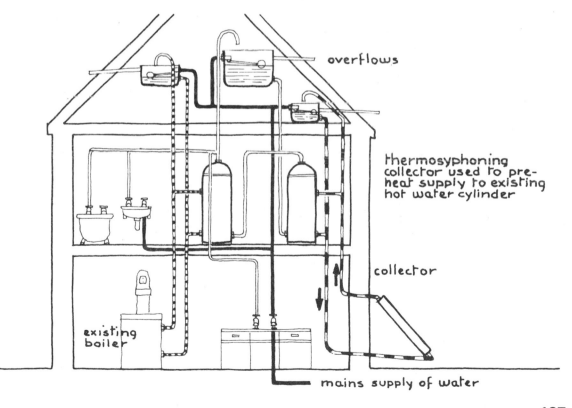

overflows

thermosyphoning collector used to pre-heat supply to existing hot water cylinder

collector

existing boiler

mains supply of water

The base of the hot water cylinder must be at least 600mm above the top of the collectors, and can be put considerably higher than this. All the pipes must be well insulated so that you do not lose all the heat collected before it passes into your hot water cylinder.

Where the pipes are outside the house the insulation must be water resistant so you should probably use the pre-formed cylindrical insulation (strips of glass fibre will not be water-proof), but check with the suppliers that it is really waterproof. Inside the building you can use anything as long as it will insulate. Do not forget to insulate the solar hot water cylinder, preferably with about 150mm or 200mm of glass fibre or mineral wool.

It is possible to save money on pipework for a thermosyphoning system by using polythene (Alkathene) pipe, the black heavy duty type used for water supply on farms and the like, not garden hosepipe. This pipe has a larger outside diameter than the same internal diameter of copper pipe because the polythene pipe has thicker walls, and to avoid spending large sums on fittings you can buy plastic Hozelock fittings similar to those sold for garden hoses but more robust for the thick polythene pipe. If you are able to find a supplier of these fittings they will be very useful, but not many places seem to keep them. It is worth asking around. You should use polythene pipe with an *internal* diameter of 25mm or 32mm for a thermosy-phoning system. The pipe is safe for water as hot as 60°C, and your solar panels are unlikely to produce water as hot as that; but as the pipe becomes hot it will become quite flexible and you must support it at intervals of about 600mm with pipe clips otherwise it will sag and your carefully arranged upward slope will be lost. If you can afford it copper pipe is much easier to manage because it is rigid and can withstand hot water, but plastic is good for temporary and experimental systems.

If you decide on a thermosyphoning solar system you should spend some time planning the location of collectors and tanks so as to keep the lengths of pipe between collector and solar cylinder as short as possible to reduce heat loss and, more importantly, cost. The

diagram shows the layout of the components needed to connect a thermosyphoning system into an existing hot water installation, using the solar energy to pre-heat the water entering the existing hot water cylinder.

Using a pump

If you make a pumped system you will find that you can use smaller diameter pipe, 22mm if it is copper or stainless steel. The layout of the pipes will also become less critical: they can slope up or down as required to thread them through to the cylinder. You will of course also need a pump. Use the kind made for central heating installations, the important factor being the height to which the water must be pumped, which is called the head. Some pumps have adjustable heads so they can be adapted to different uses, so buy one of these if you are not sure what the head will be in your system.

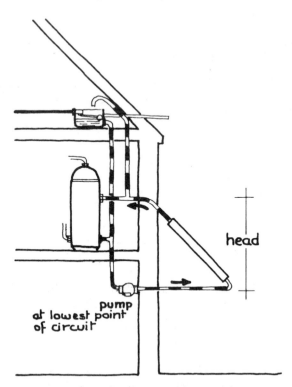

head

pump at lowest point of circuit

pumped collector – the rest of the circuit is the same as for the thermosyphoning system

138

If your system is to be efficient the pump must operate only when there is enough solar radiation to make it worthwhile, otherwise you could end up cooling the water rather than heating it. You will need a temperature differential controller which measures the temperature of the cylinder and the temperature of the collectors, and switches on the pump when the collectors are hot enough. If you know about electronics there are circuit diagrams available for building a controller, but if you cannot manage this you can buy one ready made. The controller will have long leads on it with temperature sensors on the ends. One of these sensors must be fixed securely to the absorber plate of one of your solar panels in good contact with the metal surface, and the other must be fixed to the hot water cylinder. Ask the manufacturers for their recommended fixing methods. The wire from the sensor must be led out from the back or side of the collector box, and the hole through which it passes must be sealed with silicone mastic to keep out water.

Protecting the collector

Whatever sort of system you build it will need protection from frost which could burst the collector panels, and from corrosion which could shorten the life of the solar installation. Corrosion can occur between copper fittings and iron radiators and you should use a corrosion proofer such as Fernox MB-1, available from plumbers' merchants, which is added at the rate of one part MB-1 to every twenty parts water in the solar circuit. You can see now why the indirect system must be used: you do not want corrosion proofer coming out of the hot water tap.

Fernox also make an anti-freeze called FP-1 which includes a foaming agent and a nasty taste so that if there is a leak into the hot water system you will get a warning. You should use a 25 per cent solution of FP-1 which will give protection down to −14°C which is probably sufficient for most areas. Check local weather records to see how cold it may become in a really bad winter and ask the manufacturers for their recommendations if it is colder than −14°C.

Calculating the collector's capacity

To work out the water content of your system you will need to know the water content of the radiators used in the solar panels (ask the suppliers or the manufacturers), the water content of the coil of pipe in the solar hot water cylinder (again ask the manufacturers) and the length of pipe, including fittings, in the circuit. The water content of copper pipes is as follows:

external diameter in mm	water content in litres per metre
15	0.15
22	0.32
28	0.54

Finally do not forget the volume of any header or overflow tanks. One quarter of the total calculated volume must be anti-freeze and one twentieth must be corrosion proofer, so work out the amount of proofer and anti-freeze needed, put them into the header tank, and turn on the water to fill the system up. All you have to do now is to wait for a sunny day.

You can clearly see from all this that a solar panel system will involve you in a great amount of work and expense, and it will take many years to collect enough useful energy to pay back the cost of its construction. If you decide to build solar panels take great care to do it properly so that they will last a long time, and remember to check them regularly.

20 Building a Solar Roof

An alternative to the solar panels of Chapter 19 is a solar roof, which would be particularly suitable if you have a roof that needs repairing or replacing. A solar roof is cheaper than solar panels, and acts as weatherproofing as well as a solar heater. Its disadvantage is that it is less efficient than conventional solar panels.

The solar roof, or trickle collector, consists of a black metal sheet over which water trickles from a perforated pipe at the top of the sheet. There is a layer of glass over the sheet which becomes hot in the sun and heats the water flowing down it. The hot water is collected in a gutter at the bottom of the roof, pumped through a heat exchanger in a hot water storage tank, and then back up to the top again. The system needs a pump, but it can never freeze because there is no water on the collector unless the sun shines and the pump switches on.

Access

Build the system on a suitable south-facing roof at an angle of 30° to 60° to the horizontal. To give access to the roof you will need two exten-sion ladders which you should tie to screw eyes fixed into the rafters or fascia at the eaves and to stakes driven into the ground. You will also need a roof ladder which has a special end that hooks over the ridge of the roof. There is a lot to be said for building a trickling collector on a single storey building or extension to reduce the problems of access and possible accidents. If you are keen to build on a higher roof you should perhaps hire a set of scaffolding and have it erected to provide easy access to the whole roof, or maybe reconsider the whole project.

Preparing the roof

Remove any existing roof covering to expose the rafters and give them three generous coats of wood preservative. If they are not at about 400–450mm centres nail in a few extra ones. If the roof is old check it for any signs of rot and replace any damaged timber with new treated pieces. Then cover the rafters with a layer of 18mm roofing grade chipboard, nailed down with annular nails. You can buy chipboard ready

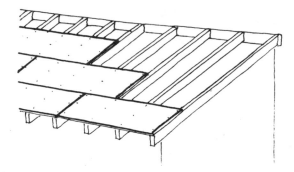

finished with a layer of roofing felt: this is worth using as it is waterproof once you have taped the joints, so you will not have the problem of rain damage. Lay roofing felt on the chipboard surface to provide protection should the collector leak and to prevent vapour from the hot water on the roof diffusing into the roof structure. The solar roof is an efficient generator of water vapour because the water is open to the air, and you must take a lot of care to keep this vapour out of your house. Starting at one edge of the roof, trowel on a thin layer of Ruberoid (or similar) cold applied mastic, which you can buy

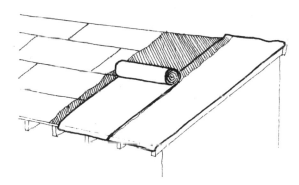

when you buy the felt, to cover the chipboard to a width slightly greater than that of the roll of felt. Unroll the felt and fix the bottom edge in place with a few galvanised clout nails. The job is best done on a warm day so that the felt, which should be a medium grade, will unroll easily without cracking.

When the first piece of felt is in place, firmly bedded on the mastic and fixed down with a few clout nails round the edges, put another band of mastic on the chipboard, overlapping

the felt by 100mm. Lay the next piece of felt with a 100mm overlap on to the piece already there and continue along until the whole roof is felted. Make sure that the whole roof is well covered with mastic and that the felt is smoothed down before nailing so that there are no wrinkles. Now lay another layer of felt, again bedded on mastic. This time it should be laid horizontally, starting at the eaves, with each layer overlapping the one below by 100mm. Both layers of felt should overhang the edges of the roof by about 100mm.

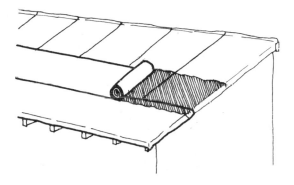

Fitting the collector

The aluminium sheets

You are now ready to make the heat-absorbing part of the collector. This should be made from corrugated aluminium, painted black. The easiest way to do this is to buy pre-painted aluminium such as Gränges Essem TRP 20 profile with Metallack black finish. The fixing screws for fastening the aluminium to the chip-

board roof can be bought from the same manufacturer. They should be of a type suitable for wood and up to 20mm long. It is essential that the screws should be stainless steel or aluminium alloy and that they have suitable sealing washers to prevent water leaking under them; if you buy them from the makers of the

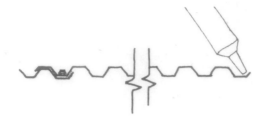

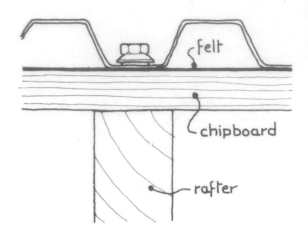

corrugated sheet you will be sure to buy the correct ones.

You will also need a tube of lap sealing stuff to seal the joints between adjacent sheets of aluminium. When you order the aluminium tell the manufacturer the length of sheet you require (up to a maximum of 13 metres) and the width of the area to be covered. Each sheet is 1123mm wide but it covers only 1050mm because of the overlap at the joint with the next sheet.

Choose a calm day to put up your aluminium and have a friend to help hold the sheets in place while you drill them. The first sheet should come in line with the side of the roof and should be carefully positioned so that it is at right angles to the line of the ridge. It should overlap the bottom edge of the roof by about 50mm. If this first sheet is not positioned correctly the whole roof will come out crooked.

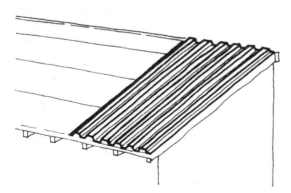

Each sheet will need a row of screws down the edge and down the middle, with the screws about a metre apart down the roof. Fix the first screws of the sheet at the top of the middle row, making a dent with a centre punch to stop the drill from sliding about. Try to drill only a short distance, say 5mm into the chipboard so that the screw has a good fixing. The

drill diameter should be very slightly larger than that of the screw. Finally tighten the screw firmly with a spanner or a socket spanner to compress the sealing washer against the aluminium. A socket spanner on a ratchet handle makes this job very much easier.

When the first sheet is fixed down at its centre line and its outside edge, smear some of the lap sealing compound along the edge where the next sheet will overlap it and then put the next sheet in place and fix it down, again starting at the middle row of screws. It will take some care to make the sheets line up properly so do not be tempted to hurry the job.

The purlins

When the sheets are all in place, attach the aluminium purlins that carry the glazing bars which hold the glass. The purlins can be aluminium Z section about 38mm high. Space them at about 1200mm centres across the aluminium sheets and fasten them to the

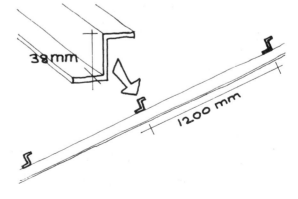

sheets with aluminium Imex rivets which are obtained from the suppliers of the corrugated sheets. It is very important to use these rivets and not steel ones so as to prevent corrosion. The purlins should be drilled to take the rivets at about 600mm centres (be sure that the holes you drill match the spacing of the corrugations in the aluminium sheets).

Stretch a string across the roof to provide a straight line to show where the purlins should go, and mark the first hole, near one end, on the aluminium. Centre punch the mark and drill the hole; then put a rivet into your rivetter, and push the end of the rivet into the hole in the purlin and the aluminium. While your helper holds the purlin in place squeeze the handles and the purlin will be rivetted in position. If you repeat the operation at the other end of the purlin it will then be fixed in place while you drill and rivet all the other holes. There should be a purlin at the top and bottom of the roof, and intermediate ones as required.

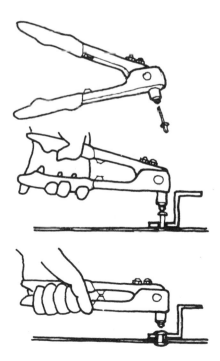

The pipe

Now is the time to put up the pipe that distributes the water over the aluminium sheet, and this is where the main problem with this type of solar water heater occurs. If aluminium comes into contact with copper, or even has water dripping on it off a copper pipe, it corrodes. It follows that the distributor pipe should not be copper, although in our experience solar roofs have been built with copper pipes and they have not corroded yet. It may be that the pipe furs up inside with mineral deposits from the water, and these prevent the water from dissolving enough copper from the pipe to affect the aluminium.

Stainless steel pipe is an alternative to copper. It comes in the same sizes as copper and is about the same price, but even if you use stainless pipe you cannot avoid the copper coil heat exchanger in the hot water cylinder. If you want to do the job properly you should use only stainless steel pipe between the heat exchanger and the top of the solar roof, with stainless steel fittings. There should be a corrosion getter between the outlet from the heat exchanger and the stainless steel pipe containing a sacrificial element of aluminium for the copper in the water to react with. However, we are all less than perfect and we suspect that a system using stainless steel pipe with normal copper joints will perform very well, although it is probably worth making the corrosion getter as described on page 148.

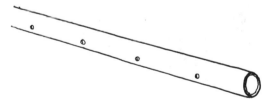

The distributor pipe should be drilled with 4mm diameter holes at 75mm centres so that the holes coincide with the valleys in the corrugated aluminium. Mark the holes with a centre punch and drill them using an electric drill, but do not press too hard or the bit will become red hot. Take care that the holes are in a straight line along the pipe. If the collector is wider than 4 metres the pipe should be jointed as shown in

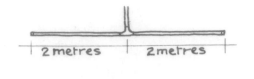

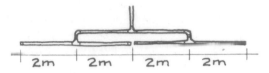

the diagram so that no piece is longer than 2 metres, as this will help give a more even flow of water through the holes.

The ends of the pipe should have removable access caps so that you can poke a stick through if any of the holes become blocked up.

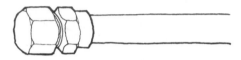

The manufacturers of the screws for holding down the aluminium sheet say that they are weatherproof but if you are worried at the idea of hot water pouring over them you can omit the holes in the pipe at each row of screws. The connection to the distributor pipe can either come up from below through the aluminium, or can be brought in from one end as shown. The perforated pipe should be about 150mm below

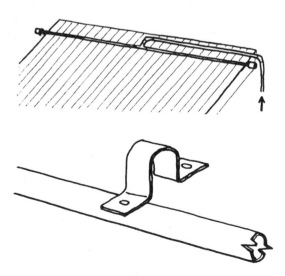

the top edge of the aluminium sheets to prevent water running behind the sheets. Fix the pipes to the sheets with strips of aluminium about 15mm wide bent to form saddles as shown, drilled and rivetted through the corrugated sheets. Space them about 900mm apart.

The fascia board

Finally make a Tanalised softwood fascia board for the bottom of the roof, using 25mm thick wood planed all round. Before you fix the board

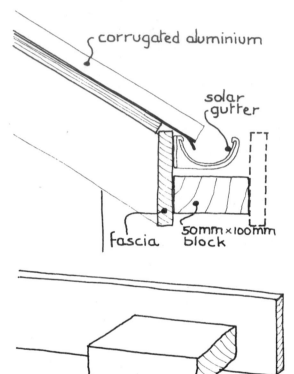

corrugated aluminium

solar gutter

fascia

50mm × 100mm block

in place, screw and glue (using waterproof glue) some blocks of Tanalised wood 50mm×100mm and about 200mm long to the fascia. These should be fixed at 900mm centres. They are to support a second fascia which will carry the rainwater gutter. It is not worth painting the inner fascia, because you will not be able to reach it to redecorate it, but the outer one, which should be made from 25mm thick Tanalised wood (19mm when planed) can have three coats of preservative stain before it is fixed.

Nail the inner fascia into place and fix a 75mm diameter half round PVC gutter to it to collect the water from the solar roof. The aluminium should overlap the edge of the gutter, and so should the felt which must be trimmed with a Stanley knife as required. The gutter will need an outlet, the position of which will depend on the layout of the building and the placing of tanks. The gutter should be supported by gutter brackets at 500mm centres to prevent it drooping when full of hot water. Do not fit the other fascia at this stage.

The glazing bars and glazing

You are now ready for the glazing bars. These should be aluminium greenhouse bars as described in Chapter 21. Before fixing them you will need some pieces of thin aluminium sheet, say 16 gauge, bent at right angles and fixed to the end rafter of the roof as shown in the diagram. These are to seal the ends of the solar roof and should be well smeared with mastic and fixed to the rafter with round head galvanised screws. You can have these pieces made up by any local small metal workshop, or you could go to evening classes in metalwork

and make them yourself. The pieces of aluminium should be overlapped by 50mm at the joints and sealed to one another with mastic.

Drill holes for the glazing bar bolts using a 6mm drill. The first glazing bar must be fixed through the aluminium edges described above and bedded on mastic to seal any gaps underneath. The glazing bar should be long enough to overlap the outer fascia board by 25mm at the eaves. At the top of the roof the glazing bars

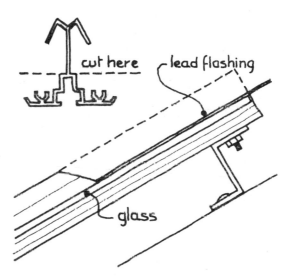

should be cut as shown so that a piece of no 6 lead sheet can be fixed over the top edge of the glass to keep the water out. See Chapter 21 for details of how to put in the glass. Fix the bottom edge of the lead with strips of lead about 25mm wide fixed to the wall or to the ridge board with galvanised clout nails. Bend the ends of the lead strips to hold the bottom edge of the flashing.

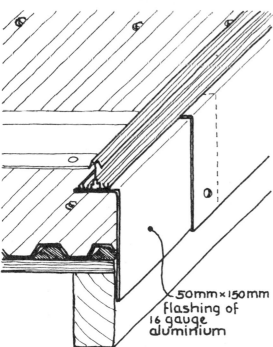

50mm × 150mm flashing of 16 gauge aluminium

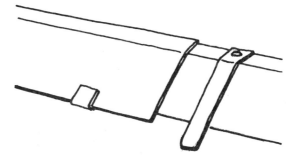

If the other side of the roof is tiled or slated, you can then mortar a row of ridge tiles into place over the top of the flashing, taking care not to break the glass. The diagrams show additional detail for lean-to roofs.

Finally, before you are finished, you must fix the fascia board in place under the glazing bars

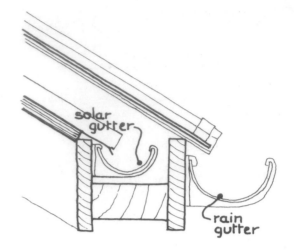

solar gutter

rain gutter

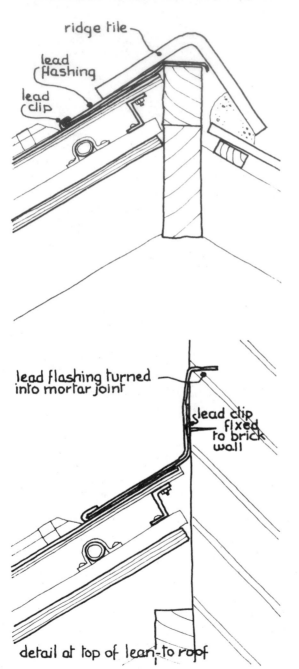

ridge tile

lead flashing

lead clip

lead flashing turned into mortar joint

lead clip fixed to brick wall

detail at top of lean-to roof

at the eaves. Fix it with cups and screws (plated of course) so that it can be removed easily to give access to the solar gutter when required. Fit a gutter of your choice under the glass, arrange it to discharge the water into a rain-water butt or soakaway and the solar roof is nearly finished.

Behind the chipboard put at least 100mm of insulation: be sure that you do not use expanded polystyrene in case the roof ever becomes hot enough to melt it. Choose glass fibre or mineral wool. If the collector is on a roof with a ventilated attic you need do nothing else, but if the back of the roof is a ceiling it will need a vapour barrier of heavy duty polythene, foil-backed plasterboard or special vapour barrier foil, to protect the insulation.

PVC glazing
If you want to build a really cheap solar roof you can use corrugated clear PVC sheet for the glazing instead of glass. This will not last so long, and it may have a tendency to melt, or at least sag, in very hot weather, but it does allow you to put up a solar roof very easily. If you want to use PVC, follow the construction of the solar roof as far as the aluminium sheet; but instead of aluminium purlins, use wooden purlins so that the PVC can be screwed to them. The purlins should be of 25mm×50mm hardwood such as iroko if you can find some, or else of Tanalised 25mm×50mm softwood. Screw them through the aluminium into the chipboard

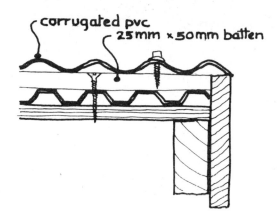

corrugated pvc
25mm x 50mm batten

of the PVC with a piece of lead sheet just the same as the glass, and you will need some aluminium edges as used on the roof with glazing bars. Alternatively you can screw the edge of the PVC sheet into a 25mm wide Tanalised softwood board at the edge of the roof as shown in the drawing.

The PVC-covered solar roof will work perfectly well, and will provide hot water, but after about ten years you will probably find that you must replace the PVC as it will have become brittle and discoloured.

Connecting the system to the plumbing

Once the roof is glazed you can connect it up to the plumbing. Do not be tempted to connect up the solar gutter before the roof is glazed because you will flood the house if it rains. The gutter should have a conventional downpipe discharging over an expansion tank with a capacity of about twenty litres. Support the downpipe with clips to prevent it sagging when

with countersunk head no 12 screws 63mm long. The screws must be bright zinc-plated or cadmium-plated to prevent corrosion.

Space the purlins about one metre apart down the roof, and fix the PVC sheets to them with the special screws and waterproof caps sold for this purpose. Drill the holes for the screws in the plastic very carefully so that you do not crack the sheet, and do not overtighten the screws. You will need to flash over the top

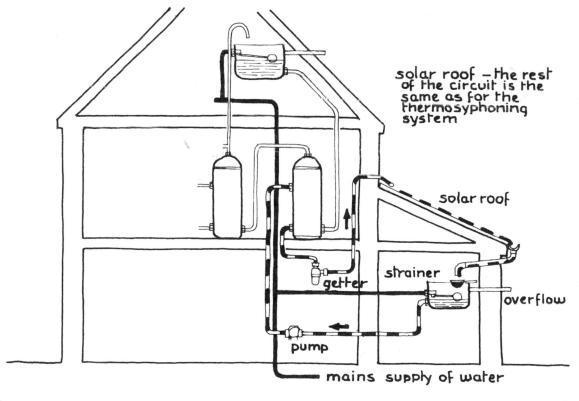

solar roof — the rest of the circuit is the same as for the thermosyphoning system

solar roof

getter

strainer

overflow

pump

mains supply of water

full of hot water. When the pump is switched off all the water in the system will drain back into this tank, so if your collector is large you had better calculate the volume of water involved by using the pipe volumes given in the section on solar panels.

This overflow tank is also the water supply for the collector circuit and it should be connected to a conventional cold water header tank up in the roof by a 15mm pipe with a low pressure ball valve in the solar tank. This is done to prevent possible contamination of the mains supply; if there is any problem the header tank alone – which is used only to supply this solar tank and should be of the same size – will be affected.

The header tank will need a mains water supply through a high pressure ball valve, and an overflow pipe to warn of any problems with the ball valve. The solar tank should also have an overflow pipe. The ball valve for this tank should be about halfway down the side rather than near the top, so that there is room for the extra water when the pump switches off. Put a nylon kitchen sieve under the outlet from the gutter downpipe to catch any bits and pieces that may fall into the system and clog the holes in the pipe at the top of the collector.

Near the bottom of the solar tank fit an outlet to take a 22mm pipe and connect up to a central heating pump of a suitable head capacity for the system you have designed. The pump must be at the lowest point in the circuit so that it is always full of water, otherwise it will not work properly. From the pump the water goes through the indirect hot water cylinder (buy one with a coil type heat exchanger) and up to the perforated pipe at the top of the collector. All pipework should be in 22mm stainless steel, and you can use conventional compression fittings on all the pipes from the tank to the hot water cylinder.

When the pipe comes out from the cylinder heat exchanger it should go into a corrosion getter. This is a plastic bottle trap as used for wash basins and sinks with a 75mm seal. You will need fittings to connect 22mm stainless steel pipe to both sides of the trap. Bring the water in at the top of the trap and out at the

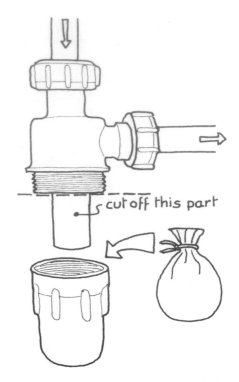

cut off this part

side, just as if it was being used in a sink, but cut off the projecting pipe inside as shown. Then make a muslin or nylon bag and fill it with little bits of aluminium, or aluminium shavings from a workshop. Put the bag, like herbs in a stew, in the base of the trap and screw the base back on. The idea is that any copper in the water will react with the sacrificial element in the trap rather than with the collector itself. You should check the trap occasionally when the collector is not operating and renew the aluminium as required.

Between the trap and the perforated pipe all joints as well as pipe ought to be in stainless steel. For the perfectionist stainless steel pipe joints are available and have the added advantage that they are assembled with glue which makes the whole job very easy. The special glue and primer are supplied by the makers of the fittings together with instructions on their use. The important thing (as with all pipework) is to cut the pipe square using a proper pipe cutter and to clean it well with emery cloth. Clean the inside of the joint as well, then spray pipe and joint with the special primer and allow to dry for a minute or two.

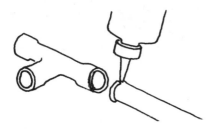

Squeeze a bead of adhesive round the end of the pipe and the mouth of the fitting. Insert the pipe, pushing it right into the fitting, and give it a very slight twist. Leave it to set at room temperature for five or ten minutes before you handle it. Leave it to set overnight before running water through it. The only stainless steel fittings that seem rather expensive are the stop ends with access caps for the ends of the distributor pipe, so you could use a normal copper stop end compression fitting and take a chance.

The rest of the solar roof plumbing is the same as that for a solar panel system. You will need a connection to the existing hot water cylinder and a pump controller. Fit the temperature sensor from the controller to the top of the collector plate with an aluminium strap, or wedge it in behind with a piece of wood.

Now the solar roof is ready to run. It has the advantage over solar panels that you can actually *see* the hot water coming out of the gutter into the tank, you can put your hand under the stream of water and feel all the heat coming from nothing but the sun. It is a great way to convince sceptics who say that solar energy does not work.

21 Building a Conservatory

The conservatory first became popular as a plant-filled extension to a living-room when the Victorians developed the design of glasshouses, encouraged by the new availability of mass produced glass and glazing bars. The present revival of interest in conservatories among alternative technologists has less to do with the production of out-of-season vegetables and exotic fruit than with the collection of energy. Because of the greenhouse effect, the conservatory is often considerably warmer than the outside air so it can reduce the heat loss from a building and save conventional fuels. Its effectiveness will depend on the area of glazing — which should face south — but generally the bigger the better.

We do not have any figures to prove it, but we suspect that money spent on a conservatory will provide more useful energy than the same sum spent on solar panels. The problem is that you cannot measure the energy collected by a conservatory; if you have solar panels at least you have a tank of hot water (when the sun shines) which you know you have not paid the electricity or gas boards for.

You can also use the conservatory as a greenhouse to grow tomatoes, and if you are adventurous you can produce aubergines, figs, nectarines and other delicacies.

The legal aspects

If you want a small conservatory there are prefabricated ones on the market in aluminium or cedar wood, sold with instructions for their installation. These are up to 2100mm wide, reach a maximum height of 2500mm, and come in various lengths. If you want something bigger than this you will have to design your own.

You will need planning permission for a conservatory with a volume greater than 50m³. If it is near the edge of your land you may have to consider various regulations concerning fire resistance in addition to the other building regulations. One regulation which you will have to consider is no K4 which deals with ventilation. It states that if a room is ventilated through a conservatory (in other words if the conservatory covers the window of the room) the

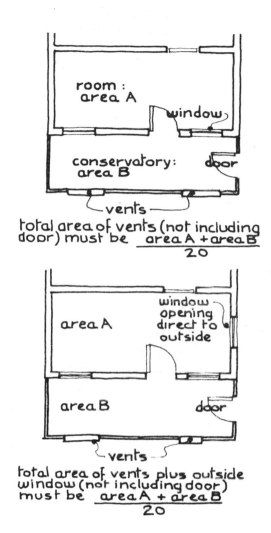

room :
area A

window

conservatory:
area B

door

vents

total area of vents (not including door) must be $\dfrac{\text{area A + area B}}{20}$

area A

window opening direct to outside

area B

door

vents

total area of vents plus outside window (not including door) must be $\dfrac{\text{area A + area B}}{20}$

ning permission, except in the case of an off-the-peg conservatory which you could probably put up without asking anyone. If you build *anything* without permission you run the risk of having to take it down again, so it is always worth checking before you start.

Choosing the materials

The two common materials for building conservatory frames are aluminium and timber. Glass is not essential: you can use corrugated PVC for a cheaper job, although this will last only about ten years because it is degraded by sunlight. We automatically seem to build everything to last a hundred years, and glass is the most durable material unless you live in an area of frequent hailstorms. The glass must be supported by glazing bars and it is here that you make the choice between wood and metal.

Wooden glazing bars tend to need a lot of maintenance, especially if you paint them and use putty to hold the glass. To overcome these problems a group at the Architecture Department of Sheffield University have devised a system using Tanalised wood glazing bars 38mm wide: the top edge is planed and the bar is covered with three coats of preservative stain on top of the Tanalising, to help throw off the water. The bars are positioned at 616mm centres and two strips of self-adhesive draught strip (Schlegel VS 9mm×6mm) are stuck to the

conservatory should have ventilation openings, excluding doors, equal in area to one twentieth of its floor area plus the floor area of the room. If the room also has another window open directly to the outside air the area of this vent plus the conservatory vents must be one twentieth of the floor areas of the room and the conservatory combined.

The regulation does not say if roof ventilators in a conservatory count towards the total vent area but it would be a very churlish building inspector who did not allow you to include them in your calculations. The inspectors tend to be keen on ventilation, so if you can prove to them that you have enough you will avoid one source of conflict. You need building regulations permission even if you do not need plan-

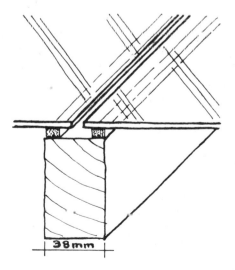

38mm

top of them as shown in the diagrams. The draught strip has a shiny PVC covering over the foam part and a reinforcing cord running down inside.

The glass used is standard 3mm thick horticultural glass, 610mm×610mm. It is fixed with a gap of about 6mm between the adjacent panes forming a narrow gutter on top of the bars for rainwater. The panes of glass are held down at the corners by clips of cadmium-plated galvanised 26 gauge mild steel, 38mm wide and 45mm long. The clips could be aluminium, but it was found to be slightly cheaper to have

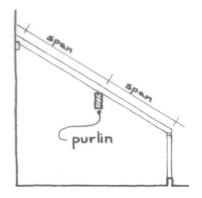

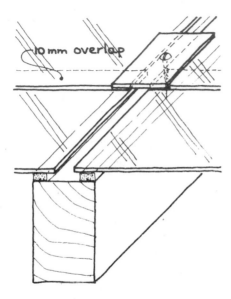

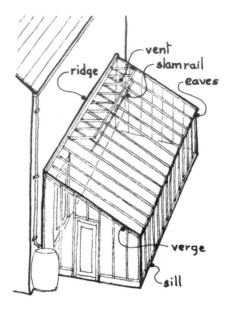

them plated specially. One end of the clip is turned down about 2.5mm to support the end of the glass. Each clip is drilled with a 6mm hole for a 50mm no 12 bright zinc or cadmium plated round head screw. No sealing is used round the screw head as it does not matter if there is a leak. Each pane of glass overlaps the one below it by about 10mm.

This system certainly appears to have overcome most of the problems of wooden glazing bars and it is well worth trying. The bars used at Sheffield were 63mm deep when finished which would mean that they could span about 2.5 metres; 100mm deep bars could span about 3 metres, and 150mm about 4.5 metres. You could always use a purlin to reduce the span as shown in the diagram. The pitch of the

roof should be no less than 25°; the one built at Sheffield was 45°.

The advantage of using aluminium bars, apart from avoiding putty and maintenance, is that you can fit ventilators into them easily without having to worry about waterproofing. The place to buy the bars is a commercial greenhouse manufacturer, who will also sell you lots of other useful pieces such as bolts, glazing strip and clips, vent assemblies, sills and ridges, and even the glass.

Assembly

Laying the foundations

You start your conservatory by digging the foundations. We will assume that you have decided to use aluminium; yes, it does take a lot of energy to make it, but once made it will last a lifetime and can be melted down and re-used in the future. We used bars made by the Cambridge Glasshouse Company who also supplied the glazing bars for the famous BRAD solar roof in Wales.

The bars have to be spaced a standard 24½ in apart centre to centre, which is 622.3mm (the glasshouse industry has not really gone metric yet), to take the standard 610mm (2ft) square panes of horticultural glass. The roof slope should be 26° or up to about 30°. If it is steeper than this you will not be able to use standard greenhouse parts. If you want to avoid cutting narrow strips of glass at one end of the conservatory, try to make its length a multiple of 622.3mm. The standard pieces of aluminium purlin, sill and ridge section are eight of these 622.3mm bays long, so it is a good idea if your conservatory is 8, 16 or 24 bays long rather than 9, 17 or 25. Otherwise you will have to buy a whole extra lot of aluminium, most of which will be wasted, unless you can persuade the manufacturers to cut you off a shorter piece.

When you have fixed this dimension add 50mm, to give you the outer edge of the foundation wall if you are having glazed ends, or the inner edge of the wall if you intend building brick ends. The foundations for a large conservatory are a matter for discussion with your building inspector. Our foundations would

support a three-storey house, but we live on clay which tends to shrink in hot weather. A typical foundation might go down 900mm into the ground and be 300mm wide to support a 225mm thick brick foundation wall; it all depends on the soil. Set out the foundations as shown in the drawings; be sure to check that the diagonal measurements are the same, as this will ensure that the corners meet at right angles. You will find it is not easy to dig a narrow trench with a spade, but try to keep the bottom 200mm the right size as this is where the concrete will go, and the larger you make it the more concrete you will use.

When the trench is dug, level off the bottom and drive some sharpened stakes (about 50mm×50mm) into it so that they stick up 200mm above the bottom of the trench. Fix them quite firmly so that they do not move when you pour in the concrete. Using a long straight board and a level, set the stakes so that the concrete will have a horizontal surface for the brick base walls of the conservatory. Now is the time to contact the ready-mixed concrete people and have friends ready with shovels to move the concrete along the trench until it is level with the tops of the stakes all the way round.

Building the brick wall
The next step is to build a 225mm brick wall off the concrete to support the conservatory itself. If you are no good at bricklaying you could ask a builder or a friend to do this. The wall should

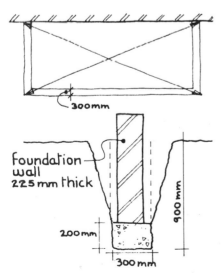

foundation wall 225 mm thick

300mm

200mm

900mm

300 mm

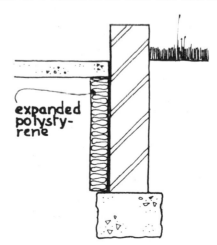

expanded polysty-rene

finish at least 150mm above ground level, with gaps where there are to be doors. Now you can shovel some of the enormous pile of earth that you so laboriously dug out back into the trench, but before you do this put some 50mm or 75mm thick expanded polystyrene against the inside of the brickwork, resting it on the concrete at the bottom. The insulation will help to hold heat in the floor slab of the conservatory in cold weather.

The timber frame

The glazed walls of the conservatory are built off a 50mm×100mm Tanalised timber sill which should be rested on top of the base wall.

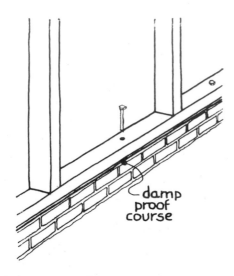

It should sit on a 100mm wide strip of damp proof course (available from your builders' merchant) and both the damp course and the sill should be bedded on mortar. Check with a level that the sill is truly horizontal. Fix it into the brick wall with Fischer bolts at about 1200mm centres. To use these, drill a hole with a masonry drill the same diameter as the bolt straight through the wood and 50mm at least into the brick. Drop in a 100mm bolt and tighten the nut which will expand the end of the bolt so that it grips into the brick. Do not do this until the mortar has dried, and try to drill into the centre of bricks rather than into a joint.

Next, fix the vertical posts, which should measure 50mm×100mm, preferably Tanal-

ised or at least painted thoroughly with preservative. They go at 1245mm centres so that they line up with the glazing bars. Skew nail them into the sill with 100mm nails and ask someone to hold them roughly upright while you nail them. When you have put up the first upright at one end of the conservatory, prop it with pieces of scrap timber nailed to it and to posts driven into the ground so that it is fixed vertically in both directions.

When three or four posts have been nailed to the sill and are propped or held more or less upright you can put on the top plate. This is another piece measuring 50mm×100mm (Tanalised of course) and should be nailed on to the tops of the uprights, which should all be the same length, with 100mm nails. Check that each post is vertical before you nail the top piece to it — mistakes will be hard to correct later — and check that the top plate is horizontal. Joint the sections of the top plate as shown with additional pieces of 50mm×100mm, nails and coach screws so that the whole length will act as one piece of wood.

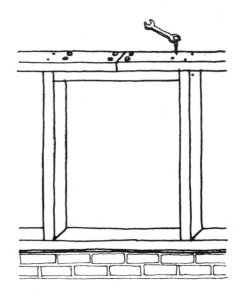

When you have four or five uprights nailed to the sill with the plate on top you can put up the first rafters. Make sure that the wall framework you have just built is very firmly propped and that it is vertical in both directions.

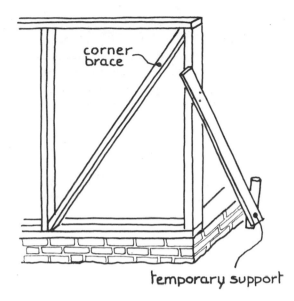

corner brace

temporary support

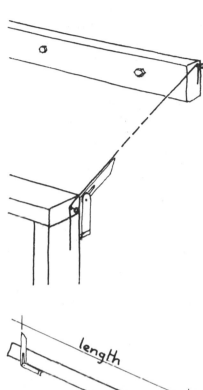

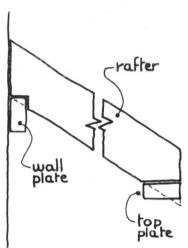

rafter

wall plate

top plate

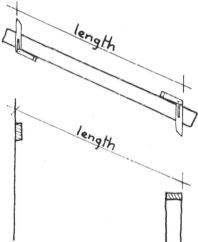

length

length

Then nail in a diagonal corner brace of 50mm×100mm timber, cut accurately to fit into the angle as shown, to keep it steady in one direction. Now bolt a horizontal wall plate of Tanalised wood, 50mm×100mm, to the wall of the house, using 150mm long Rawlbolts or Fischerbolts at 1200mm centres. Make sure that the plate is level. It will support the rafters which can be 50mm wide and of a depth suitable to the span. A glass roof with glazing bars puts a dead load of about 15kg/m² on the rafters, so you could probably use 50mm×150mm for a span of 4 metres, or 50mm×100mm for a span of 2.5 metres.

To cut the rafters you will need a good saw and an adjustable bevel to mark the angles. Stretch a piece of string between the wall plate and the top plate as shown to give you the angle to set the bevel, then mark the angle to cut the top end of the rafter. Measure from the wall of the house to the outer edge of the top plate: mark this dimension on the top edge of the rafter, then mark the angle of the bottom end. Notch the ends of the rafters to fit over the plates. Put the rafter in place and check that it is at right angles to the wall of the house, then skew nail it to the plates with 100mm nails. Provided you have put a diagonal brace in the vertical wall frame you will have a rigid structure once you have put up a few rafters.

Brick end walls

If you decide to have brick ends to the conservatory the construction of the timber part becomes much easier. Build the end walls which should be of 225mm thick brickwork before you make the timber part, putting in doors and windows as required. We recommend a bricklayer for this job unless you are very good at it yourself. Try to position any openings so that there are several courses of brickwork above them otherwise you will

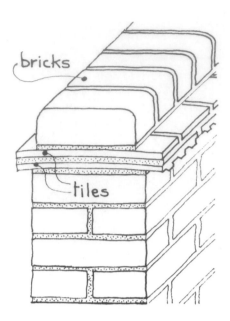

bricks

tiles

The brick ends should project half a course beyond the front brick foundation wall as shown in the drawings. Once they are up, the

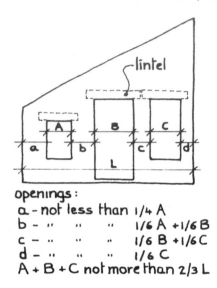

lintel

openings:
a - not less than 1/4 A
b - " " " 1/6 A + 1/6 B
c - " " " 1/6 B + 1/6 C
d - " " " 1/6 C
A + B + C not more than 2/3 L

weaken the structure. Follow the diagram regarding widths of openings. Every opening must have a reinforced concrete or steel lintel to carry the brickwork over it. Where the brick end meets the house bond in the bricks to make a strong joint.

Stop the brickwork 110mm above the intended line of the tops of the rafters and cap it with a coping to throw off the rainwater. This can be made either with precast concrete sections, or with two courses of plain clay or concrete roofing tiles laid as shown with a capping of hard engineering bricks. The 'double bullnose' type which have curved edges are probably the best to use as they will shed rainwater more effectively. But, if you cannot find them, the ordinary square ones will do the job.

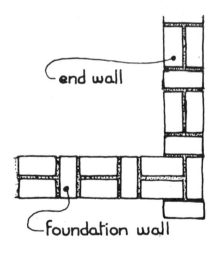

end wall

foundation wall

erection of the timber is very easy. Put in the sill and screw and plug the first upright to the brickwork with 75mm no 12 zinc-plated screws. There should be a piece of damp proof course material between it and the bricks. Now fix a second upright and nail the top plate between them both. Now fit in the intermediate uprights. With this method only one end of the

156

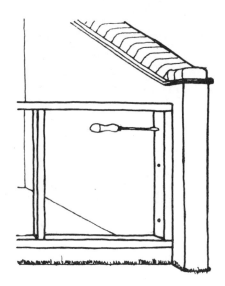

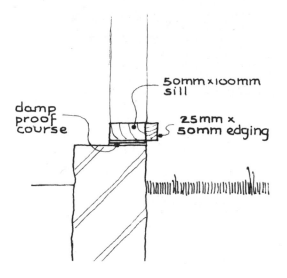

50mm×100mm sill

damp proof course

25mm × 50mm edging

timber wall must be propped up to stop it falling over, and it will not be trying to fall in two planes at once. If you fix a rafter in place at the end furthest from the brick wall the whole structure will be rigid.

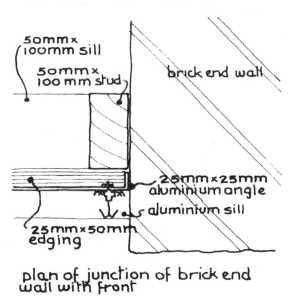

50mm× 100mm sill

50mm× 100 mm stud

brick end wall

25mm×25mm aluminium angle

aluminium sill

25mm×50mm edging

plan of junction of brick end wall with front

Completing the frame

Whatever sort of ends you have used you should now finish putting up the timber for the front wall and the rafters. Do it methodically and carefully, checking that the posts and rafters are all at 1245mm centres. You should also check from one end that the dimensions are

multiples of these measurements in case any errors are adding up as you go along from one measurement to the next. When the front wall is complete nail a piece of 25mm×50mm Tanalised timber along the front edge of the wall as shown.

If you are building glazed ends you can finish them now, using the details shown in the next three drawings. Screw or bolt the final upright of the timber end to the wall of the house. If you are using a standard door and door frame you must put in an extra glazing bar above the door,

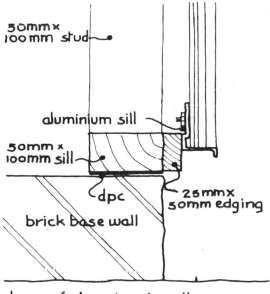

50mm× 100mm stud

aluminium sill

50mm × 100mm sill

dpc

brick base wall

25mm× 50mm edging

base of glazed end wall

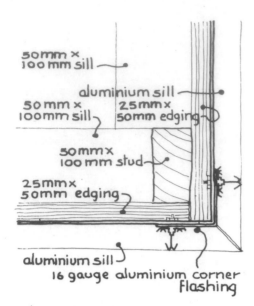

50mm ×
100 mm sill

aluminium sill

50 mm ×
100 mm sill

25 mm ×
50 mm edging

50 mm ×
100 mm stud

25 mm ×
50 mm edging

aluminium sill

16 gauge aluminium corner
flashing

**plan of junction of glazed end wall
with front wall**

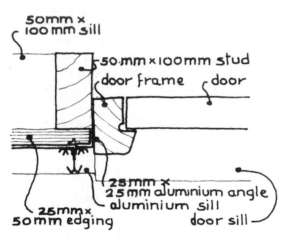

50mm ×
100 mm sill

50 mm ×100mm stud

door frame   door

25 mm ×
25 mm aluminium angle
aluminium sill

25mm ×
50mm edging

door sill

**plan of junction of glazed end
wall with door frame**

and the glass will have to be cut down to this
reduced width. As an alternative to glazing you
might consider cladding the end walls with
wooden boarding and putting in conventional
ready made timber windows.

When all the wooden framing is in place, give
it another coat of preservative, if it is not Tanalised, in addition to the preservative each piece
should have received after it was cut and
before it was fixed into place. If you want to
change the colour of the wood give it all three
coats of preservative stain at this stage. It will
be quite difficult to repaint some of it once the
glass is in place so it is wise to choose a colour
that will look alright even when it has faded
rather than one which relies on its brightness
for effect. The cost of the timber framing will be
reduced if you use secondhand timber, which
will be perfectly satisfactory if you choose the
pieces carefully. Pull out all the nails and then
use it as if it were new, but be careful when
sawing that you do not hit a hidden piece of
broken nail and ruin your saw. Secondhand
timber should of course be given the full
preservative treatment.

Inserting the aluminium framing
You are now ready to put up the aluminium
framing. When you buy the framing and glazing
bars ask for a set of drawings and assembly
instructions so that you can see how the bits go
together on a normal greenhouse. Our comments below are intended as an addition to the
makers' instructions to explain how the parts
are used on a conservatory.

The first parts are the U-section purlins
which carry the glazing bars. They should be
spaced no more than 1800mm apart. You will
see that the purlins are drilled with holes at the
correct centres for the glazing bars. Take the
first one and cut off the end to leave 20mm between the centre of the hole and the end. If you

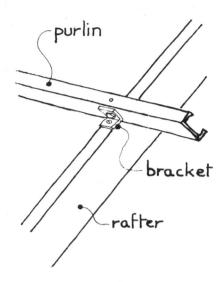

purlin

bracket

rafter

use a hacksaw with a fine tooth blade you should find that the aluminium is no harder to cut than wood. Be sure that the purlin is the right way round before you decide which end to cut, with the holes at the top and the open end of the U facing the ridge of the conservatory.

To fix the purlins you will need some 50mm×50mm aluminium angle, and some 10mm diameter aluminium nuts and bolts, all of which you buy from the greenhouse makers.

joining plate

If your conservatory is longer than 8 bays of glazing you will need purlin joining plates as well, as the purlins are only this long. To make the fixing brackets cut some 50mm lengths from the aluminium angle; drill a 10mm hole in one side for a bolt, and a 6mm hole in the other for a screw.

You will now need some round head no 12 screws about 50mm long to fix the brackets to the rafters. The screws should be stainless

steel if you can get them. Otherwise use cadmium-plated or bright zinc-plated ones. Measure up from the bottom end of the rafter to find where you want the purlin to go, and screw the bracket to the rafter at this position. Fix another bracket on the rafter at the other end of the purlin length, making sure that both brackets are the same distance from the rafter ends so that the purlin will be parallel to the front and back of the conservatory. Lay the purlin in place across the brackets with the holes for the glazing bars aligned on the centre lines of the rafters. Then hold it firmly and drill through the hole in the first bracket with a 10mm drill and fit the first bolt and nut.

When the purlin is fixed at both ends you can put in the intermediate brackets. If you have to join on another length of purlin use the joining plates to ensure that the spacing of the holes for the glazing bars is maintained correctly. If you use more than one line of purlins be sure that the holes line up so that the glazing bars will be at right angles to the purlins.

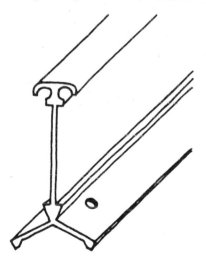

After the purlin or purlins, fix the ridge to the existing house wall. Slide a bolt into a glazing bar and bolt it to one end of the purlin. Bolt another glazing bar to the purlin so that the bars are about the length of a section of ridge apart. Bolt the upper ends of the bars to the first piece of ridge, which you should have cut to give a dimension of 20mm from the centre of the first hole to the end. You may find that if you have

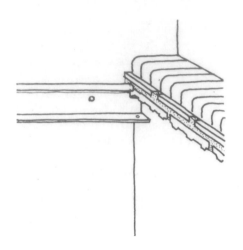

built a brick end wall you now have to cut off a piece of the top of the ridge to clear the overhanging tiles at the top of the wall. Prop the glazing bars up off the top of the rafters with the pieces of purlin that you cut off earlier, to give the correct spacing between the bars and the rafters.

This then gives you the height at which to fix the ridge. You will need help from friends to prevent it all sliding off the roof at this stage. Find a piece of Tanalised 25mm×50mm timber to make up the gap between the ridge and the wall. You do not need a piece all the way along. The ridge should be screwed to the wall at 1200mm intervals and the pieces of wood need only be 400–500mm long. With the ridge

held in place by the glazing bars, slip a piece of wood behind where it is to be fixed and drill through the ridge and the wood with a 6mm diameter drill. When you hit the bricks change to a 6mm masonry drill and go a further 50mm into the brickwork. Put a plasplug in the hole in the ridge, insert the screw, tap the screw head to drive the plug right to the bottom of the hole in the brick and tighten up. The screws should be 75mm round head no 12, plated or stainless.

An alternative is the screws made for fixing aluminium roofing as described in Chapter 20. These are stainless steel with a waterproofing washer under the head, and are obtained in 75mm lengths from the suppliers of the roofing sheet. They are tightened with a spanner. The screws must go about 20mm up from the small projection on the ridge. The glass sits on this projection and the screw heads could prevent it from seating properly.

Adding a roof ventilator

If you are planning to have a roof ventilator, which is essential unless you aim to use your conservatory as a solar cooker in the summer, it should be fitted now. The standard unit supplied by the manufacturers is seven bays of glazing long or a multiple of this. It is worked by a chain from the ground. It is a simple matter to

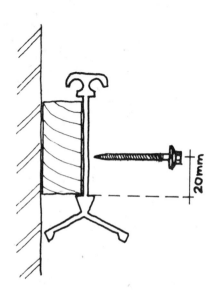

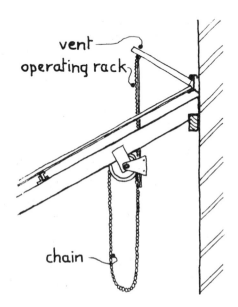

vent

operating rack

chain

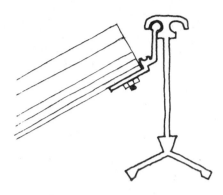

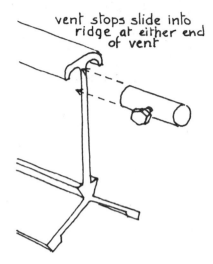

vent stops slide into ridge at either end of vent

cut it down to make it smaller as required. The hinging part of the ventilator slides into a groove in the ridge, and the assembled ventilator section should be fitted once the first length of ridge is in place with its glazing bars. This only applies if the conservatory is 16 bays long. If it is shorter you will have to slide the top piece of the ventilator into the ridge before you screw the ridge to the wall, and then assemble the rest of the ventilator in position once the glazing bars and the ridge are in place.

Make up the whole vent unit on the ground before you do any of this so that you can check that you have cut the top and bottom sections correctly to make the thing fit together. Then take it apart and fit the top section and its locating stops into the ridge as described. If you use more than one section of ridge buy a joining plate to attach the next piece to it so as to maintain the spacing of the glazing bar holes. In

order to be able to put the bolts through the holes in the ridge, you will have to attach the plate before screwing the end of the ridge to the wall; but it is easy enough to slacken off the other screws sufficiently to allow the ridge to be pulled away from the wall so that the bolts can be fixed.

Attaching the glazing bars
When all the ridge sections have been fixed to the wall you can attach the glazing bars. On a conservatory with wooden glazed ends the end glazing bar of the roof should be fixed on top of a specially formed piece of 16 gauge aluminium as shown in the drawing. Have this made up by

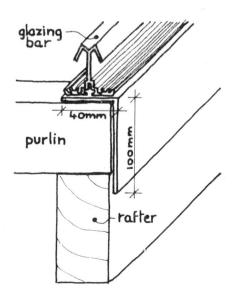

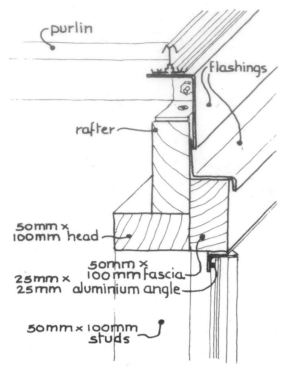

purlin

flashings

rafter

50mm × 100mm head

50mm × 100mm fascia

25mm × 25mm aluminium angle

50mm × 100mm studs

junction of glazed end wall with roof

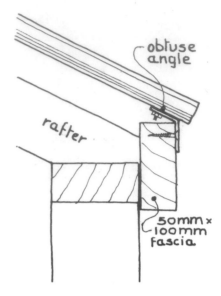

obtuse angle

rafter

50mm × 100mm fascia

a metal workshop, bed the bars on mastic and overlap the edging pieces at the joints as shown. At the bottom of the conservatory roof pack up a few of the glazing bars off the top of the rafters with pieces of offcut purlin and posi-

tion the 50mm×100mm fascia which should have been preservative treated and stained, if required, before you put it up. This is nailed to the rafter ends so that its top edge is about 5mm below the bottom edge of the glazing bars. You will then need a piece of 14 or 16 gauge aluminium about 80mm wide bent to an obtuse angle which should be the pitch of your roof plus 90°. You can buy the angle from the greenhouse manufacturers along with the other parts. The angle should be screwed with 38mm or 50mm no 12 round head stainless screws to the fascia so that it supports the ends of the glazing bars at the correct level.

Where joints in the fascia occur the screws should be put in as shown to try to prevent the wood from warping, otherwise the angle should be fixed at the glazing bar positions.

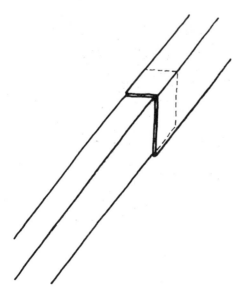

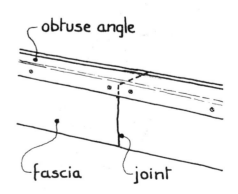

obtuse angle

fascia

joint

Finally drill 6mm holes at 622.3mm centres in the top of the angle for the bars; you can push the bars to one side while you drill the holes, but you should sight along the bars to make sure that they are straight before drilling the holes. This will allow for any inaccuracies in the fixing of the other parts.

Flashing

At the top of the ridge you will need a flashing to stop the rain coming down the wall and running behind the ridge. The flashing will also help to make the conservatory draught-tight which is essential if it is to work properly as a

source of solar heat. Have the flashing made up from 16 gauge aluminium by a local metal workshop to the approximate dimensions given in the drawing. You should be careful to make the turned down edge no greater than 5mm so that it does not obstruct the hinged ventilator. Put a section of flashing in place on top of the ridge and mark the positions for holes in it at 900mm centres to fix it to the brickwork. Avoid having holes where there are mortar joints. The pieces of flashing will be about 2 metres long each because small firms do not have metal bending machines larger than this. Squirt a line of mastic along the top of the ridge and along the back top edge of the flashing. Then put it in place, drill the wall for 50mm stainless screws and plugs, and screw the flashing up. Butt the next piece up to it with mastic in the joint between them.

Turning to the front wall of the conservatory, the vertical glazing bars should not be longer than 1800mm, otherwise they will need supporting in the middle. Screw the sill to the piece of 25mm×50mm wood at the bottom of the wall, making sure that the first hole is vertically below the first roof glazing bar by using a weighted piece of string as a plumb line. Fix the sill so that the part with the holes in it sticks up above the top of the piece of wood as shown.

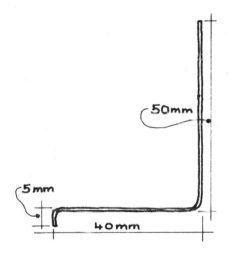

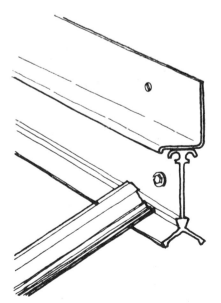

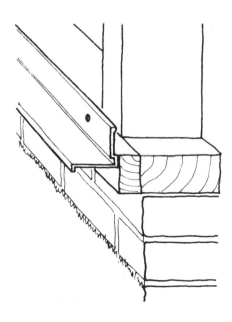

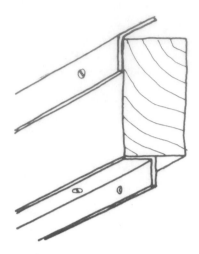

Seelastrip, which looks like strips of plasticine and can be obtained from greenhouse makers. This will keep out draughts. Slide the slam rails up the glazing bars to the ventilator, open it slightly and push the first one under it. Shut the vent and pull the slam rail back against the edge of the bottom section of the vent.

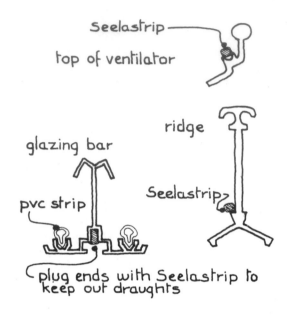

To the underside of the fascia fix a piece of 25mm×25mm aluminium angle with screws at 600mm centres. Drill this piece with holes to come directly above the holes in the sill so that the glazing bars are vertical, and bolt the bars into place.

Fit the ventilator operating gear as described by the manufacturers, but drill the brackets which hold the operating tube and screw them to the sides of the rafters. If they are hung from the glazing bars as they are designed to be the tube will foul the rafters. The rest of the vent operating gear can be fixed normally.

Glazing

Now you are ready for the glazing. Put the PVC glazing gasket into the grooves in the bars and put Seelastrip along the groove in the ridge and along the top of the ventilator as shown in the manufacturers' instructions. The PVC strip should go up as far as the slam rails on the bars where the ventilator is fitted. Put PVC strips also on the glazing bars of the vent. Before

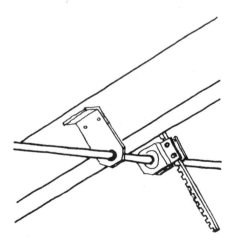

Finally seal all the gaps between the glazing bars and the rest of the structure with mastic, and plug the ends of the glazing bars with

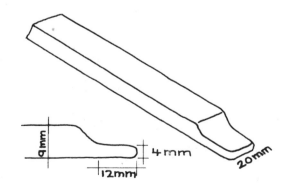

164

starting the glazing make a wooden tool to push the glazing clips into place from a piece of hardwood to the dimensions on the drawing. Shape it with a knife to a smooth curve. You are supposed to be able to push the clips into place with your fingers but the tool will make the job easier.

Now is the time to unpack the first crate of glass, which you should have kept under cover. Put on a pair of leather gloves to protect your hands, take out the first sheet of glass and lay it on the glazing gasket, setting it level with the bottom edge of the glazing bars. Put a plain glazing clip on one side of the glass and push the curved part of it with the tool to press it into the gap between the surface of the glass and the underside of the bar. Try not to put downward pressure on the tool or you may crack the glass. You will have to expect to crack several

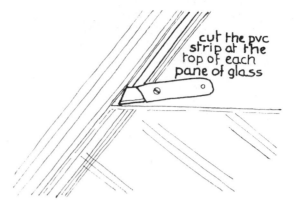

cut the pvc strip at the top of each pane of glass

sheets when you start the glazing but you will get the hang of it eventually.

Cut through the PVC gasket with a knife at the top edge of this piece of glass. Then fetch another pane from the crate and put it in place, overlapping the lower one by about 15mm. The clips at the overlap have their edges turned over to stop the glass from slipping, and they are a little thinner to accommodate the double thickness of glass. Fit them in the same way as the other clips; you may find that it helps if you slacken off the bolts holding the glazing bars to the purlins so that everything can move a bit when you are pushing the clips into place. The glazing is easier if you can do it in warm weather as the glass will be less brittle.

When you have fixed the last but one sheet you will have to measure from the edge of the glass to the ridge, and add 15mm for the overlap. This gives you the dimension for the last sheet, which you will have to cut to fit. You should perhaps check before you start glazing that this top sheet will not work out very short: if it does you will have to start at the bottom of the roof with a half sheet of glass.

Glass cutting is a craft which seems very difficult when you first try it but you will improve with practice. Put the glass on a flat surface such as a sheet of chipboard and make a mark on the glass with the cutting wheel of a glass cutter at the correct distance from the edge. Lay a straight edge or straight thin piece of wood a little in from the marks so that the wheel of the cutter is on the mark when the flat side of the cutter is against the straight edge. Press the straight edge firmly on to the glass.

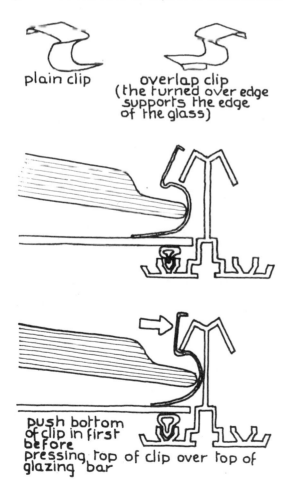

plain clip

overlap clip (the turned over edge supports the edge of the glass)

push bottom of clip in first before pressing top of clip over top of glazing bar

Hold the glass cutter vertically and press it down hard on the glass close to, but not on, the edge of the glass furthest from you. Draw it along the straight edge continuing to press firmly, but stop when you are within a couple of millimetres of the other edge of the glass. Hold the glass as shown and bend it to make it break

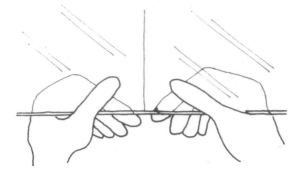

along the line. With luck you will now have a piece of glass that will fit at the top of the roof. Do not be afraid to press the cutter down hard on the glass otherwise the glass will break but it will not break along the line.

When you come to glaze the ventilator you will be able to use a whole pane of glass for each section of it. You may have slight difficulty fitting in the glass because of the flashing at the top of the ridge; but if you remove the vent glazing bar adjacent to the glass position, you can slide it in and then refit the glazing bar and clip the glass in place. The glass below the vent should be pushed into the slam rail and held by a plain clip, and a special narrower clip should be used above the slam rail to hold it in

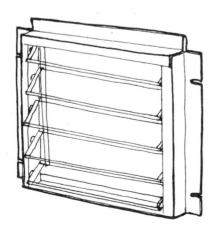

place against the glass. When the glazing is complete fit the PVC sealing strip provided over the top of the slam rails for the vent to shut against. The louvered vents in the front wall are fitted into the glazing bars intead of a pane of glass. You will find that they will fit only to the right of a timber post (seen from inside the conservatory) otherwise the operating handle will hit the post and the vent will not open.

Draught sealing and drainage

When all the glass is in place buy some neoprene sealing strip. This can be obtained from Sealmaster Ltd who use it in their draught seals. You will need a piece 13mm in diameter and 590mm long for each bay of glazing. Push it under the glass to seal the gap between the glass and the obtuse angle. It is important that

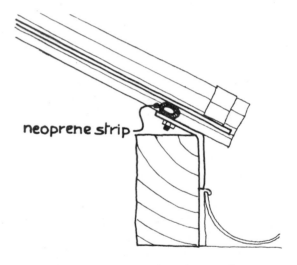

neoprene strip

the conservatory is as draught proof as possible: one way to find out is to stand in it on a windy day and feel where the draughts are, then take your trusty mastic gun and try to stop them. You will never make it completely draught proof so do not despair if the air inside is never quite still. The final step is to fix a gutter to the fascia and lead the downpipe into a convenient rainwater butt.

Inserting vents

Your conservatory is now finished and you can start ordering the grapevines and the peach trees. If you want to make use of the heat from it you may want to vent it into the house. To do this you must make holes in the house wall, near the ridge of the conservatory. The holes must go right through to the rooms to be heated. Knock out half a brick with a cold chisel and lump hammer, making sure that bits of brick do not fall down and block the cavity in a cavity wall. To make a neat hole mortar in a piece of 100mm plastic soil pipe. In the rooms, you will need to fix something to allow you to close off the flow of air. This can be a hit-and-

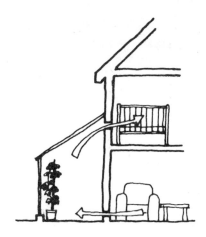

miss ventilator or a more elaborate insulated flap like an insulated window shutter. In one room you should have two sets of holes, each consisting of four pieces of pipe more or less next to each other (so that you can cover four holes with one shutter). In theory there should be the same number of holes leading into the conservatory from the downstairs rooms as there are leading into the rooms upstairs, so that air can circulate as shown in the drawing.

It is obvious from all this that the aluminium and glass conservatory is not something that you knock up over the weekend. It is perfectly possible to build a conservatory of recycled materials – old windows, secondhand timber and a transparent PVC roof. When we moved we inherited just such a structure on the back of the house. At the same time, we have watched it slowly disintegrate year by year. Rather than constantly patching up the old structure we opted for building a conservatory that would have a long life and would not need maintaining. At the same time we have built useful extra floor space for only a quarter of the price per square metre of a traditional brick and timber construction; and there are many days in the year when the conservatory is warm enough to sit among the plants, sipping elderflower wine in elegant alternative comfort.

22 Alternative Cooking

Solar ovens

If you build a solar oven as described below, you should be able to use it to bake bread on a sunny summer's day and even meringues in January offer a positive demonstration of the power of solar energy.

Materials and construction

You will need some 19mm blockboard or 12mm plywood, or any similar rigid sheet, and a pack of 80mm Foamglas insulation. Foamglas is used because it is rigid and because it will not be damaged by the high temperatures that you hope to get inside the oven.

Go outside to work on the Foamglas as it gives off a smell of rotten eggs when cut. Using a fine toothed saw, cut the pieces to the shapes and measurements given in the drawings. Take great care as the material is fragile and it is easy to cut it wrong.

Next, make a box to fit round the Foamglas, using the blockboard or ply for the top, bottom and sides, and a piece of 4mm ply for the back. Glue and nail the sides and base together, fit on

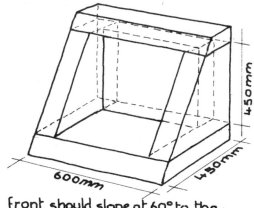

front should slope at 60° to the horizontal

the back, put the Foamglas inside, and fix on the top. Now you need a piece of 14 gauge aluminium sheet cut to fit over the front as shown. If you have access to a tilting circular-saw table or can saw angles with a hand saw, cut the top and bottom pieces of the box at a 60° angle so that the aluminium fits flush against them. Alternatively you can have the aluminium bent to fit the straight cut box, or

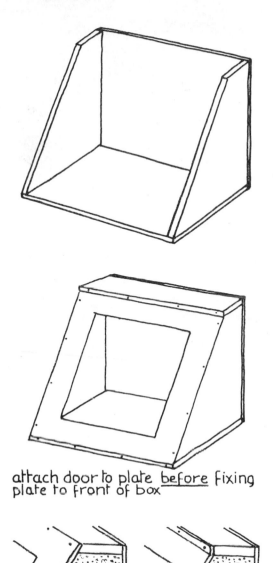

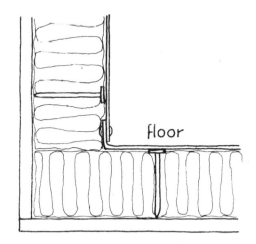

attach door to plate **before** fixing
plate to front of box

cut to fit on top of the Foamglas. A refinement would be to make a complete metal lining for the oven as shown in the drawing, riveted together and removable for cleaning. The insulation is quite fragile and produces a fine dust when handled, but if you take care not to knock the inside of the oven with pots, and if you cover your cooking with lids or foil, you should be able to manage with only a floor. If you do make the lining, you should be able to use glass fibre or mineral wool instead of the more expensive Foamglas: as these materials are not rigid the lining is needed to hold them in place. You could support the floor of the lining on four 75mm nails pushed through the insulation as shown in the drawings, and perhaps use nails in the sides and back to prevent movement in these directions as well.

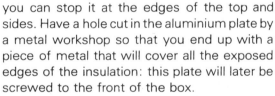

floor

you can stop it at the edges of the top and sides. Have a hole cut in the aluminium plate by a metal workshop so that you end up with a piece of metal that will cover all the exposed edges of the insulation: this plate will later be screwed to the front of the box.

You will also need a piece of aluminium for the floor of the oven. This can be 16 or 18 gauge

The oven door is made from a piece of 25mm×25mm aluminium angle. Cut out notches as shown, making sure that the cuts are at 45°, and then bend the angle to form a square frame. Mark out all the dimensions very

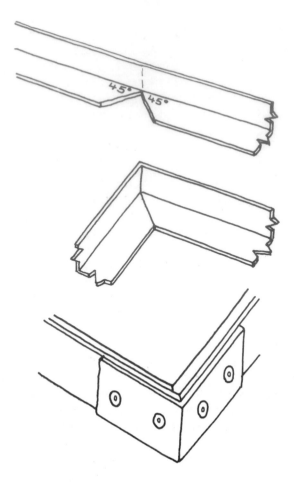

Bolt a pair of hinges to one edge of the door as shown: use very short countersunk head bolts so that very little of the bolt protrudes into the door. Galvanised or plated hinges are preferable as they will not rust. Using similar short bolts fix a handle to the bottom edge of the door. Bolt the door hinges to the piece of aluminium that forms the front of the oven, using the same short bolts that you used to attach the hinges to the door. Fit the door centrally over the opening in the oven front. Now screw the front plate to the oven box, putting screws into the wooden edges to hold it in place.

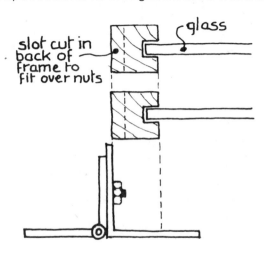

carefully and bend the metal on a flat surface, so that you end up with a door that will lie flat. Check that the frame is square at the corners. Join the open end of the frame with a bent piece of aluminium riveted in place as shown. Drill the holes for the rivets before you bend the aluminium angle.

The door must have glass in it so that the sunlight can shine into the inside of the oven. Use a couple of lengths of the wooden section made for sliding glass doors for cupboards to hold this glass. A d-i-y shop should stock these: buy a section to fit 4mm glass. Cut the wood as

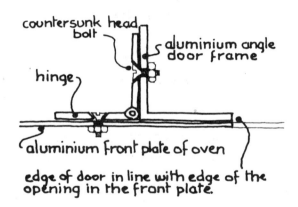

countersunk head bolt

aluminium angle door frame

hinge

aluminium front plate of oven

edge of door in line with edge of the opening in the front plate.

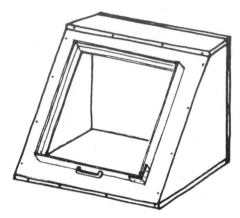

glass

slot cut in back of frame to fit over nuts

shown to fit into the frame, and put the pieces in place. Measure across the wood from side to side and from top to bottom. Check that the frame is square and then measure the depth of the slot in the wood section. Add one and a half times this slot dimension to the measurements across the wood frame. This allows space for the glass to expand in the heat of the sun.

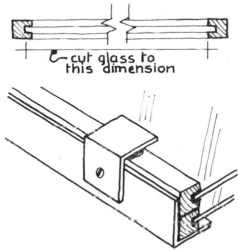

Cut the glass to these dimensions; it should be 3mm glass to fit loosely in the wooden frame. Fit the pieces of wood round the first pane of glass, lay it in the aluminium door frame, then lay in the second sheet of glass in its wooden surround on top of it. Finally fit the clamps which are pieces of 25mm×25mm aluminium angle 25mm long. The clamps should be fixed to the aluminium with very short self-tapping screws to hold the wooden frame in place. Under each clamp put four thicknesses of old cycle inner tube to cushion the frames and glass.

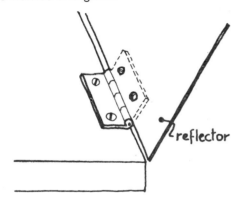

You will need four pieces of 16 or 18 gauge polished stainless steel 610mm×610mm sheet to form the reflectors that concentrate the solar radiation into the oven. Bolt a pair of hinges to each sheet of stainless steel, positioning the bolts as shown. Screw the hinges into the wooden box round the oven so that there is a reflector on each side of the oven. Take two pairs of metal angle brackets, available from an ironmonger, and bend them to an

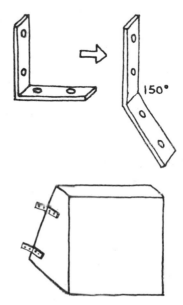

angle of 150°. Then screw a pair to each side of the box to support the side reflectors at an angle of 30° to the solar radiation.

Finally fix a small round head bolt (as shown) to the front corner of each side reflector and to

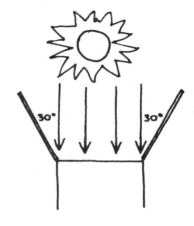

171

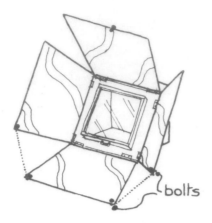

the front corners of the bottom reflector. Also fit a bolt to the middle of the front edge of the top reflector. Fix the bolts with a nut either side of the reflector so that the bolt protrudes about 10mm. Buy some chain that will just fit over the heads of the bolts and screw a round headed screw with a head the same size as those of the bolts into the middle of the back of the box near the top.

Installation and cooking

The oven is best set up outside or perhaps in a conservatory. It is a good idea to wear sunglasses because the reflections may be fairly dazzling and you will also need an oven thermometer. Face the oven towards the sun and swing out the side reflectors to rest against the brackets. You will be able to see the reflected light inside the oven and this will show you that the reflectors are in the right position.

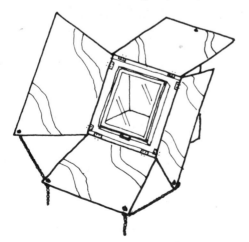

Raise the lower reflector until the reflection from it is visible inside the oven. Fix it in place by hooking lengths of chain over the bolts underneath its front edge, and then over the bolts at the bottom of the side reflectors. Once you know roughly how much chain you will need the pieces of chain can be fixed to the bolts of the bottom reflector with washers under the bolt heads. Position the top reflector to shine its contribution of energy into the oven. Hook a chain over the bolt on the reflector and then over the screw at the back of the oven, to hold the metal sheet in place.

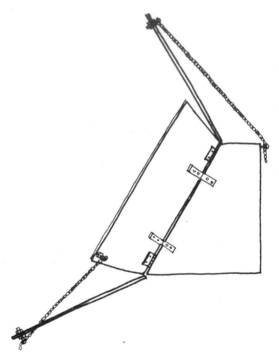

Now you can put on your gloves and open the oven door. Put in the oven thermometer to measure the temperature so that you know what sort of cooking you can do. Once you know the temperature put in the food and let it cook. You should adjust the position of the oven and the reflectors as necessary to track the sun as it moves round the sky.

Hay boxes

Materials and construction

If you are at all worried by the constant use of

the plastic insulating materials advocated throughout this book (although we believe their manufacture is the best possible way to use the remaining oil reserves), when you come to build a hay box you have a real chance to use natural materials. The purpose of a hay box is to provide a well insulated space within which hot food can continue to cook. Hay boxes were much favoured during the last war, when the obvious insulating material that came to hand was hay.

You will need about half a bale of hay: do not attempt to buy it in the small bagged quantities sold by pet shops for rabbits as this will be far too expensive. If you live in a town and want to use hay, wait until you are driving in the country and stop where you see the 'Hay for sale' sign, especially during June and July when the first cut has been baled. The worst quality hay will be good enough for a hay box. You will also need a large cardboard box, one that originally contained a small washing machine or fridge, easily obtained from your local dealer. We use a tea-chest (bought from a tea blender's warehouse) which is stronger if a little more expensive.

Simply half fill the box with the hay, leaving it fairly well compacted, form a hollow in the centre to take the cooking pot and pack the hay around this. You will find that the hay has sufficient body to retain the shape of the pot when you lift it out. Save a good slice of your bale for a lid to go over the pot when in place; if the slice is very compressed it can be fluffed out a little.

Installation and cooking

To use the hay box you will need a cooking pot with a lid that can be placed directly on top of a gas or electric cooker: a cast iron pot is ideal. Casseroles, porridge, milk puddings and soups can all be cooked in the box. However, it is probably best to stick to bean and vegetable stews as the food will be cooking below boiling point or at even lower temperatures and if you are at all unsure of your source of meat it might not be wise to keep it at temperatures ideal for the growth of harmful bacteria. Left-over meat that has already been cooked once should not be used.

Having assembled the ingredients just as if the casserole were going into an oven, bring the contents of the pan to the boil on top of your stove, boil for a minute or two and then put the lid on and quickly transfer the hot pot to the hay box, putting the lid of hay on top. The stew can then be left to cook all day if made in the morning and required for the evening. Before eating it should be brought to boiling point and kept there for two or three minutes to thoroughly warm the contents.

Hay box cookery is always something of an experiment because the effectiveness of the insulating layer will depend on how well you have packed the hay and how large a box you use. The first time we made porridge overnight – by pouring boiling milk on to the oats, covering the pot and leaving it in the hay box – we came down in the morning to cooked but cold porridge, which we would probably have achieved by leaving the pot-full of boiling milk and oats on the table. First we heated up and ate the porridge, and then we increased the thickness of the layer of hay.

The real hay box does have one advantage over the better insulated expanded polystyrene box described next: the meadow-sweet smell of warm hay fills the kitchen while it is in use, and is much more appetising than the acrid fumes of the expanded plastics if you touch the exposed material with your hot pot.

Expanded polystyrene boxes

Materials and construction

If you do decide to go for the expanded polystyrene box you will improve your standard of cooking. Using the box described below, we have taken out soup three hours after it was put in and found that, apart from being cooked, it was still too hot to drink. The top, sides and base of the box are made of 100mm thick expanded polystyrene, this being made up of two layers that are 50mm thick. One sheet 2400mm×1200mm will be ample to make a box to fit a 3.5 litre circular cast iron pot with lid. If you have insulated walls, floor and roof you should have enough left-over pieces of 50mm expanded polystyrene to knock up a hay box.

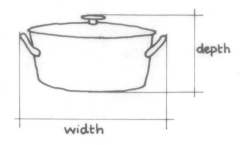

Begin by measuring the width of the pot across its handles, add 25mm, and use this as the width of the inside of the box. Similarly measure the depth and add 25mm. You will have to make the box to fit one particular pot, although it will of course take smaller pots, as you will not have the flexibility you have with compressible hay. Cut the first base, a square with sides equal to the measured width plus 25mm. Cut two sides equal to the measured depth plus 25mm plus 50mm. The polystyrene can be cut with a bread knife although an old panel saw will work quickly and more accurately, so you will have a better chance of cutting the edges at right angles, which is important when building a box shape.

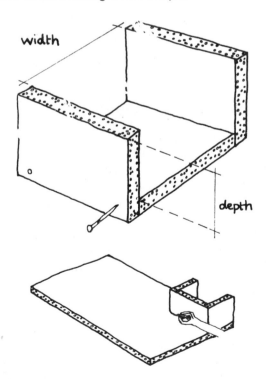

Using PVA glue and 100mm wire nails, glue the sides to the base, making sure the glue is spread well over the surface, and putting a nail through at each corner. From now on you will not have to make any more measurements. Place the glued top and sides on to the sheet of polystyrene and draw round it to mark out two pieces to fit the other two sides. Fix these into place as before. Next draw round the open end

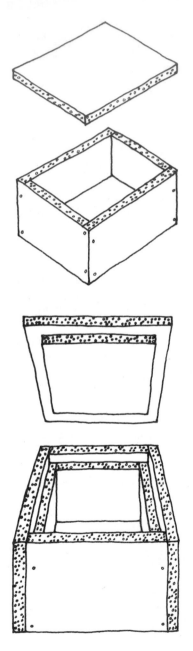

of the box and cut out a piece for the lid which should not be fixed yet. You now have a box of 50mm thick polystyrene into which your pot should fit easily.

The process is now repeated, a new base being cut and fixed and further pairs of sides and finally the lid. Fit the first lid in place, spread glue over it and place the larger lid on top, fixing through with the 100mm wire nails as usual. The finished lid should now lift on and off easily.

Protecting the box

If the polystyrene box is to be long lasting it must be protected. If it is just left in the kitchen where it will be constantly brushed against, little flakes of polystyrene will keep falling off. The polystyrene box could simply be placed inside a close fitting cardboard box although it would be better and neater to surround it with a purpose built box of cardboard, hardboard or thin plywood.

Far more important, however, is the protection of the inside of the box. We both knew that polystyrene melts when heated; that is why it can be cut with a hot wire, although the technique is not recommended since at the same time as it melts it gives off poisonous fumes. However, when faced with the completed polystyrene box we could not resist putting the hot pot of soon-to-be-porridge directly inside and as the pot sunk slowly through the bottom of the box... An inner lining or at very least an inner base can again be made of thin plywood, hardboard, cardboard (the double thickness variety is best) or even off-cuts of cork tiles if you have any. This lining will occupy some of the extra 25mm that you allowed on the initial width of the pot.

To make the inner lining you will have to measure the internal surfaces. Cut out pieces of the lining material to fit and nail or press 25mm wire nails through each corner. The lining pieces can then be pushed gently into place and the nails pressed into the polystyrene to fix them. The exposed edges of the box and of the lid should also be covered: otherwise every time you put the lid in place or lift out the pot, brushing against the exposed polystyrene, flakes will fall on to the hot pot and you will

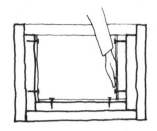

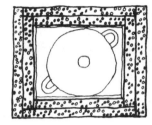

if the lining is thick the pot can be put in on the diagonal

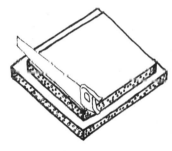

trim the lid by twice the thickness of the lining before covering the edges of the lid and box

always be aware of this because of the nasty smell.

A lining for the outside of the box could be made in the same way, using hardboard or cardboard and sealing the corner joints with 50mm wide sticky tape.

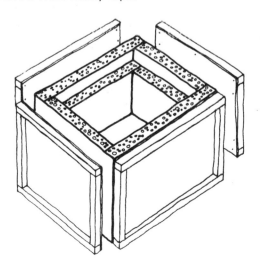

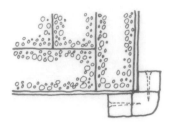

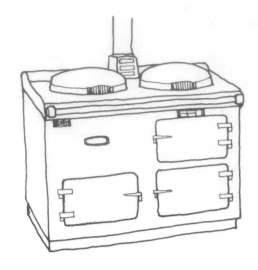

The best job would be to form a box of 4mm plywood framed with ex 25mm×25mm planed softwood. Cut pieces of ply to fit the four sides of the box. Glue these, and nail them to 25mm×25mm framing on all four sides, which is butt jointed as shown. Join the framed panels at the corners around the polystyrene box with further lengths of 25mm softwood, screwed in place as shown. Measure the base of the box, including the framing, cut a piece of plywood to fit, and glue and nail it in place.

The lid of polystyrene is treated in exactly the same way, the top of the lid being measured, cut and fixed into place when the framing is assembled. The finished plywood box can then be stained or painted. The box made in this way, especially if it has a similar interior lining of plywood, should have a long and useful life.

Cookers for space heating

Apart from attempting to reduce the energy used for cooking by using a hay box or direct solar energy where possible, it is also useful to try to save energy by combining the cooking and heating source. Once you have thoroughly insulated a house you will find that its heat demand is reduced to the point where casual gains from people, lights and appliances, including the cooker, are having an appreciable effect in heating your house. However much gas or electricity you use for cooking – and it may be possible to estimate this from your bill – this is in effect energy put directly into the house as very little is actually used in cooking the food. A typical estimation of the amount of energy put into the house by a cooker is 1400kW a year. In the insulated house it may be useful to use the cooker for space heating as the demand for energy has been reduced.

An insulated cooker such as the Aga, which runs for twenty-four hours a day and is only lit at the beginning of the heating season, will put about 1kW constantly into the house as well as acting as a stove and providing hot water. This amount of heat, especially when added to solar gain through windows, will probably be sufficient to heat the insulated house in all but the coldest months of December, January and February. Running at an efficiency of about 80 per cent when burning solid fuel (if a gas or oil burning Aga is used the efficiency drops to 60 per cent), such an installation would be burning about 1.75 tonnes of coke over the heating season.

If such an appliance were used only as a cooker, in say a centrally heated house, it would not only be expensive to install but also a very extravagant way of providing energy for cooking. In a setting where it can be used for both cooking and space heating, it is an economical solution. Other wood and coke burning insulated cookers are available, some of which, such as the Hamco woodburner and the Rayburn, will also run radiators. Unlike the Aga these are not thermostatically controlled and the fire has to be stoked up to raise the oven temperature in preparation for cooking. Between cooking periods, however, they will be ticking over and continuing to put out heat into the building.

All combined cookers and space heaters will involve a high initial cost, comparable to that of central heating and a conventional cooker; so if

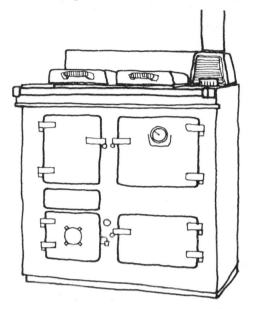

you are planning to insulate your house as it stands, it will probably not be economical to change from, say, your present gas cooker and gas fires to a gas Rayburn. If you are starting from scratch in a building that has no real heating, then it would be worth considering the combined space heater and cooker: preferably choose one that burns coal or wood as these are the fuels most likely to be around for the cooker's whole life, which might be fifty to a hundred years depending on the type and the quality of the materials used in its construction. Such a cooker, if placed centrally in the building, becomes the real heart of the home.

It would be uneconomical to run such an appliance all summer just to provide hot water and cooking. You will have to find some small back-up conventional cooker for the summer, unless you choose to convert yourself entirely and rely in summer on water heated in your solar collector, an electric kettle (wind powered naturally), a solar cooker, hay box and salads.

23 Building a Windmill

The windmill described below has a maximum electrical output of 750 Watts at 24 volts. It is partly based on two recent designs which in turn are based on the windmills used in Crete to pump water. The designs are by the National Centre for Alternative Technology at Machynlleth in Wales, and by the Steering Committee for Windenergy in Developing Countries of Amersfoort in the Netherlands. We have chosen this seemingly crude design with its wooden construction and canvas sails because of its inherent safety and reliability. We have experience of high speed windmills with blades like an aircraft propeller and have found that even apparently well designed and solidly built commercial machines frequently suffer severe mechanical failures which could be dangerous. A homemade machine may be less well constructed and might therefore be assumed to be more dangerous; at any event you do not want to be impaled by a piece of broken blade. The Cretan machine is slow, simple and safe, and can be repaired easily. It needs no complex engineering tools or skill in metalwork for its manufacture.

This chapter will consist largely of pictures as the windmill is a fairly complicated piece of three dimensional design, more easily explained in drawings.

Rotor assembly

Start by making the rotor assembly. Cut out the face plate from 25mm exterior grade plywood. The plate should be 450mm in diameter and should have a 32mm hole bored through the exact centre. If you make this hole with a brace and bit the point of the bit can be positioned in the hole made by the compass (a strip of wood, a nail and a pencil) with which you marked out the circle. Try to make this as accurate as possible, although as the rotor turns at only 50rpm, vibration from out of balance parts should not manage to shake the whole thing to pieces.

Before you drill the hole divide the ply disc into eight equal parts to mark the positions of the sail spars. The diameter of the windmill is 3.85 metres and the 8 spars of 50mm×50mm ash (ash is a very resilient wood which will stand shock loads) should be cut 1850mm long

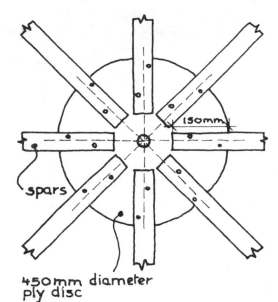

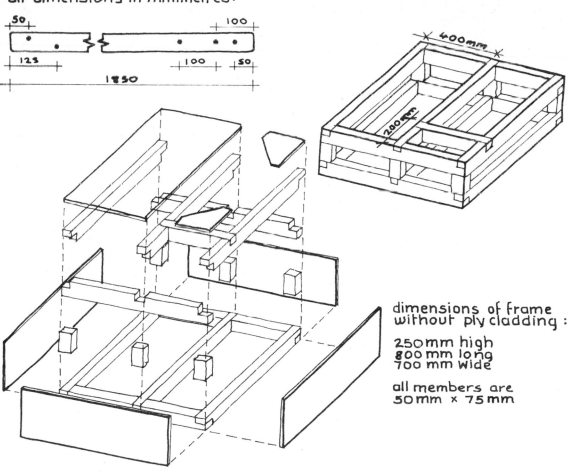

spars

450mm diameter
ply disc

all dimensions in millimetres:

50
100
125
100
50
1850

each, and the edges should be rounded off. The spars are bolted to the face plate as shown with 8mm diameter bolts. Put large washers under the heads of the bolts and under the nuts and use lock washers in addition or self-locking nuts on the bolts. It is essential that the machine does not vibrate to pieces. The spars must be drilled with 10mm diameter holes as shown to attach the sails and the bracing ropes.

Frame for the alternator and gearbox

Now make up the frame that carries the alternator and gearbox to the dimensions shown in the drawings, using 50mm×75mm timber with top sides and ends of 6mm exterior plywood screwed and glued (using waterproof glue) to make it rigid. This frame is bolted firmly to the

400mm

200mm

dimensions of frame
without ply cladding :

250mm high
800mm long
700mm wide

all members are
50mm × 75mm

179

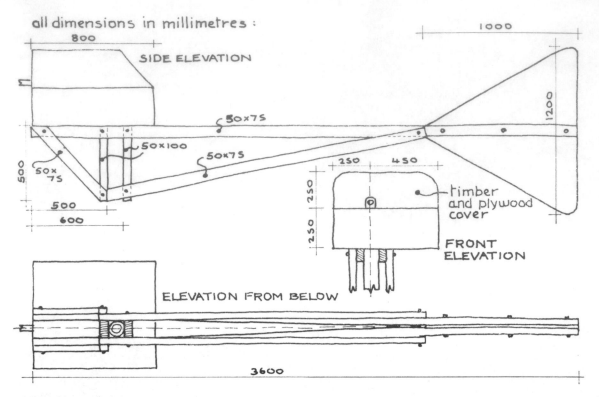

all dimensions in millimetres :

SIDE ELEVATION

800

50×75

50×100

50×75

50×75

500

500

600

1000

1200

250

250

250

250

450

timber
and plywood
cover

FRONT
ELEVATION

ELEVATION FROM BELOW

3600

main frame of the windmill which holds the tail and the pivot that allows the machine to turn into the wind.

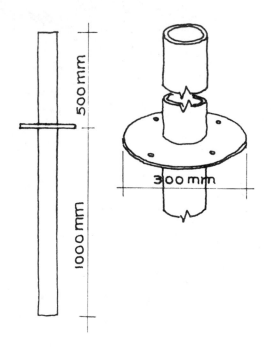

500 mm

1000 mm

300 mm

The pivot

For the pivot you will need a piece of steel tube slightly under 100mm in diameter, with a wall thickness of 3–4mm. It must be fairly strong to take the loads caused by the machine shaking about in gusty weather. Have a 4mm thick steel disc welded on as shown, to support the weight of the windmill. The frame of the windmill must be made so that it fits over this tube, so if you find a tube with a different diameter, modify the frame accordingly. When you have the tube, make up the frame to the dimensions given, employing coach screws to attach the diagonal bracing members to the vertical parts that fit over the pivot.

Building the shaft

The shaft is a length of 32mm diameter mild steel rod, which must have a keyway cut in one end to suit a Fenner C20 reduction gearbox. The gearbox is used back to front to provide a 20 to 1 step-up drive. You will need one with the output shaft bushed down to 32mm, and

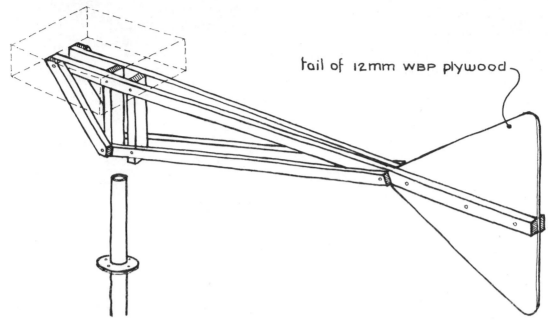

tail of 12mm WBP plywood

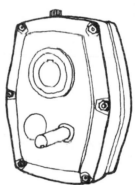

Fenners will provide the necessary specification so that you can have the keyway cut in your shaft. Perhaps the easiest thing to do is to take the gearbox along to the place where the shaft will be made and have them make it to fit. Do not forget to buy a key to fit the keyway.

You will need a 315mm diameter single belt Fenner pulley to fit the other shaft of the gearbox (the input shaft, although because you are using it as a step-up gear it will become the

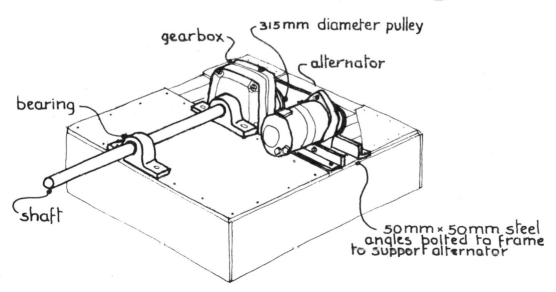

gearbox

315mm diameter pulley

alternator

bearing

shaft

50mm × 50mm steel angles bolted to frame to support alternator

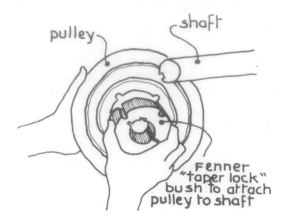

pulley　shaft

Fenner "taper lock" bush to attach pulley to shaft

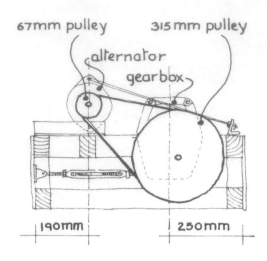

67mm pulley　315mm pulley

alternator

gearbox

| 190mm |　| 250mm |

view from rear

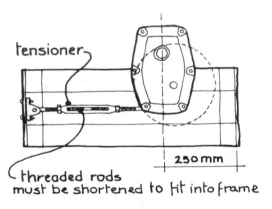

tensioner

| 250mm |

threaded rods must be shortened to fit into frame

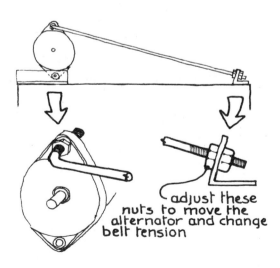

adjust these nuts to move the alternator and change belt tension

output shaft), with a Taper lock bush to hold it in place and a suitable key. Buy a second 315mm pulley to fit the main shaft with another bush and key, and have a keyway cut in the shaft to suit it. This pulley is used to attach the rotor to the shaft. It should be set about 150mm in from the end of the shaft. You will also need a pair of bearing blocks, preferably self-aligning, to fit the 32mm shaft, and a 1320mm SPZ belt.

The alternator

The alternator should be a CAV model AC5 24/R, with a V belt pulley about 67mm in diameter. If the pulley diameter is larger than this the alternator may not turn fast enough, but if it is smaller that is alright. The alternator must have a cooling fan suitable for anti-clockwise rotation when viewed from the front of the alternator. If you cannot find the CAV alternator any 24 volt alternator which gives roughly 30 amps at about 3500rpm will be suitable. If the alternator you find runs clockwise rather than anti-clockwise it is easy enough to fit the sails on the windmill the other way round so that it rotates in the other direction.

Assembling the machine

The mechanical parts are assembled as shown in the drawings, with the large pulley accommodated within the framework. The gearbox has a tensioning screw which should be shortened by cutting down the threaded parts so that there is room for the fixing bracket on the framework. Make an adjustor for the alternator from a piece of threaded rod, bent as shown and fixed through a steel plate screwed to the framework. Be sure that the main shaft bearings are very securely bolted to the frame, and attach the 315 diameter pulley to the main shaft.

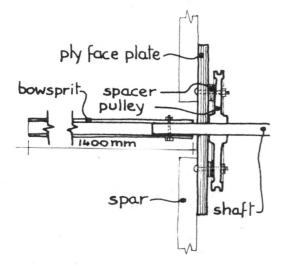

Bolt the rotor to this pulley with 10mm diameter bolts with washers under the heads to protect the plywood face plate, plywood spacers between the face plate and the pulley and lock washers under the nuts to prevent them being loosened by vibration. Make a bowsprit about 1400mm long with a metal tube; this should have an internal diameter of about 32mm to fit over the end of the shaft. Fix it to the shaft with a bolt to prevent it from fal-

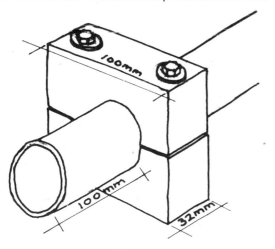

ling off. Attach a block of hardwood as shown at the end of the bowsprit to provide an anchorage for the ropes that reinforce the rotor assembly. As an alternative you can make the shaft with a fairly thick walled piece of 25mm diameter tube, extended 1400mm to form the bowsprit.

Attaching the ropes

Now you can put on the ropes. This is best done with the machine at ground level and propped up so that the lowest parts of the rotor arms are clear of the ground. Use a rope with a diameter of about 5mm made of a material that will not stretch or rot. You will need about 70 metres of rope – the best place for rope is a boat chandler's.

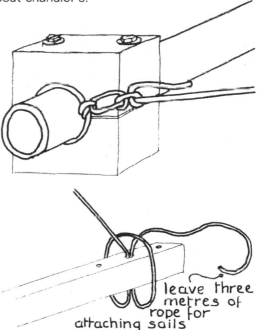

leave three metres of rope for attaching sails

Tie the rope with a loop over the block at the end of the bowsprit and then thread it as shown through the second hole from the end of the rotor arm. Pull the rope tight but not so tight as to bend the spar. Attach a second rope to the bowsprit and then to the arm directly opposite the first one; adjust the knot until the two lengths of rope are the same. This dimension can be checked with another piece of rope looped over the bowsprit tip and knotted at the required distance from the end. When the knot is level with the end of each spar the ropes are in the right positions. Attach ropes to the other spars similarly. You should leave about 3 metres of rope hanging free at the end where it is tied to the spar, to tie the sails to the spars. Finally tie another rope round the outside of the whole rotor assembly, adjusting the knots until the rotor arms are equidistant from one another.

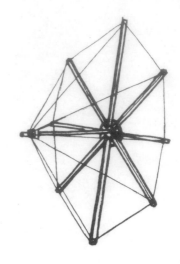

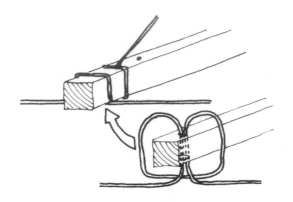

Making the sails

The sails are made next, using the strongest material you can find. The artificial fibre fabrics used for yacht sails are probably the best, but heavy canvas, tarpaulin or any other strong cloth can be used. Cut out the eight sails to the

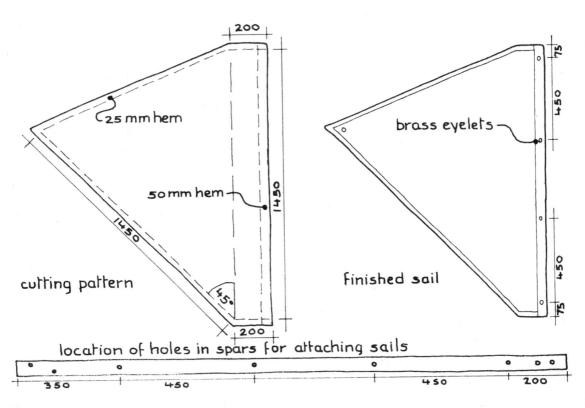

cutting pattern

finished sail

location of holes in spars for attaching sails

184

pattern in the drawings, and give them 25mm hems with three rows of stitching in waterproof thread. Make holes in the sails where shown and put in brass eyelets with holes about 20mm in diameter so that the sails can be laced on to the rotor arms. A chandler, sail maker or tent manufacturer will make up the sails if you do not feel like sewing them yourself. The sails are finally fitted when the machine is on its mast, but put them on now to check the fit, threading the ropes as shown in the drawings. The free ends of the sails should have a spring clip tied to them with a short length of rope, and the clip is then fastened to an eyebolt put through the spar as shown. If you hear on the weather forecast that there is a gale on the way, the spring clips can be unfixed so that the sails can be wrapped around the spars and tied to them. This will prevent the windmill from turning and will save the sails from damage. If the mill is not shut down in a gale it cannot overspeed but the sails may be torn depending on how well they were made in the first place.

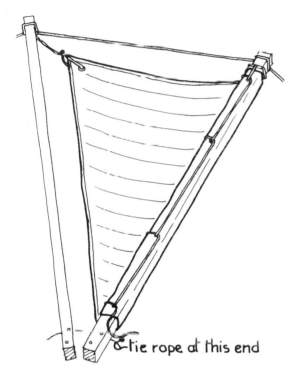

tie rope at this end

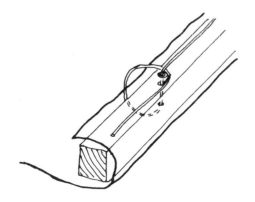

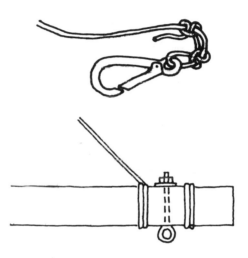

Building the tower

The tower is made of four Tanalised round poles with a top diameter of 80mm, and with 50mm×100mm Tanalised cross braces attached with 125mm coach screws or bolts.

Make the tower as shown in the drawings overleaf, and paint the whole assembly with several coats of preservative before erecting it. The parts of the legs that will be under ground should have four coats of creosote before being concreted into holes 900mm deep and 600mm×600mm square. You will need the help of eight to ten people to erect the tower. Choose a dead calm day, follow the drawings and do it very slowly and carefully. Check that the pivot pipe at the top of the tower is vertical before concreting; the tower legs can be packed up with pieces of broken brick to make it right.

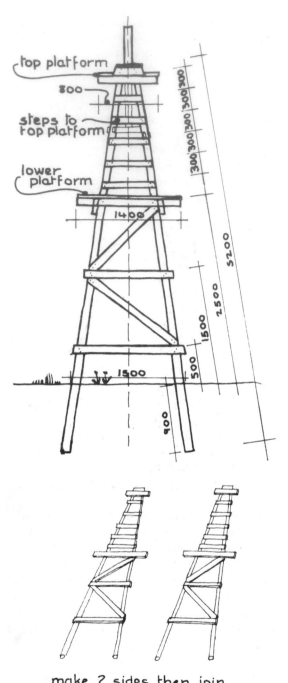

top platform

800

steps to top platform

lower platform

1400

300 300 300 300 300

5200

2500

1500

500

1500

400

make 2 sides then join them to form tower

six people pull it up. There should be a second rope tied to the windmill so that it can be manoeuvred as necessary before being lowered into place.

detail of top of tower:

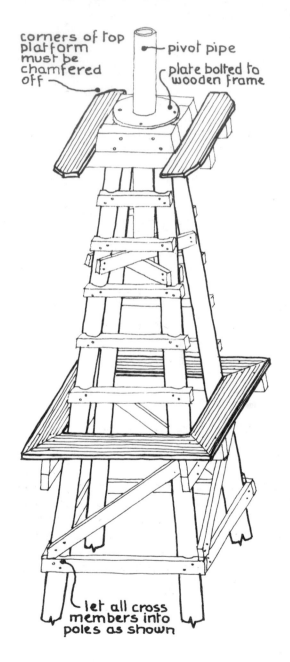

corners of top platform must be chamfered off

pivot pipe

plate bolted to wooden frame

let all cross members into poles as shown

When the concrete has set, the windmill can be hoisted to the top of the tower using a ladder roped to the tower as a crane. One person should be at the top of the tower, wearing a safety harness, to position the mill while five or

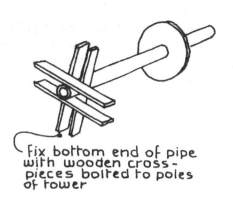

Fix bottom end of pipe with wooden cross-pieces bolted to poles of tower

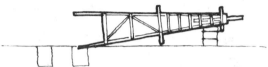

position legs in foundation holes and prop up end of tower.

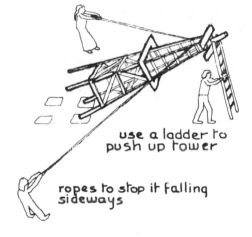

use a ladder to push up tower

ropes to stop it falling sideways

Connecting the alternator

Connect the alternator as recommended by the manufacturers, making sure that the output cables from alternator to batteries have a low resistance (use a wire with a cross-section area of 10mm²). The cables should run from the alternator down the pivot pipe and they must pass through the wooden frame so that they do not rub on the pipe and get damaged. Allow

plenty of slack in the cables at the foot of the tower so that they can become twisted as the mill turns to follow the wind.

ladder tied firmly to tower

Windmill designs are open to many modifications, and improvements to this one will probably occur to you. A brake on the shaft for example would be a useful addition so that the mill can be stopped for repairs. At the time of writing we have not built this design, although we fully intend to, and we may well be able to improve it while we are making it. If you do decide to make a windmill do it slowly and carefully, and spend a lot of time working it out and even drawing it so that you are sure how it will go together before you start. The design here is really intended to give some ideas rather than to act as a blueprint.

24 Collecting Rainwater

Water-butts have, for a long time, offered an example of recycled materials: usually an empty wooden beer barrel, tapped at the bottom, this is set up on enough bricks so that a watering can may be comfortably placed under the tap; and it is covered to keep out leaves that would otherwise sink to the bottom as they rotted, eventually blocking up the tap. So pervasive is this image that the standard 170 litre plastic water-butt for sale in every garden and hardware shop retains the barrel shape. If

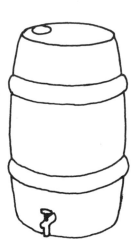

you are satisfied with storing a little rainwater for use in the garden, allowing the surplus to flow to a ditch or soakaway, then two water-butts, one at the front and one at the back of the house, will be all you need. However, if you aim to provide the recommended storage volume of 25 per cent of the estimated collected rainfall, for the example quoted in Chapter 9 you will be talking of a storage volume of about

4000 litres, which would be equivalent to about twenty-four plastic water-butts, an expensive and impractical idea. In this case some kind of large underground cistern might be the best solution.

Using oil drums

The cheap alternative to the water-butt is a 250 litre oil drum, direct descendant of the old recycled beer barrel. Our oil drum was left by a

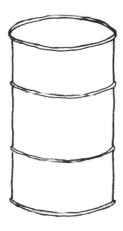

friendly builder, but we have seen them advertised in the small-ad column of a local paper and you may know of a source anyway. If you can, get one from which the top has already been cut. Our knowledge of metalwork is limited and we could not think of an obvious way of removing the top, beyond using a cold chisel and a hammer. Do not use any form of hot cutting tool: this would be disastrous if there was any oil left in the drum.

The tap

To fit a tap in the bottom of the drum, the first

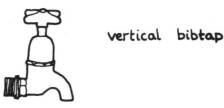

vertical bibtap

step is to make a hole. Use a normal tank cutter (sold for cutting holes in the side of a cold water cistern) on a brace and bit. You will need a vertical bibtap, either chromium-plated or brass if you can buy it, and a back nut to fit. The wall of the oil drum is thin so there will be sufficient thread projecting inside it on which to fix the back nut. Alternatively it is possible to buy an urn or wash-boiler tap which comes complete with back nut and has a long thread which makes it easy to fit it into an urn or wash-boiler.

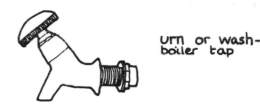

urn or wash-boiler tap

Fitting the tap is a job for two people. One of you stays outside the oil drum and holds the tap in the hole whilst the other person crawls inside with the back nut and the stilson. Before the tap is inserted wind PTFE tape round the threaded shaft. Resisting the temptation to roll your friend or life partner over inside the drum, and this is the hard part, hold both the tap and drum steady whilst he or she tightens up the back nut on to the PTFE tape in a very confined dark space. If you want to prolong the life of the oil drum water-butt, paint it inside and out with bituminous paint.

Setting the drum up

Set the drum up on three or four courses of brick and arrange a shoe on the bottom of your downpipe so that the water from the gutter discharges into the drum. It is wise to provide some kind of lid made from scrap boarding or exterior grade plywood with a hole cut out so

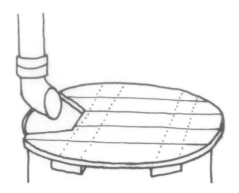

that the water discharges through it. This will have to be weighted down with a couple of bricks to prevent the wind blowing it off.

Many alternative vessels may come your way that can be used as water-butts: galvanised tanks, especially those which were once used for cold water supplies in the older type of plumbing system; or plastic cold water cisterns, which can be fitted with taps as described and which are available with a capacity of up to 227 litres. In fact, anything that will hold water can be used and you do not even need the refinement of a tap if you are prepared to dip your watering can directly into the top.

The site
The most obvious place to site the water-butt is directly under the existing discharging downpipe but if you are planning, or have built, a conservatory along the south side of the house, it would be worth considering rearranging the guttering to bring the water-butt inside the conservatory. The mass of water inside the conservatory, apart from being handy for watering the melons and tomatoes, helps to store heat which is released when the conservatory cools down at night.

It can also serve to avoid wasting energy: on clear sunny days, especially in spring, the air temperature inside the conservatory may reach a point where you need to open ventilators to avoid overheating. If you have arranged for hot air from the conservatory to be vented directly into the upstairs rooms of the house you will be able to use the heat this way, otherwise it is so much energy lost. A large

volume of water inside the conservatory could be heated up by this surplus, releasing the heat once the sun goes down and the structure begins to cool.

It is hard to judge exactly how much heat can be stored, but experiments have been carried out, especially in America, to store heat in this way in conservatories and greenhouses. The vessels used have included black-painted containers with capacities ranging from 4 litres to the more familiar 250 litres of the oil drum, and transparent containers filled with dyed water. These have succeeded in keeping the temperatures up within the structure on cold, overcast days. A single 170 litre water-butt is not going to make a major contribution to heat storage but ten of them or a single tank of equivalent size probably would. And the lid will also provide a warm spot on which to stand your germinating seedlings so that they do not suffer too wide a temperature fluctuation.

Fitting the down-pipe
If your conservatory has brick ends then it will be a simple matter to guide the downpipe through a hole in the end wall. To make the hole you will need a lump hammer and a cold chisel.

The speed at which you make the hole will depend on the age of the brickwork and the type of mortar. If you are worried drill a few holes through the wall first, in the place where the pipe is to pass, using a masonry drill; then knock out the brickwork left between the holes with the chisel. Once the downpipe has been fitted it should be mortared into the brickwork.

If your conservatory has glass ends it would be best to replace the pane of glass the downpipe will pass through with a sheet of WBP plywood or perspex cut to the same size. A hole to take the downpipe can be cut in either of these materials with a padsaw once a pilot hole has been drilled first. Make the diameter of the hole match the external diameter of the downpipe as closely as possible, and seal around the gap when the guttering is assembled with silicone mastic to stop the draughts.

For serious heat storage the water-butt should be a dark colour – the black-painted oil drum is ideal – and set so it intercepts the light through the vertical panes of glass. If it receives light only from the top, only the top layer of water will be heated and as hot water rises there will be no mixing of hot and cold water within the drum. The aim is to set up convection currents within the water-butt so that all the water becomes as uniformly heated as possible and thereby stores the maximum amount of heat.

Using a series of butts

If you want to store large quantities of rainwater and use the mass as a heat store it is possible to connect up tanks or oil drums in series. To cope with the flow of water from the roof during heavy rain the tanks will have to be connected with a wide diameter pipe and Bartol Plastics Ltd make 41mm external diameter waste pipe and a tank connector to fit. You connect all the water-butts either at the bottom or at the top. The former will mean that all the butts will fill simultaneously and only one tap need be fitted to draw water from them all; but you will have to crawl inside to wrench on the back nuts. It is easier to make the connection at the top of the butts when they will fill

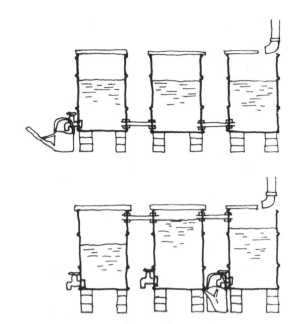

one after the other; but each will then have to be emptied with its own tap.

The latter is probably the better solution from the point of view of heat storage as once the tanks have been filled they can be emptied in turn starting with the one directly under the downpipe which will be the first to be refilled. The others, meanwhile, sit there quietly storing more heat in their filled state than if they were only half full.

If you are using old flat-sided galvanised tanks then make holes in them using a suitable diameter tank cutter on a brace and bit. Ideally the tanks should stand as close together as possible: the surface area of the storage should be minimal so that it loses heat to its surroundings more slowly, which may be important in periods of prolonged cloudy weather. In practice, unless you are good at lining up tank connectors on a horizontal level to within 1–2mm, this will be impossible and it will be easier to space the storage tanks about 300mm apart. You can always grow tomatoes in pots between them. Having cut the hole, push the tank connector through from the outside, wind PTFE tape around the threaded part, screw on the back nut and tighten it into place. Now push the 300mm length of plastic waste pipe into place if you are using the Bartol

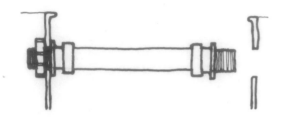

system (other systems may require solvent welding).

In the next tank cut a hole the same height above ground level. With the tank connector fitted on to the end of a short length of pipe, manoeuvre the tank into position so that the connector passes through the hole. Since both tanks will probably be supported on bricks if they are fitted with taps, you will need help at this point. The tanks can be levelled with pieces of broken slate placed on top of the bricks and, although the 300mm length of pipe will absorb some discrepancy, it would be best to line the tank connectors as near level as possible before screwing on the last back nut; and do not forget the PTFE tape.

If you are using oil drums rather than flat sided tanks you may find that the curvature of the drum prevents you from obtaining a water-tight seal. Take a mallet and bash the side of the drum to give a flatter surface against which to tighten the back nut. This will help relieve the frustration of trying to juggle large tanks so that the holes you have cut in them line up.

Using a storage tank

As an alternative to the series of connected butts, doing double service for storage of rain-water and heat, it might be worth considering building a purpose-built rainwater storage tank. If featured inside your conservatory and fitted with a few water plants it might also be called a pond. Unless you are a proficient amateur concreter and preferably already own a concrete mixer it would be better to stick with the old oil drums, but even with the method described below you could at least supply the labour whilst employing a builder to do the concreting. If you do intend to go to the expense and trouble of building a concrete tank you will have to be fairly dedicated about the need for storing rainwater.

Digging the hole

From the example quoted earlier the volume of storage required is about 4000 litres or 4m³, that is a tank 2m×2m×1m. Although it is possible to build a concrete tank of this size above ground, it would be more sensible to make use of the ground as a support for the mass of the water. So the first job will be to dig a hole the appropriate size. Depending on the ground water table of the area in which you live, you will generally find that if you make the excavations and do the concreting in summer you will be less likely to be digging out the last 300mm under water.

The exact dimensions of the tank will depend on how much water you want to store and whether you want to use it as an optional indoor paddling pool/boating lake for young children (under supervision) in which case it should only be 300–400mm deep. Whatever the proposed size of the tank the bottom of the excavation should be 200mm greater all round

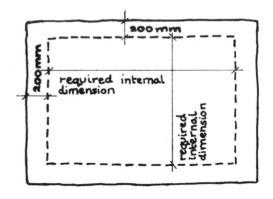

to provide the space in which to build the con-crete block walls of the tank. The type of soil will determine how much wider the hole will be at the top than at the bottom as the sides of the excavation may have to slope outwards.

When you have done the digging and disposed of the soil (a skip which is 7m³ in volume is useful for this purpose but a rock garden somewhere nearby might be an alternative) you will have to level the bottom off reasonably

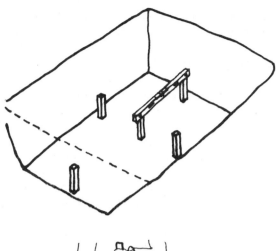

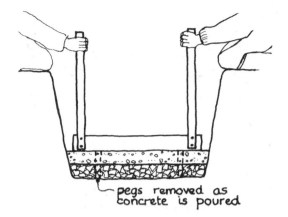

accurately. Fix timber pegs across the width and along the length of the tank. These should be 250mm above the ground – 100mm for the hardcore and 150mm for the concrete slab. By laying a level across the tops of the pegs you will be able to line them up. Once the pegs are fixed in place put in a 100mm layer of broken brick and ram it well down. The pegs will inevitably get knocked so check that they are level again, but it is still easier to put them in first rather than trying to bash them through the hardcore.

The cement

The concrete for the tank should be a mix of one part by volume cement to two parts sand to three parts coarse aggregate. This can either be ordered ready-mixed or if you have a concrete mixer you can make it in batches. Fill the excavation slightly above the top of the pegs and then tamp it down with a length of say

pegs removed as concrete is poured

50mm×200mm timber used on edge to compact the concrete. You will have to fit handles on to this timber so that it can be used from the top of the excavation; otherwise you may find your wellingtons concreted into the bottom of the tank. Do not worry about smoothing the outer 100mm around the edge of the tank as this should be left fairly rough so that the concrete which forms the sides bonds with the bottom slab.

The day after making the bottom of the tank you should be ready to build the concrete block walls. It is important that the work be done on consecutive days so that the whole thing bonds together properly. Use solid dense concrete blocks 400mm×200mm×100mm and lay these in a mortar of one part cement to three parts sand. Start laying the blocks at the

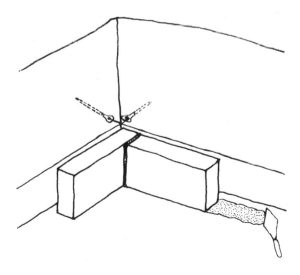

193

corner and use stretched strings fixed to pegs knocked into the sides of the excavation to keep the work level. The dimensions between the inside faces of the blocks will be the finished dimensions of the tank. With the blockwork built up to the top of the excavation, the mortar should be left for twenty-four hours to harden.

The following day mix another batch of concrete, the same mix as used for the bottom. The rough edges of the concrete bottom beyond the block wall should be dampened before this fresh concrete is poured in. Fill up

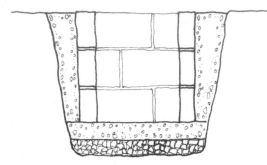

between the block wall and the top of the excavation with concrete. If you cannot face doing all the blockwork and pouring the concrete side walls on consecutive days you could do the work in stages, building a course of blockwork and pouring the concrete behind, dampening the junction between the old and new concrete. The courses must be laid on consecutive days. The concrete should be left

for at least a week to cure and the surface of the concrete blocks should then be sealed with a mortar of one part cement to one part fine sand which should be brushed in by hand with a small brush.

Alternative versions

Lawrence Hills of the Henry Doubleday Research Association has devised another method for making a concrete rainwater tank. The slab at the base is formed in the same way but after it has set overnight cardboard boxes are placed on it so that there is a margin of approximately 150mm between the sides of the boxes and the sides of the excavation. The boxes are then filled with soil and concrete is poured around them. When the concrete has set after a week the soil is dug out and the cardboard removed. Finally the inside surface of the

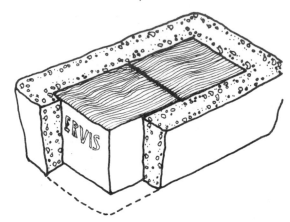

tank is given a rendering of three parts sand to one part cement. The disadvantage of this method is that having completed the initial excavation you have to shovel a great part of the earth back and then dig it out again, but it would be very invigorating exercise.

If you really cannot face the bother of making a permanent concrete rainwater storage tank you could just dig the hole and then line it with a garden pond liner, preferably one of butyl rubber, which would have to be held down around the edges with stone or thick baulks of timber. Polythene sheet is unsuitable as it degrades in sunlight. Providing you were never careless with your garden fork such a construction should have a reasonable life.

However you form the underground tank arrange your downpipe to feed into it and provide some kind of cover lest you step backwards unthinkingly. The cover can be formed by building your greenhouse staging over the tank, thereby bringing the plants directly above the water heat store.

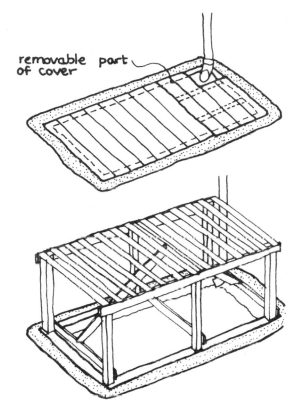

removable part of cover

Overflows

Building an overflow system into your underground tank is difficult, and impossible if you have used the hole and liner system. The easiest plan is to keep an eye on the level and to bale the tank out with a bucket if it becomes too full, pouring the water on the garden. The excess water should not really be poured down the drain as this is usually designed only to take foul water. For normal use watering cans and buckets can be dipped into the tank. If you are going to the trouble of providing underground storage it is likely that your tank is going to be as large as possible, otherwise all the effort is not going to be worthwhile; as long as you use the water it is unlikely to become so full that it starts to overflow.

An overflow should be provided if you have only one or two water-butts to take the whole of the flow off the roof. It should discharge into a nearby ditch or a purpose built soakaway, designed so that the water permeates into the surrounding soil. The normal diameter of pipe discharging into a soakaway would be 75mm; but as the pipe has to be connected to the top of the water-butt it will have to be 41mm as it is limited by the size of tank connector available. Because of this it would be best to provide two such pipes, perhaps discharging from separate water-butts to the same soakaway. Check with your local building inspector to see what they will accept: they will probably also have some suggestions for the way to make a soakaway acceptable to your particular local authority.

Typically it is a hole 1m×1m×1m (yes, more digging), filled with broken hardcore and covered at the top with 150mm of earth. The 41mm pipe from the water-butt travels under ground and discharges into the hardcore somewhere near the top of the soakaway. The soakaway should not be dug anywhere near the foundations of the building it is to serve, or any other building, and it should also not be dug in ground which is higher than that on which the building stands.

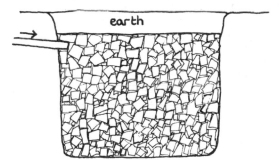

earth

The inevitable pile of soil you will be left with presents the usual problem; by now the rock garden is probably beginning to resemble a tumulus. However, even if you leave it where it was dug out nature will eventually take over and we have already had a crop of onions and carrots off what was once the soil from our foundations.

25 Windbreak Hedges and Shelter-Belts

Unless you happen to live in a farmhouse in the middle of a bleak fen, your attempts to alter the windspeed around your home will probably concentrate on the planting of a windbreak hedge rather than a true shelter-belt of trees. Before deciding on the type of hedging plant to use you will have to consider the local soil (clay, loam, peat, etc.); the degree of exposure of the site; the speed of growth of the hedge, and the final height required; whether the hedge is to be clipped or unclipped; the relative costs of the different plants; and finally, of course, your own personal preference. Whatever its relative merits, if you love the snowy blossom of the damson in springtime, then plant a damson hedge and enjoy it.

Windbreak hedges

If you are starting with a recently abandoned building site, where the earth is a typical mixture of sub-soil, brick bats and empty crisp packets, you must provide a bed of topsoil, with perhaps some well rotted manure or compost in which to start the young plants. In an estab-lished garden most hedging plants (e.g., hawthorn, blackthorn, holly and cherry plum) will accept a variety of soil conditions and grow well. If the soil is very acid the hardy purple rhododendron can be grown as a windbreak. For a chalky soil the common beech can be trained into a hedge; indeed, the beech can be so grown anywhere that is not wet. In wet soils the goat willow will grow rapidly into an untidy hedge, and the common alder would also be suitable.

The common alder, blackthorn and hawthorn all withstand strong winds, although hawthorn is not suitable for high altitudes, and will not grow under the shade of other trees. On very high ground and if the soil is thin and sandy, gorse will thrive and can be made to form an untidy hedge. The sea buckthorn makes a good windbreak hedge, will thrive in sandy areas and is useful for exposed coastal sites. Other hedging plants that will withstand salt laden winds include the maple, which is often seen in hedgerows in southern England, and elaeagnus. Not all hedging plants will thrive in shade but hornbeam will grow as long as the soil is not thin and holly will also tolerate a shady position.

In establishing something as long lasting as a windbreak hedge the rate at which the plants first grow may be an unimportant guide to the choice of species. However, for the impatient, hawthorn, willow and Leyland cypress will soon produce a hedge. The latter when grown as a tree will reach a height of fifteen metres and is characterised by a thin leading shoot which must be clipped to round about 300mm below the required final height in order to make the side shoots branch and thicken the top. At the other extreme, a hedge of common holly will grow very slowly.

For a formal clipped hedge, evergreens with small leaves, such as privet, cypress and holly, can all be trimmed to a precise shape. Beech can also be clipped as a formal hedge and, if trimmed in late summer, it will keep its russet leaves until the next spring. Plants with larger leaves are better kept as informal hedges and these need only minimal pruning with secateurs. Rhododendron, the outdoor fuschia, and cotoneaster (although the last two are actually small leaved) will all make useful informal windbreak hedges.

The table below shows the present comparative cost of some of the most suitable species for windbreak hedges together with some of their other characteristics.

For ourselves, we wanted a hedge to hide the view of the main road from the garden and to provide some shelter for new fruit trees. We decided on a damson hedge, Farleigh damson, because there was already a mixed hedge of damson and hawthorn to the neighbouring field, which always produced some fruit, and

we are very fond of damson jam. In the end it must be a personal choice.

The rules for hedge planting are much more established than those for selecting a suitable species. Deciduous hedges should be planted in the autumn but evergreen are best left for the spring. For both types the ground where the hedge is to be established should be dug over deeply and all the roots of perennial weeds (such as bindweed and ground elder) should be removed. The prepared bed should be about 600mm wide and a layer of well rotted manure or compost should be put in about 300mm below the surface of the soil. With very wet ground, apart from choosing a water tolerant species of plant, it will help if a ridge about 300mm high is built up over the bed.

When buying the plants make sure that they are small enough not to need staking, say about

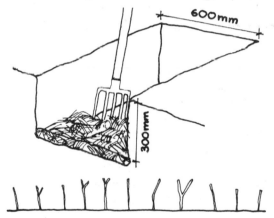

300mm high. It is also wise to sort the plants into similar sizes for planting as a large, strong plant placed next to a smaller specimen will grow faster and eventually suffocate the weaker plant, leaving gaps in the hedge.

comparative cost	species	deciduous or evergreen	clipped or unclipped	relative growth rate
cheapest	{ hawthorn	deciduous	clipped	fast
	{ willow	,,	unclipped	fast
	beech	,,	clipped	average
	holly	evergreen	clipped	slow
most	{ rhododendron	,,	unclipped	average
expensive	{ cypress	,,	clipped	fast

197

staggered row

Using a garden line as a guide, the specimens can be planted in a straight line or staggered, the exact spacing depending on the plant you have chosen (hawthorn 200–300mm apart; cypress 600-900mm apart); take advice on this when you are buying. Using the soil mark on the stem as a guide put the plants in to the same depth as they were in the nursery. Spread the roots when planting, cover them with fine earth and press the earth firmly round the stems with your heel.

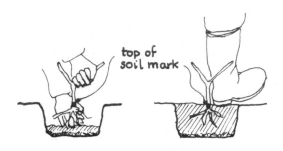

top of soil mark

The following spring and summer, if the weather is dry, you may need to water the plants: don't just shower them briefly with a watering can, soak each plant with a whole can of water. Remember to keep young plants free of weeds. In very exposed sites it may be necessary to shelter them with a temporary fence or to support them by putting in stakes at either end of the row with string stretched between.

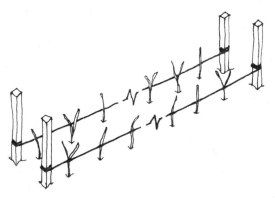

The general principles outlined will apply to all hedging plants, but when buying the plants it would be wise to enquire about the best way to set them out. The nursery should also be able to advise you about how and when to do the pruning to ensure a bushy hedge. As the idea is to encourage side branching at the expense of the growing tip, pruning will usually consist of cutting back all growths by half or a third of their length either at planting, leaving you with a very expensive handful of twigs, or in the first spring. An unclipped hedge should be left to grow up after this, although another severe pruning in the second year may help. Formal clipped hedges require more attention to achieve a better shape.

Shelter-belts

The difference between a windbreak hedge and a shelter-belt of trees is not clearly defined as the same plants can be used for both (e.g., common alder and Leyland cypress). However, trees in a true shelter-belt will be planted 1800-2400mm apart, in two or three staggered rows. The types of trees to use are pines (the Austrian pine) which is useful on exposed sites; cypress (Lawson's cypress, Leyland cypress); poplars (Lombardy poplar); alders (common alder); and, on wet soils, the white willow, the aim always being to grow a screen of trees as quickly as possible.

The trees should be planted very young so that the rapid root growth common to all young trees is made in the tree's permanent position rather than in the nursery. This ensures that the tree is anchored firmly into the soil; it is especially important in the case of the cypress which should always be planted young and always in deep soil. The remarks about the preparation of the ground and the planting of the young specimens discussed for hedges also apply here although the spacings will be different. Again, the young plants should be well heeled in and looked after during the first year.

Before planting a windbreak hedge or a shelter-belt, you can probably get the best information on what specimens to choose by looking at what grows best in your area. In our own garden, on an area of heavy soil that is rather poorly drained, a line of willow fence posts that once supported the netting of a chicken run have now reached maturity as a fine screen of white willow 8 metres high.

Insulating with creepers

A creeper grown up the side of your house to provide some insulation will have to be a permanent feature, so colourful annuals such as morning glory and nasturtium are no good. The choice of creeper will depend on personal preference, on the speed of growth required, the type of soil and the orientation of the particular wall. Wisteria will only grow well on a sunny south or west wall and will establish itself slowly. It will also need hard pruning if it is to flower well. It is not self-clinging and will require some support, and when fully grown and covered in leaf and flower, it will be heavy. The Russian vine will thrive in any soil, including chalk, and on any wall whether north- or south-facing. It does, however, still require supporting wires but grows three or four metres in a year.

Supporting wires are best arranged before planting. Fix galvanised screw eyes in the wall

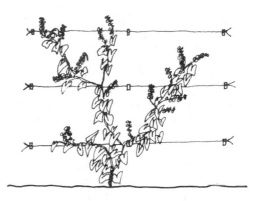

at 600mm centres; screw them into holes drilled in the wall and filled with plastic plugs. Alternatively galvanised vine eyes can be banged into the mortar joints. Thread 13 gauge galvanised wire through the eyes and fasten it by twisting it over the final eye with pliers. The lines of wire should be 200–300mm apart up the wall. You could use a length of galvanised chain link netting instead of the wire, in which case the fixings would be along the top and bottom edges and the netting would be tied to the eyes with galvanised wire.

If you prefer a self-clinging creeper, the common ivy will thrive in any position or soil. Beware of using a self-clinging creeper on old brickwork as the aerial roots may work their way into the old mortar joints, allowing rainwater to run along them and penetrate the brickwork. Many other species of plant can be trained or encouraged up a wall, some with flowers such as clematis, others with splendid autumnal foliage such as the Virginia creeper. As yet there is no official recognition of the insulating value of the various types available, so there is no pseudo-scientific reason for selecting any particular species. Nor does such a simple alteration of the external appearance of your house require official permission.

Building a trellis

When planning a trellis to shade a south-facing window in summer choose a deciduous creeper such as a rose (select a climber or a rambler), a honeysuckle, or a clematis. All the wood used for making the trellis should be

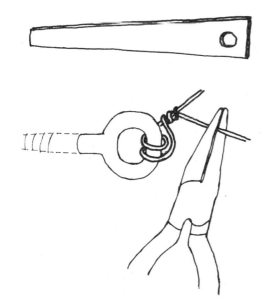

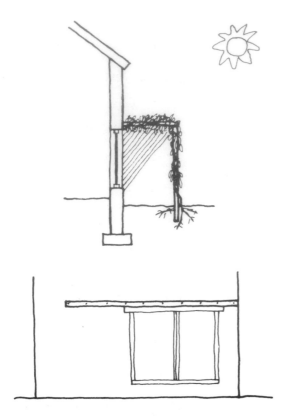

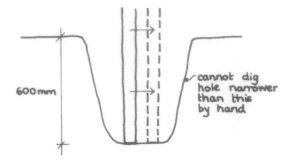

The holes will automatically be large enough to allow some tolerance in the exact positioning of the posts. Working on the ground you should screw the 75mm×75mm posts to a second 50mm×100mm member the same length as that fixed to the wall, again using 75mm no 12 zinc-plated screws. Now lift this framework into place with the help of a friend; fill the holes in and firm the earth around the posts.

A 50mm×50mm piece temporarily nailed between the framework and the wall member can be used to check that the structure is at right angles; the posts should also be checked with a level so that they are set vertically in the ground. Then nail 50mm×50mm pieces, cut to give a projection, at 600mm centres on top of the 50mm×100mm members using 75mm galvanised wire nails. The addition of wires stapled to the underside of the 50mm×50mm pieces will provide support for the climbers.

Tanalised or treated with three liberally applied coats of creosote.

Over the window to be protected fix a 50mm×100mm member allowing an overhang of approximately 2 metres either side of the end of the window, or as wide as the building will allow. The fixings can be made with 75mm no 12 zinc-plated screws and plastic wall plugs at 600mm centres. Mark out the positions for the uprights which should be spaced at 2 metre centres, 1.5 metres away from the wall of your house.

Dig holes at these points so that the posts can be let into the ground to a depth of 600mm.

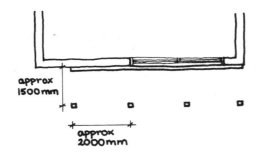

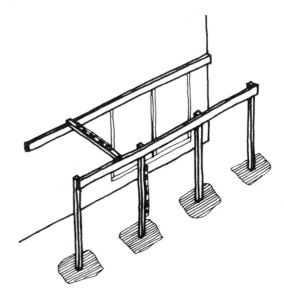

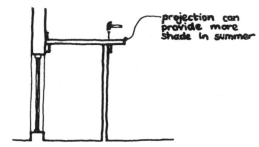

projection can provide more shade in summer

The plants can either be put in at the foot of the posts or against the wall, in which case additional wires will be needed to train the plant up the framework.

It may be difficult actually to affect the climate around your home with new planting, but in planning a new house the planting of the garden should be an integral part of the design. However, it is not so much the single house that may be usefully protected but rather groups of houses that could benefit by the protection of a wide shelter-belt of trees.

Planting is not the only thing that could be considered with the cooperation of your neighbours. Other schemes discussed in this book may work better on a larger scale. It would be easier to add external insulation to a whole terrace of houses at once than to insulate each house separately; a solar heating system serving a village might be easier to control and operate than fifty sets of solar panels; a windmill large enough to provide the lighting needs of a group of houses will have less visual impact than a number of smaller ones, and be only a single maintenance problem. At this point d-i-y begins to move outwards to co-operation between individuals, or community self-help, but that is another story...

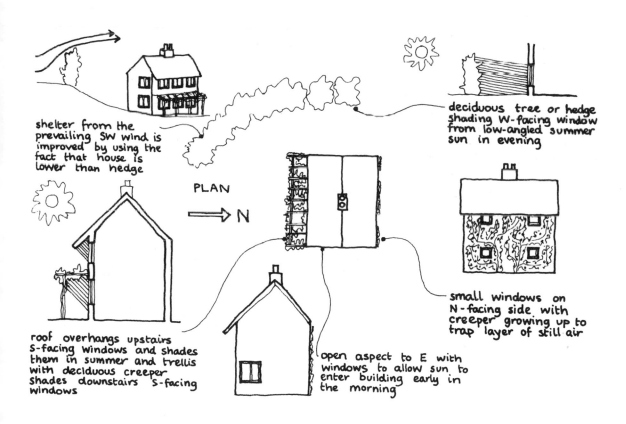

shelter from the prevailing SW wind is improved by using the fact that house is lower than hedge

deciduous tree or hedge shading W-facing window from low-angled summer sun in evening

PLAN → N

roof overhangs upstairs S-facing windows and shades them in summer and trellis with deciduous creeper shades downstairs S-facing windows

open aspect to E with windows to allow sun to enter building early in the morning

small windows on N-facing side with creeper growing up to trap layer of still air

Further Reading

The Guide to the Building Regulations
A. J. Elder, The Architectural Press, London, 1976

Keeping Warm for Half the Cost, Complete Guide to Home Insulation
Phil Townsend and John Colesby, Prism Press, Dorchester, 1976

The Solar Home Book, Heating, Cooling and Designing with the Sun
Bruce Anderson, Prism Press, Dorchester, 1977

Practical Solar Heating
Kevin McCartney with Brian Ford, Prism Press, Dorchester, 1978

The Solar Greenhouse Book
edited by James McCullagh, Rodale Press, Emmaus, PA, USA, 1978

The Woodburner's Encyclopedia
Jay Shelton and Andrew Shapiro, Vermont Crossroads Press, Waitsfield, Vt, USA, 1976

Wood Heat
John Vivian, Rodale Press, Emmaus, PA, USA, 1976

Construction Manual for a Cretan Windmill
N. van de Ven, Steering Committee for Windenergy in Developing Countries, Amersfoort, Holland, 1977

The Reader's Digest Complete Do-it-yourself Manual
The Reader's Digest Association Ltd, London, 1976

Radical Technology
edited by P. Harper and G. Boyle, Wildwood House Ltd, London, 1976

The Energy Question
Gerald Foley *et al.*, Pelican, London, 1976

Energy Primer, Solar, Water, Wind and Biofuels
Portola Institute, Prism Press, Dorchester, 1975

Fuel's Paradise, Energy Options for Britain
Peter Chapman, Penguin, London, 1975

The Woodburning Book
published by *Practical Self-Sufficiency*, Leys Publishing Company, Widdington, second edition — 1978

Fuel Efficiency Booklet 7-Degree Days
Department of Energy, Thames House South,
  Millbank SW1P 4QJ

The National Centre for Alternative
  Technology, Machynlleth, Powys, in Wales,
  sells information sheets on, among other
  things, building a Cretan type windmill and
  homemade solar panels. They also have an
  excellent mail order book service.

The Open University, Walton Hall, Milton
  Keynes, Bucks, offers a short course called
  Energy in the Home.

Useful Addresses

For general enquiries contact
Building Research Establishment, Garston,
Watford WD2 7JR
tel: Garston (092 73) 74040

*Information on all building materials as well as
wood-burning stoves and commercial solar
collectors can be obtained free from*
The Building Centre, 26 Store St, London WC1
tel: 01-637 8361

*All types of insulating materials including
Foamglas can be obtained from Sheffield
Insulations. They have depots all over England,
Scotland and Wales, but the head office is*
The Sheffield Insulating Company Ltd,
Hillsborough Works, Sheffield S6 2LW
tel: Sheffield (0742) 340781

*The Neoprene gap sealing strip described in
Chapters 15 and 21 can be obtained from*
Sealmaster Ltd, Pampisford,
Cambridge CB2 4HG
tel: Cambridge (0223) 832851

*The solar differential controller that we used for
our solar roof was made by*

Sunsense Ltd, 1 Lincoln Rd, Northborough,
Peterborough PE6 9BL
tel: Peterborough (0733) 252672

*Corrugated aluminium sheet, stainless fixing
screws and alloy rivets can be obtained from*
Granges Essem (UK) Ltd, Leon House,
233 High St, Croydon CR0 9XT
tel: 01-681 0061

*Stainless steel pipe can be bought from
plumbers' merchants; stainless fittings and the
special adhesive to join them are available from*
Lancashire Fitting Ltd, County Works, Claro Rd,
Harrogate HG1 4AF
tel: Harrogate (0423) 67981

*Condensation control equipment and dewstats
are available from*
Aidelle Products, Lancaster Rd,
High Wycombe HP12 3QP
tel: High Wycombe (0494) 25252

Aluminium conservatory parts
Cambridge Glasshouse Company Ltd,
Comberton, Cambridge CB3 7BY
tel: Comberton (022 026) 2395

Aluminium Z sections
British Aluminium Stockholders Ltd,
32-6 Station Rd, Gerrards Cross SL9 8EL
tel: Gerrards Cross (49) 88424

Alternators
CAV Ltd, PO Box 36, Warple Way,
London W3 7SS
tel: 01-734 3111

Gearboxes, pulleys and V belts, and Taper lock bushes
J.H. Fenner and Company Ltd,
Marfleet, Hull
tel: Hull (0482) 781234

Large diameter overflow pipes
Bartol Plastics Ltd, Edlington,
Doncaster DN12 1BY
tel: Rotherham (0709) 863551

'Red Rib' expanded metal lath for external render is made by
Expamet Building Products Ltd,
1 Butler Place,
London SW1H 0PS
tel: 01-222 7766

Preservative stain for wood, in various colours, can be obtained from
Sadolins (U.K.) Ltd, Shire Hill Industrial Estate,
Saffron Walden, Essex CB11 3DA
tel: Saffron Walden (0799) 27501

Breather paper is made by
St Regis Coating and Laminating Division,
British Sisalkraft Ltd, Knight Road, Strood,
Rochester, Kent ME2 2AW
tel: Medway (0634) 74171

Bartol Plastics Ltd have just introduced the 'Acorn' range of push-fit plastic connections for *hot* water pipes which should make the plumbing of solar collectors very much easier as well as cheaper.

Glossary

Acrow props (trade name) Adjustable supports used when alterations are being made.

Aggregate The stones and sand that are mixed with cement to make concrete.

Angle L-shaped section of metal strip.

Annular nails Nails with ridges round the shaft which make them grip.

At 100mm centres The distance from the centre line of one component to the centre line of the next. Used to measure the spacing of, for example, rafters.

Back nut A nut to allow a tap or connector to be fastened to a tank or other container.

Baffles Metal plates inside a stove which guide the flow of air and other gases within it.

Battens Thin lengths of wood, no larger than 50mm×50mm.

Bearing blocks Components which support a shaft and allow it to rotate.

Bevel A tool for marking various angles.

Bibtap A conventional tap.

Blanking-off disc A metal disc used to close off the end of a compression fitting.

Blinding A layer of sand spread over the top of hardcore to make a smooth level surface.

Blockboard A sheet material consisting of a core made of wooden strips, with a plywood sheet glued to each side. Available in greater thicknesses than plywood.

Boss A projecting plug (or spigot).

Bowsprit A projecting spar at the front of a Cretan windmill.

Brace A type of drill for making holes in wood.

Bush The part of a component which allows it to be fitted to a shaft.

Butt hinges Conventional hinges that are recessed into the door and frame.

Butyl A kind of artificial rubber sheet.

Clout nails Short nails with large flat heads.

Coach screws Large screws with heads that fit a spanner rather than a screwdriver.

Compression fitting A plumbing connection which is made waterproof by tightening it with a spanner (as opposed to soldering).

Conduction The transfer of heat through the substance of a material.

Convection The transfer of heat by the movement of heated fluids.

Coping Waterproof capping to a wall.

Countersunk head A screw head designed to be recessed into the surface of a material.

DPM Damp proof membrane, a waterproof layer under a floor designed to stop damp rising into the concrete.

Expanded polystyrene A very light, white plastic insulating material.

Extruded polystyrene A light plastic insulating material slightly more water resistant than expanded polystyrene.

Feather edged Overlapping boarding, thicker at the bottom edge than at the top.

Fischerbolt (trade name) A German expanding bolt.

Flange A flat rim surround.

Flashing Pieces of metal used to cover gaps between building components so as to exclude rainwater.

Float A tool used for putting plaster on to walls and ceilings.

Floorbrads Flat rectangular section nails used for fixing floorboards to joists.

Flush hinge A hinge designed to be screwed to the face of the door and frame so that no recess is needed. Not as strong as butt hinges.

Galvanised Coated with zinc to reduce the chances of corrosion.

Getter A replaceable element to remove corrosive properties from water.

Hardcore Lumps of broken brick used to form a solid base before laying concrete.

Header A brick used with the short face showing.

Iroko A tropical hardwood.

Keyway A slot cut in a shaft and the component which is to be fixed to it. A metal 'key' fitted in the slot prevents rotation of the component round the shaft.

Lintel A member that supports a wall across an opening.

Lost head nails Circular section nails with very small heads which are driven in flush with the surface of the wood.

Lump hammer A small heavy hammer used one-handed.

Male A fitting that screws into a female fitting.

Masonry bit A drill bit specially made for drilling holes in brick, stone and concrete.

Mastic A sticky, flexible sealing compound.

Metal lath A type of wire netting that provides a base for plaster or rendering.

Neoprene A very durable artificial rubber material.

Oval wire nail Oval section nail with very small head. Not as strong as lost head nails.

Padsaw A long, very thin saw with replaceable blades.

Parliament hinges Projecting hinges which allow a door to swing out to clear a wall or other obstruction.

Pivot draught control Rotating inlet used to adjust the flow of combustion air entering a woodstove.

Plasplug (trade name) An expanding wall plug used for fixing screws into masonry.

Plasterers' nails Glavanised nails for fixing up plasterboard.

PTFE Tape Polytetrafluorethylene, used for sealing screw type plumbing connections.

Purlin A horizontal beam in a roof.

Radiation The transfer of heat by electromagnetic waves across an intervening space.

Rawlbolt (trade name) An expanding bolt for making very strong fixings to masonry.

Rendering A plaster containing cement for use externally on walls.

Resin-bonded glass fibre An insulating material made of spun glass treated to make it water resistant.

Screed A thin (50mm-75mm) layer of cement and sand mortar laid on top of a concrete floor to form a smooth surface.

Screw eyes Screws with rings on the end instead of the normal head.

Shiplap Interlocking boarding for the exterior cladding of buildings.

Skew nails Nails driven in at an angle to join two pieces of wood when you cannot nail straight through one piece to the other.

Soakaway A stone-filled pit that allows water to soak into the surrounding ground in a controlled manner.

Softwood The type of timber normally used in building (spruce, hemlock, deal, etc.).

Spirit level A tool used to determine

whether something is truly horizontal or vertical.

Step-up drive A gearing system used to increase rotational speed.

Stilson A large spanner with adjustable jaws used by plumbers.

Stretcher A brick used with the long face showing.

Stud partition A timber-framed internal wall clad with plasterboard.

Studs The vertical members in a timber-framed wall.

Taper lock bush (trade name) A proprietary bush for making a very firm connection of a component to a shaft.

Tensioning screw An adjusting screw to allow a belt to be tightened or loosened.

Thermal break A method of reducing the heat loss through a metal window frame by incorporating an insulating material between the inside and outside sections of the frame.

Tile hung wall A wall to which plain roofing tiles are fixed to form a water resisting exterior finish.

Trimmer A length of wood used to support joists or rafters when an opening is formed.

Vertical twist wall ties Specially shaped metal pieces used to tie together the two halves of a brick or concrete block cavity wall.

Vine eye A strip of metal with a hole in one end designed to be driven into brick walls to support wires for climbing plants.

Wash boiler A container for boiling clothes in soapy water.

WBP plywood The exterior grade of plywood ('Water and Boil Proof'), not as good as marine grade but cheaper.

Weatherboard A shaped piece of wood that throws off the rain at the bottom of a door.

Wire nails Round section nails with flat heads, used for timber frame building construction.

Z Section Metal formed into a Z shape but with 90° angles.

Index